The
Naturalist's
Garden

The
NATURALIST'S
GARDEN

RUTH SHAW ERNST

Illustrations by Robin Brickman

Rodale Press, Emmaus, Pennsylvania

Dedicated to all who love flowers and gardens
and the wild creatures that come to visit them

Printed in the United States of America on recycled paper,
containing a high percentage of de-inked fiber.

Book Design by Glen Burris

Library of Congress Cataloging-in-Publication Data

Ernst, Ruth Shaw.
    The naturalist's garden.

    Bibliography: p.
    Includes index.
    1. Wildlife attracting.   2. Gardening to attract
wildlife.   I. Title.
QL59.E76   1987   635   87–23227

ISBN   0–87857–730–0   hardcover
ISBN   0–87857–731–9   paperback

2 4 6 8 10 9 7 5 3 1   hardcover
2 4 6 8 10 9 7 5 3 1   paperback

Contents

Preface   vii

Acknowledgments   ix

Introduction *What Is
   a Naturalist's Garden?*   xi

**Part One
Creating a Naturalist's Garden**

Chapter 1   Landscaping for Wildlife   1

Chapter 2   Trees and Shrubs   8

Chapter 3   The Naturalist's Flower Garden   28

Chapter 4   Wildflowers in the Garden   75

Chapter 5   Pools and Water Gardens   101

Chapter 6   On Growing Vegetables   112

**Part Two
The Garden as Backyard
Nature Center**

Chapter 7   Birds in the Backyard   129

Chapter 8   Butterflies and Friends   157

Chapter 9   Backyard Wildlife   174

v

Part Three
How to Keep the Garden Healthy

Chapter 10   The Stuff of Life   193

Chapter 11   Battling Bugs and Diseases . . .
                    Naturally   210

Chapter 12   Weather or Not   228

                    USDA Hardiness Zone Map   238

                    Resources   239

                    Bibliography   253

                    Index   264

Preface

I learned about gardening soon after I learned to walk. Tagging after my grandpa with my little watering can, I sprinkled where he hosed, jabbed at the earth with my toy shovel where he cultivated the soil, peered at the flowers that he examined. "Now be very still," he would warn. "Here comes a hummer!" And I would hold my breath and gaze in awe at the tiny iridescent blur hovering above a morning glory. Grandpa told me wonderful stories about the caterpillars that spun cocoons or wrapped themselves in leaves and emerged later as beautiful butterflies and moths—"turned-intos," he called them—and taught me to recognize and respect the ones in our garden. "Leave some seeds," he said, when I was old enough to snip off dead flower heads. "Some for the birds, and some for us. Nature will make them take root and bloom next year."

Many years of city living were to pass before I could walk about my own garden, aware now of bird and insect behavior patterns but still filled with wonder. A flash of yellow and the sway of a stem show me where a goldfinch is gorging on cosmos seeds. Butterflies wing over to the butterfly bush, which lives up to its name, luring them with its purple, perfumed florets. A persistent cardinal dive-bombs a tomato plant half a dozen times before he is able to pry a fat hornworm from a leaf and carry it off. The bright-eyed chipmunk that lives under the garage wall peeks out warily from his burrow, then makes a dash for the bushes to forage for food.

It is not possible for the naturalist/gardener to view the landscape as purely aesthetic or boundary defining or shade producing; although it is all these things, for her or him it functions as the setting for developing relationships with the creatures that inhabit or pass through it. When buying or transplanting flowering plants or shrubs, consider their appeal to wildlife. That's easy to do, for there is such a marvelous diversity of color, scent, size, and design; of nectar, pollen, and fruit; of shelter and brood-rearing attractions, that the difficulties lie in narrowing down the choices.

In writing this book, I too must narrow down my choices, for if I were to attempt to do full justice to organic gardening and backyard wildlife in all regions of the country, the reader would not be able to lift such a weighty tome. A pared-down selection of well-known, readily available and reliable flowers and other plant life and the most commonly encountered forms of wildlife had to be made. Thus, if I have omitted your favorite wildflower or denizen of the backyard, forgive me. There just isn't room for all of them in these pages.

My hope is that I can help you to create and maintain a beautiful garden with natural methods, or enhance the one you have, with an awareness of the needs of the winged and other creatures that may visit or inhabit it. The pleasures of gardening include sharing with wildlife. And taken altogether, these amount to some of the greatest, most rewarding pleasures life has to offer.

 # Acknowledgments

Rita Napolitano, Horticultural Consultant, Agricultural Division of Cornell Cooperative Extension in White Plains, New York, has been most generous in providing information on horticultural subjects and on controls of insects and diseases. The New York State Department of Environmental Conservation has also been helpful with data on pest controls and IPM. To Peter J. Woodcock, Urban Forester, Superintendent of Highways and Scarsdale Village naturalist, my thanks for sharing his knowledge of wildflowers and wildflower plantings with me.

Valuable aid was provided by BobbiJo Jarvis, Public Horticulture Specialist of the Missouri Botanical Garden, and by the Missouri Department of Conservation on wildlife, plantings, and food for birds and backyard wildlife. I am greatly indebted to Nan Chadwick of the National Audubon Society, Northeast Region, for information on the New York Nest Box Network for Bluebirds, of which she is Project Director. More helpful data on the bluebird program in the state of Arkansas came from Mel White, Managing Editor of the *Arkansas Times,* and from Jay S. Miller, Administrator of Program Services, and Lisa Hlass, Field Interpreter, both of the Arkansas Department of Parks and Tourism.

Special thanks and appreciation go to my editors, Suzanne Nelson and Ellen Cohen, whose expert guidance has been invaluable.

Introduction

What Is a Naturalist's Garden?

Imagine a garden brimming with a wide diversity of plants and flowers flourishing in rich, fertile soil—a colorful, blossoming, and fruitful plot of land where various forms of wildlife come to visit or to live. Picture a place where you, the naturalist/gardener, can find pleasure not only in the landscape but also in observing and providing for the wildlife that lives there. Think about the garden as a small community of plants and animals coexisting with one another and with human beings, interrelating with the environment, reflecting the ecology in miniature.

This tiny but significant part of the vast web of life is the naturalist's garden. It is not just a collection of flowers, trees, and shrubs, but a beautiful, varied landscape where birds, butterflies, bees, moths, and other insects and animals come to seek food and drink, nesting and breeding places, shelter from the elements, and hiding places from enemies. It is a sanctuary and a safe harbor for many creatures and a temporary way station for others on the move.

In this garden you can get excited about the different species of birds and butterflies that you see by day, the magnificent big moths that arrive at dusk, and the swift, cellophane-winged dragonflies that dive down to rest on a lily pad in your little pond. Squirrels and chipmunks scurry about for seeds and berries and, perhaps, to mooch a crumb or cracker from you. Other small animals visit the garden to see what's in it for them in the way of grubs and insects. Honeybees, drawn to certain blossoms by their vivid colors or inviting markings, buzz intently about their nectar-gathering business, dusting flowers with life-renewing pollen as they go. A handsome caterpillar is consuming a sprig of parsley, and you let it share the wealth, knowing that it will turn into a gorgeous black swallowtail butterfly. Freckled red ladybugs methodically munch their way along a line of destructive aphids on a tender shoot. Pink, rose, and white cosmos, bold, multicolored zinnias, and maroon-and-yellow marigolds are blossoming, self-sown or grown from seed you saved from last year's annual flowers.

You try your hand at all sorts of new things that will increase the diversity and richness of your yard. You interplant pungent nasturtiums, marigolds, and strong-scented herbs such as mint, chives, and basil among the vegetables, both for their insect-repellent value and for the colorful, varied look they give the vegetable beds. After Christmas, you set your tree outside and watch the grateful birds take shelter from winter storms and cold-hardy cats between raids on the feeder. This is the year you start a compost pile, tucked in a corner of the backyard vegetable plot, and you find yourself saving every carrot top and wilted lettuce leaf to add to the heap.

You are jubilant when a pair of bluebirds decides to nest in your bluebird box and raise a family there, entranced when a ruby-throated hummingbird hovers over a red bee balm, delighted when a robin splashes blissfully in a big saucer of water. *You* put up the nest box, *you* planted the bee balm, *you* set out the saucer "birdbath" and kept it filled and fresh. It's all your doing!

A sudden small movement nearby catches your attention and you see a praying mantis devour a hapless beetle it has just grabbed with lightning speed. The big insect turns its head and looks at you, as mantids do, and you think how well nature's own system of checks and balances works without the interference of hazardous synthetic substances.

Your garden is a place as favorable to plant and animal life as it is pleasing to the human eye . . . and nose, for the myriad sweet scents; and ear, for the chatter of birds; and mouth, for the harvest-fresh flavors of berries and vegetables; and hands, for the velvety feel of the petals of a pansy or wild poppy. Your efforts are richly rewarded by the presence of a variety of wildlife, many of which visit or remain because their own natural habitat and food supply have been destroyed or polluted. Your place looks mighty good to them. And *you* feel good about having them there!

No matter how hard you work in your garden, find time to relax, reflect, and observe. Awareness of the continuous process of birth, growth and bloom, death, decay, and renewal going on all about you gives rise to a feeling of kinship with all living things. These tranquil, harmonious observations nourish and refresh the mind and emotions and bring you joy. And this, too, is part of the naturalist's garden.

Part One

CREATING A NATURALIST'S GARDEN

Chapter 1

Landscaping for Wildlife

The grass, the thicket, and the fruit-tree wild;
White hawthorn, and the pastoral eglantine;
Fast fading violets covered up in leaves;
And mid-May's eldest child,
The coming musk rose, full of dewy wine

John Keats,
"Ode to a Nightingale"

Open the back door and take a fresh look around!

Chances are you'll see a venerable oak, maple, or hickory, a tall pine or two, a clipped hedge or fence on a boundary line, a well-kept lawn, a few shrubs. Perhaps there's a garden bed where every spring you set out tomato plants and annual flower seedlings just to have a patch of color out there, a bumper crop of vine-ripened tomatoes, and some cut flowers to bring into the house. Maybe there's a bird feeder hanging from a bough near the kitchen door. All in all, it's an attractive and orderly scene that greets your eye.

But could your pleasant backyard be something more? Could it be doing more for birds and other kinds of wildlife that are in need of steady sources of food and water, shelter from wind, storm, or cold, respite from weariness and hunger? Could your yard help to offset the "dispossessed notices"

1

that confront so many creatures as more and more woodland, swamp, and meadow fall prey to development and urbanization? And at the same time, could it present you with a more handsome landscape and more enchanting flowers than you ever dreamed possible?

Certainly it could, and this part of the book is going to tell you what elements you can provide to make your yard a beautiful haven for birds, mammals, water creatures, butterflies, and other interesting wildlife. By combining all the good elements now existing on your property with well-chosen and well-placed new features, you can create a valuable and appealing habitat for wildlife. As you add new trees and shrubs and plant more flowers, the sources of food, shelter, and reproductive or nesting areas will increase. If a supply of water isn't available naturally, you'll supply it. The word will spread ... and the wildlife will fly, flutter, run, crawl, or amble in! All the while, you will be learning a great deal about feathered, furred, and scaly creatures, many kinds of plants and flowers, and the relationships between them.

What to Add

Once you have committed yourself to the exciting concept of being a backyard naturalist, the first thing to do is to see what you need to add to your landscape to make it more inviting to wildlife. Start by looking at what you already have in a new way. The oak that is a joy to behold in autumn, when its leaves turn copper and bronze, bears acorns that are an excellent winter food for squirrels, blue jays, woodpeckers, game birds, and many small mammals. The luminous red, peach, pink, and white azalea blossoms extend a "welcome back" in spring to nectar-seeking bees, butterflies, and northward-migrating hummingbirds. That honeysuckle with the sweet scent you love is also loved by bumblebees, butterflies, and other long-tongued insects. But in order to become a lush, flowery, fruitful haven for wildlife, the backyard will benefit

You begin to be a naturalist/gardener by observing the wildlife that is already in your yard.

from additional plantings to satisfy the requirements of many species.

Adding Trees and Flowers

If the perimeter of your property has a number of bare spots, or few big trees, the first thing to consider is adding some trees that will grow tall. Deciduous trees, which shed their leaves in autumn, generally bear the most fruit, nuts, and seeds for a variety of wildlife and offer shelter and leafy, shady nesting sites. The evergreens, which hold their leaves all winter, offer year-round shelter and protection, some breeding sites, and food in the form of berries and seed-filled cones. You'll find plenty of trees and shrubs to choose from in Chapter 2, Trees and Shrubs.

Flowers are an essential part of the naturalist's garden. The sheer beauty of garden flowers is reason enough to grow a great many, even if they serve no other purpose than to be a feast for the eyes and the soul. But as the hummingbird siphons up nectar, the butterfly alights and sips, and the bee

loads her bags with pollen, the observant gardener glows
with satisfaction, knowing that these blossoms are also helping to fulfill the needs of wildlife and are in turn pollinated
by them.

Whether you enlarge your existing herbaceous (flower)
border or make a new one, locate it where it will get full sun
for at least six hours a day, where it will not be shaded by
trees or invaded by their roots, and where you can enjoy seeing it from the house. You'll learn what to plant for wildlife
and beauty in Chapter 3, The Naturalist's Flower Garden.

Coping With Problem Sites

Problem areas need be problems no longer. Create a woodland wildflower garden in a shady damp spot near pines or
oaks. A wet, low-lying, or boggy place where nothing you
ever tried to grow did well is highly suitable for a number of
unusual and attractive plants. A stretch of lawn that is weedy
or sparse—demanding time, energy, and money to maintain
and improve—can be transformed into the centerpiece of
the backyard: a colorful, carefree wildflower garden or
grassy meadow studded with wildflowers. These native flowers have enormous appeal for a throng of nectar-, pollen-,
and seed-seekers. Details on growing wildflowers in sun or
shade are provided in Chapter 4, Wildflowers in the Garden.

Easy Water Gardening

Lucky you and your wildlife friends if you have a stream or
pond on or adjacent to your property. Otherwise, you will
need to supply water for drinking and bathing. You can create or build your own pool or install a prefabricated one in
almost any size. Water can also be supplied in birdbaths,
large plant saucers, or shallow dishes. The pool and plants
within and alongside it will be a focal point in the landscape.
Birds, small mammals, insects, amphibians—they'll all flock
to your watering hole. Position water so that it is near protective vegetation for quick escapes and so that you can have a

good view from the house. Water gardening is the focus of Chapter 5, Pools and Water Gardens.

Adding Vegetables

If you plan to grow vegetables, consider planting them in an extension of the flower border or interspersed with flowers and herbs. There are a number of insect-repellent flowers that add a bright and useful note. Wildlife enjoy vegetables, but a vegetable patch is not usually considered an integral part of the habitat plan. Unless you are willing to share with caterpillars, rabbits, deer, woodchucks, and other wild visitors, you'd better be prepared to fend them off with various preventive measures. You'll learn how in Chapter 6, On Growing Vegetables.

An Overall View

Don't get so carried away by individual features that you forget the overall picture. You don't want to add a pool here, a vegetable garden here, and a wildflower meadow there like a child splatting finger paints on a sheet of paper. After all, a garden is not merely a collection of plants and trees. It should be a pleasing expanse of natural landscape, however small. Harmony and scale, sunshine and shade, views and aspects at the present time, and visions of future growth should all be taken into account.

In addition to integrating the individual wildlife attractions, don't forget to plant for a succession of bloom and fruit so that there will be flowers and fruit, berries, nuts, or seeds during most of the year. Different creatures have different food preferences and come and go at different times. The greatest diversity of food-producing plants will attract the greatest number of birds and other wildlife. In winter, you may wish to set up feeders to implement the birds' food supply.

Making Shelters

But remember, it isn't just food that wild creatures are after. If they can't find a cozy, sheltered spot to roost or rest, hide or breed in, they may just eat and run! Your mixture of tall and short trees and shrubs, dense evergreens, flowers, wildflowers, vines, sources of water, meadow, and brush pile (if you have the space) all add up to a naturalistic, hospitable landscape that wildlife can call home.

Whether ¼ acre or 5 acres, with or without a stream, woodland, or meadow, your property can become a miniature ecosystem where plants and animals coexist and interrelate as they do in nature. The naturalist's garden reflects the larger environment of which it is a small but important part—important because it helps compensate for relentless habitat destruction. A flourishing wildlife sanctuary will be a source of joy, pride, and entertainment—right in your own backyard.

A variety of cone- and berry-bearing trees and shrubs will make your garden attractive to hungry wildlife in winter. Evergreens provide shelter as well.

Chapter 2

Trees and Shrubs

Why are there trees I never walk under
but large and melodious thoughts descend upon me?

Walt Whitman,
"Song of the Open Road"

I have an immense sugar maple that causes "large and melodious thoughts" to "descend upon me." Noble trees do seem to inspire noble and pleasurable ideas.

In the naturalist's garden, the relationship of trees to the herbaceous border (or flower garden), as well as to each other and to the property as a whole, must be considered, for trees are the lords of the plant community. They have the *droit du seigneur*, the right to demand the space and attention they need. They require huge amounts of water, a feeding every four or five years with a high-nitrogen fertilizer such as cottonseed meal, bloodmeal, or guano, and pruning as needed. In return, they draw carbon dioxide from the air as they release oxygen and moisture into it, offer blissful shade and coolness in summer heat, give food and shelter to birds, insects, and many other creatures, and immeasurably enhance the appearance of yards and streets.

Why Plant Trees and Shrubs?

Strategically placed, trees and shrubs benefit the homeowner by shading and cooling the house in summer and protecting it from winter wind and storms. They add a measure of privacy, besides increasing the value of the property. But be careful not to place trees where they might interfere with your view of the backyard from the house.

Big, deciduous shade trees such as maples, sweet gums, oaks, and beeches need the most space of all. In return, they display a rich variety of autumn colors and provide samaras, gum balls, acorns, and beechnuts for wildlife feasting. Conifers and broadleaf evergreen shrubs—azaleas, rhododendrons, and mountain laurels—stay green all year round, and a clump of them provides needed shelter for birds in cold and windy weather. Flowering shrubs (such as the viburnums, honeysuckles, and butterfly bush) and dwarf fruit trees make good borders and accents, as well as sources of food for birds and wildlife.

Before you buy any tree or shrub, think carefully about where it should be located and what its size will be at maturity. As trees grow large, they cast more shade, extend their roots farther out, and may even tap at your windowpane or bump into each other. Border or background bushes, small and shapely when young, can grow to overhang and encroach upon a flowerbed. The joy of selecting and planting trees and shrubs can be dimmed after a few years when they start to spell disaster to your flowers, depriving them of sunlight, nutrients, and water; when leaves clog gutters and drains; and when branches reach out into the driveway or over the neighbor's property and must be cut.

Roses and White Pines

I can illustrate this point with a personal backyard tragedy. Many years ago, I planted a row of young 5-foot-tall white pines along a boundary of my yard without realizing what their eventual size (over 100 feet!) would be. Not far away, I

put in a rose bed. The rosebushes flourished in good soil and full sun; they were my pride and joy. But as the pines shot up and spread, the roses began to decline. The more I fed and watered the roses, the more nourishment the pine roots gobbled up, and the bigger the trees grew. Plunged eventually into shade most of the day, undermined by ravenous tree roots, sprinkled liberally with pine needles, my precious roses weakened and many died. Replacing them with strong, healthy bushes was an exercise in futility. I gave up trying to grow roses there. The huge pines live on, taking up space I begrudge them mightily. However, they do provide shelter and nesting sites for many birds.

When you plan your garden, do not locate a flowerbed near big trees or plant trees too close to an existing bed. Do some research on the size of trees and shrubs when they are full grown, then plant trees that will mature in a scale appropriate to your landscape and other plantings.

Adding Shrubs and Small Trees

Since a young 10- or 15-foot-tall maple or cedar may take 30 or 40 years to become a mature tree, smaller trees and shrubs should be planted in front of and between them. Lower plantings can also fill the gaps around older trees if there are large, empty spaces. Good choices are ornamental trees such as crabapple, plum, cherry, dogwood, and hawthorn, which bear pink, white, rose, or red blossoms in spring and fruit or berries in fall.

Group some evergreen shrubs in dense clumps near trees, and plant them as a boundary hedge or background for a flowerbed. They provide cover, nesting sites, and food for many birds and other creatures. Be sure to plant some flowering deciduous shrubs such as lilac, mockorange, and quince, which have nectar and pollen that appeal to a host of winged visitors, and beauty and fragrance that will appeal to

Trees and shrubs give us shade and beauty, and provide our wild friends with food, cover, and nesting sites. They are the cornerstone of the naturalist's garden.

you. And don't fail to include some bushes—hazelnuts, raspberries, blueberries, currants, gooseberries, and cherries, to name a few—with delicious nuts and berries that you can share with your wildlife!

Pointers on Planting and Pruning

All plants, including shrubs and trees, need planting holes properly prepared and wide enough so that roots can be spread out, if bare-root, or can spread with ease, if within a ball of soil or peat. The hole should be at least 18 to 24 inches wider than the root ball. Cut off any damaged or broken roots, and loosen the soil or peat ball around them if it is very compacted. If a shrub is balled and burlapped, cut the burlap and lay it in the hole, where it will decompose. If the spade has compacted the sides of the hole, loosen the soil. Fill the hole with the unamended soil you took out of it, or you'll hinder root growth.

Water as you backfill to get rid of air pockets, again several hours after planting, then every seven to ten days—unless there's adequate rainfall—for the first season. Newly planted shrubs and trees need a great deal of water. In a drought, save as much "used" household water as possible for thirsty trees and shrubs that have been recently planted. (The older ones will need it too, of course, but since their roots can search for moisture at deeper levels, they can wait longer.)

Immediately after planting, apply a mulch to help retain water and keep soil temperature even. Use peat or compost, which will improve the structure and fertility of the soil as it slowly decomposes. The mulch should be 3 to 4 inches deep and extend as far out as possible—5 feet out from the tree trunk is ideal. Fertilize after planting.

Aftercare

Young shrubs and trees don't need much care if the planting hole has been well prepared *and if they get sufficient water* (this point can't be stressed enough). As they grow, the best way to keep them looking and feeling good is to remove any

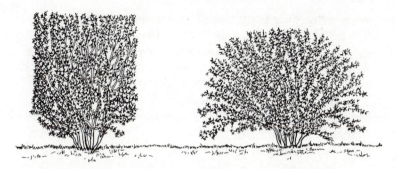

Prune shrubs lightly, removing older wood to promote flowering. The naturally lovely forsythia on the right looks better than its boxy, mechanically trimmed counterpart on the left. Birds also prefer the natural shape for nesting and shelter.

dead wood and cut down old, thick, less productive stems from shrubs.

Prune lightly for shapeliness—*never* to create stiff, formal shapes. There's a world of difference! The artificially rounded or sharply angled electric-hedge-trimmer look is ugly and unnatural, and birds and other creatures find such a bush hard to get into and out of. Besides, overpruning may eliminate desirable buds, flowers, and berries. Do what seems necessary *after* the shrub has bloomed, never shortly before, or you will surely decrease blooming and fruiting. Pruning seems to have an almost irresistible attraction for some people—here a snip, there a snip, everywhere a snip, snip. Keep a tight hold on the clippers!

Unless you're an expert, it's best to leave tree pruning to the tree surgeons. And please don't rush to cut down a dead tree, unless it presents a hazard. Dead trees offer wonderful homes to bluebirds, woodpeckers, chickadees, titmice, nuthatches, and other cavity-nesting birds, as well as some small mammals; places for all birds to perch and survey the terrain; and banquets of insects in the bark.

Variety Is the Spice of Wildlife

Your choice of trees and shrubs should be based on the following considerations: pleasing flowers, fragrance, and foliage; yield for wildlife; blossom time and fruiting time; tolerance of heat, cold, and shade; proximity to the existing greenery and the house; suitability to your soil and climate. Fruit is of interest to almost all forms of wildlife, and nearly every tree or bush ending in "-berry" is a source of food.

All flowering shrubs like sun, but many will tolerate light shade or dappled shade from taller trees. Bear in mind that, as with flowers in the herbaceous border that bloom a few weeks earlier in warm areas, flowering shrubs will bloom

Washington Hawthorn

Trees for the Naturalist's Garden

Species	Fruiting Season	Birds or Wildlife
Allegheny serviceberry (shadbush) (*Amelanchier laevis*)	Summer	Bluebird, cardinal, catbird, flicker, mockingbird, oriole, scarlet tanager, thrush, woodpecker
American holly (*Ilex opaca*)	Fall, winter	Bluebird, brown thrasher, catbird, cedar waxwing, flicker, mockingbird, robin, thrush, 37 other species
Beech (*Fagus* spp.)	Fall	Blue jay, cardinal, titmouse, towhee, many others; squirrels, other mammals
Birch (*Betula* spp.)	Fall– spring	Black-capped chickadee, goldfinch, grouse, redpoll, siskin, tanager, titmouse, vireo, warbler, woodpecker; butterflies
Black walnut (*Juglans nigra*)	Fall	Squirrels
Callery pear (*Pyrus calleryana*)	Fall, winter	Many birds; bees

earlier in the South than in the North, and their berries will ripen sooner.

In the tables that follow, many wildlife-attracting trees, shrubs, and vines are listed. In addition to these are the immense Northwest conifers, including Douglas fir, Colorado spruce, Ponderosa pine, and others that reach heights of from 100 to 300 feet and offer cover and nesting for many forms of wildlife, plus cones that provide fall and winter food for songbirds, gamebirds, and mammals.

Attractions and Notes	Mature Height	Hardi- ness Zone
Drooping clusters of white flowers in spring; purplish black fruit like small apples; bright green, oval, 3½-inch-long leaves, which turn bright yellow, orange, and red in fall	20–30 feet	3
Pea-sized, usually single red berries; evergreen spiny leaves 1¾–3 inches long; shrubby; good cover, nesting	To 45 feet	6
Huge, stately trees with smooth gray bark; leaves are shiny green, oval, toothed, 4–7 inches long; some cultivars have copper or purple leaves; beechnuts in prickly burrs 1 inch long	90–100 feet	2–3
Beautiful bark on many birches, white on paper birch, reddish brown on black and river birch; double-toothed, oval, 1⅓–5-inch-long leaves turn clear yellow in fall; birds enjoy small cones, catkins, insects in bark; cover	30–75 feet	2–4
2-inch, round, thick green shells enclose walnuts; compound leaves with 2½–5-inch-long oval-toothed leaflets; good shade tree; hampers growth of other plants in its vicinity	70–150 feet	3
Extremely ornamental tree with glossy green leaves and splendid scarlet to wine red fall color; fine upright form; covered in late spring with single white flowers; marble-sized pears relished by birds	30–50 feet	4

(continued)

Species	Fruiting Season	Birds or Wildlife
Cherry (*Prunus* spp.)	Summer, fall	Bluebird, cedar waxwing, finch, flicker, mockingbird, robin, rose-breasted grosbeak, towhee, vireo; some wildlife; butterflies
Crabapple (*Malus* spp.)	Fall, winter	26 species of bird, including cedar waxwing, hummingbird, mockingbird, robin, and game birds; browsing wildlife
Eastern hackberry (*Celtis occidentalis*)	Winter	Bluebird, brown thrasher, cardinal, flicker, mockingbird, robin, 29 other species; some wildlife
Eastern hemlock (*Tsuga canadensis*)	Fall, winter	Black-capped chickadee, blue jay, eastern phoebe, goldfinch, junco, mourning dove, pine siskin, robin, wood thrush; squirrels, other wildlife
Eastern red cedar (*Juniperus virginiana*)	Fall, winter	Bluebird, cardinal, flicker, mockingbird, purple finch, robin, sparrow, many others; some wildlife
English holly (*Ilex aquifolium*)	Fall, winter	45 species of bird; bees
Flowering dogwood (*Cornus florida*)	Late summer–winter	Bluebird, brown thrasher, cardinal, catbird, cedar waxwing, kingbird, purple finch, robin, towhee, vireo, woodpecker, 75 other species; squirrels, other wildlife; butterflies
Hawthorn (*Crataegus* spp.)	Fall, winter	33 species of bird, including cardinal, cedar waxwing, flicker, hummingbird, mockingbird, yellow-bellied sapsucker; some wildlife; butterflies

Attractions and Notes	Mature Height	Hardi-ness Zone
Numerous 1–1½-inch-wide white to rose pink, single or double spring flowers; red, yellow, or black cherries ⅓–1 inch in diameter; oval to elliptic, 1½–5½-inch-long toothed leaves; young bark glossy and reddish; some weeping forms; hundreds of cultivars	5–40 feet	1–4
Gorgeous clusters of fragrant 1–1½-inch-wide flowers in spring; blooms are white, pink, or rose; ⅓–1-inch-wide red, purplish red, yellow, or greenish crabapples; toothed oval leaves 1¼–4 inches long; some cultivars have purple leaves; others have yellow and orange fall color; cover, nesting	15–40 feet	2–4
Elmlike tree with warty bark; oval, 3–5-inch-long toothed leaves turn yellow in fall; shiny green pea-sized berries turn dark purple when ripe; excellent food source	50–100 feet	2
Handsome evergreen with graceful drooping branches; dark green, shiny needles; smooth ¾-inch-long cones; can be trimmed as a hedge; excellent cover, nesting, food source	25–60 feet	2
Candle-flame shape, aromatic wood and foliage; ⅜-inch needles or scalelike leaves; red-brown, peeling bark; pea-sized, bluish bloomed fruit; dense cover, nesting	40–80 feet	4
Clusters of pea-sized red berries; oval, toothed leaves, shiny green with wavy margins, 1½–2½ inches long; can be grown as a shrub; over 100 cultivars; good cover, nesting	30–50 feet	4–5
Showy flowers with 4 white, pink, or red bracts, 3½–5 inches wide, in spring; elongated scarlet berries in clusters ripen in October; green, oval leaves are wavy, 3–5 inches long, turning deep red in fall; distinctive dark, blocky bark	35 feet	5
Showy 2–3-inch-wide flower clusters in spring; flowers are white to deep red; strong scent; very showy clusters of ½–¾-inch-wide scarlet to bright red berries; lobed and toothed leaves can have excellent orange and scarlet fall color; dense, thorny branches	15–35 feet	3–4

(continued)

Species	Fruiting Season	Birds or Wildlife
Kousa dogwood (*Cornus kousa*)	Late summer, fall	Many birds; squirrels, other wildlife
Linden (*Tilia* spp.)	N/A°	Bees
Maple (*Acer* spp.)	Summer	Bobwhite, cardinal, goldfinch, grosbeak, oriole, pine siskin, purple finch, robin, song sparrow, vireo, woodpecker, yellow-bellied sapsucker, yellow warbler; squirrels, other mammals; bees
Mimosa (*Albizzia julibrissin*)	N/A	Hummingbirds; butterflies
Mountain ash (*Sorbus* spp.)	Late summer, fall	Catbird, cedar waxwing, flicker, robin, 11 other species, including game birds; wildlife; bees
Mulberry (*Morus* spp.)	Summer	Cardinal, cedar waxwing, cuckoo, indigo bunting, oriole, tanager, thrush, vireo, warbler; opossums, raccoon, squirrels
Oak (*Quercus* spp.)	Fall	Blue jay, brown thrasher, crow, grackle, nuthatch, titmouse, woodpecker; squirrels, other wildlife
Pecan (*Carya pecan*)	Fall	Squirrels, other wildlife
Plum (*Prunus* spp.)	Summer	Many birds; some wildlife; browsers (deer, fox, rabbits) eat bark, twigs; butterflies; bees
Shagbark hickory (*Carya ovata*)	Fall	Squirrels, many small mammals; some birds

Attractions and Notes	Mature Height	Hardi-ness Zone
Showy flowers with 4 white, pointed bracts, 2½–3½ inches wide, appear about 3 weeks after the flowering dogwoods; fruit resembles big red raspberries; horizontal habit; scarlet fall color	20 feet	4
Dense, handsome, heart-shaped dark green foliage, 1½–5 inches long; whitish to yellowish, highly fragrant blooms, in clusters of 3 to 7, in summer; hard, pea-sized fruit; fine shade tree	50–120 feet	3
Glorious form and foliage, from the small, palmately leaved Japanese maples to the stately sugar maple; red, yellow, and orange fall color; winged seeds; bark insects; cover, nesting	10–120 feet	1–3
Cotton-candy pink, tufted flowers 1–2 inches wide, in summer; ferny, much-divided foliage, 12–18 inches long; attractive horizontal branching; decorative but messy 5-inch-long pods	20–30 feet	5
Showy, dense clusters of ¼–½-inch-wide red to yellow berries; white flowers in flat-topped clusters 4–7 inches wide, May–June; compound leaves turn red in fall; cover	20–50 feet	2
Blackberrylike white, pinkish violet, red, or purplish red fruit is a favorite, also a mess; broad oval or lobed, coarsely toothed leaves 3–5 inches long; early food for nestlings; good cover, nesting	30–50 feet	1–3
Handsome, long-lived trees with willowlike, fingered, or sharp-lobed shiny green leaves; some species develop striking bronze, scarlet, or deep red fall color; acorns provide winter food; good cover, nesting	40–125 feet	2–6
1½–2½-inch-long, delicious smooth-shelled nuts enclosed in 4-sided husks; compound leaves with 5–7-inch-long oblong leaflets; furrowed bark; over 100 varieties; good shade tree	60–150 feet	5
Profuse ¾-inch single or double white, pink, or mauve flowers in spring; oval, toothed, 1½–2-inch-long leaves; some cultivars have purple leaves; plums from 1 inch in diameter, green, yellow, red, or purple; cover, nesting	15–25 feet	3
Light gray, shaggy bark splits off in plates; compound leaves with 5 oblong leaflets 6–9 inches long; rounded, sweet nuts	80–150 feet	3

(continued)

Species	Fruiting Season	Birds or Wildlife
Sour gum (tupelo, black gum) (*Nyssa sylvatica*)	Fall, winter	Bluebird, brown thrasher, cedar waxwing, flicker, purple finch, robin, towhee, woodpecker; wildlife
Spruce (*Picea* spp.)	Fall, winter	Black-capped chickadee, blue jay, cedar waxwing, evening grosbeak, goldfinch, junco, mockingbird, mourning dove, pine siskin, purple finch, robin, sparrow, yellow-bellied sapsucker, warbler; squirrels
Sweet gum (*Liquidambar styraciflua*)	Fall, winter	Cardinal, chickadee, goldfinch, junco, mourning dove, purple finch, towhee, white-throated sparrow
Tulip tree (tulip poplar) (*Liriodendron tulipifera*)	Fall	Some birds; squirrels, other wildlife; butterflies; hummingbirds may sip from flowers
White pine (*Pinus strobus*)	Fall, winter	Blue jay, brown thrasher, chickadee, grosbeak, nuthatch, warbler, game birds; squirrels, other mammals

Blueberry

Shrubs for the Naturalist's Garden

Species	Fruiting Season	Birds or Wildlife
American cranberry bush (highbush cranberry) (*Viburnum trilobum*)	Fall, winter	Bluebird, cardinal, cedar waxwing, mockingbird, robin, white-throated sparrow, 28 other species

Attractions and Notes	Mature Height	Hardiness Zone
Graceful tree with shiny green leaves, 3–5 inches long, that turn brilliant scarlet or brick red in fall; dense greenish flower clusters in late spring; blue-purple, ⅔-inch-long fruit in small clusters; good cover, nesting	60–90 feet	3
Highly ornamental evergreen trees; also dwarf forms; needles ½–1 inch long, shining dark to bluish green; cones are 1½–7 inches long, greenish brown, glossy brown, or brownish violet; excellent cover, nesting; food source	50–150 feet	1–3
3–7 lobed starlike leaves, 5–7 inches long and toothed, turn brilliant yellow, orange, scarlet, red, and purple in fall; fruit is a macelike ball 1½ inches wide	70–120 feet	3
2½-inch-wide orange and greenish tuliplike flowers in summer, followed by a conelike cluster of seeds; splendid shield-shaped 3–5½-inch notched leaves turn clear yellow in fall; straight, handsome trunks with distinctive plated bark	80–150 feet	3
Massive evergreen with tiers of branches; blue-green, 4–5-inch-long needles in clusters of 5; cylindrical 4–7-inch-long cones; impractical for small property; good cover, nesting; favored roost of owls	90–150 feet	2

Attractions and Notes	Mature Height	Hardiness Zone
Clusters of scarlet berries; 4-inch-wide, flat, white flower clusters; 3–5-inch, bright green maplelike leaves turn scarlet in fall; nest site	4–10 feet	3–7

(continued)

Species	Fruiting Season	Birds or Wildlife
Autumn olive (*Elaeagnus umbellata*)	Fall	Cardinal, catbird, finch, mockingbird, thrush, tree swallow, waxwing, several game birds, 15 other species; some wildlife; bees
Azalea (*Rhododendron* species and hybrids)	N/A°	Bees; butterflies; hummingbirds
Bayberry (*Myrica pensylvanica*)	Fall, winter	Catbird, chipping sparrow, junco, song sparrow, thrush; wildlife
Blackberry (*Rubus allegheniensis*)	Midsummer, fall	Catbird, oriole, pheasant, sparrow, thrush, towhee, vireo, woodpecker, many others
Black haw (*Viburnum prunifolium*)	Fall, winter	Bluebird, cardinal, cedar waxwing, mockingbird, robin, white-throated sparrow, some game birds
Buckthorn (*Rhamnus cathartica*)	Fall	Many birds
Butterfly bush (*Buddleia davidii*)	N/A	Butterfly banquet; bees, many other insects
Common lilac (*Syringa vulgaris*)	N/A	Butterflies; hummingbirds
Doublefile viburnum (*Viburnum plicatum* var. *tomentosum*)	Fall, winter	Bluebird, finch, flicker, robin, thrush, waxwing, woodpecker
Elderberry (*Sambucus canadensis*)	Late summer, fall	Bluebird, blue jay, brown thrasher, cardinal, catbird, mockingbird, robin, rose-breasted grosbeak, many others; butterflies; some wildlife

Attractions and Notes	Mature Height	Hardiness Zone
Fragrant, yellowish white, ¾-inch flowers in spring; brown berries turn red in fall; elliptic 3½-inch-long leaves are silvery on the undersides; a heavy-fruiting cultivar is Cardinal; thick cover, nesting; excellent food source	To 18 feet	4
1½–2½-inch funnel-shaped flowers borne in clusters in spring; white, pink, red, magenta, lilac, yellow, apricot, orange; some forms are evergreen; deciduous varieties have lovely bright yellow, orange, or red fall color; an early feast	3–10 feet, depending on species and cultivar	5–7
Aromatic 3–4-inch-long leaves remain on plants until winter; highly aromatic waxy grayish berries in clusters; a favorite food source	3–10 feet	3
Delicious purple fruit to 1 inch long; lovely white appleblossom flowers in spring; good nesting and cover when thick but viciously thorny unless a thornless cultivar is planted; a favorite food	1–9 feet	5
4-inch-wide, half-moon-shaped, creamy white flower clusters in spring; clusters of white berries ripen bluish black; broad oval, finely toothed leaves 2–3 inches long	10–15 feet	4
Oval, dark, glossy green 1⅗- to 3-inch-long leaves; small yellowish green flowers in umbels in May; ¼-inch-wide black berries	12–15 feet	3
Slender, nodding 5–12-inch-long flower spikes summer to fall; lilac with orange throats, pink, white, dark purple, and reddish purple; fragrant; 6–9-inch-long finely toothed green lance-shaped leaves with felty white undersides	6–8 feet	5–9
Highly fragrant 6–8-inch-long clusters of lilac, white, pink, purple, or blue flowers in spring; heart-shaped to oval 2–6-inch-long leaves	To 15 feet	4
Horizontal branches bear highly ornamental flat clusters of 3-inch-wide creamy white flowers in spring; red fruit turns black when ripe; excellent reddish purple fall color on 4-inch-long leaves	8–10 feet	5
Clusters of ⅙-inch purple-black berries are an excellent food source; white flower clusters to 4 inches wide in summer; toothed compound leaves	6–10 feet	4

(continued)

Species	Fruiting Season	Birds or Wildlife
Firethorn (*Pyracantha coccinea; P. fortuneana*)	Fall	Bluebird, brown thrasher, catbird, mockingbird, purple finch, robin, sparrow, many others; bees
Highbush blueberry (*Vaccinium corymbosum*)	Summer, fall	Bluebird, blue jay, catbird, flycatcher, grouse, mockingbird, oriole, sparrow, tanager, thrush, towhee, turkey, waxwing, woodpecker; some wildlife
Japanese barberry (*Berberis thunbergii*)	Fall, winter	Cardinal, catbird, cedar waxwing, evening grosbeak, mockingbird, robin, sparrow
Mockorange (*Philadelphus coronarius* and *P. ×lemoinei*)	N/A	Butterflies; bees
Raspberry (*Rubus idaeus; R. occidentalis*)	Early summer; some cultivars bear again in fall	Black-capped chickadee, bluebird, blue jay, brown thrasher, cardinal, cedar waxwing, evening grosbeak, hermit thrush, orioles, phoebe, robin, numerous others; bees
Rhododendron (*Rhododendron* species and hybrids)	N/A	Hummingbirds; butterflies
Rugosa rose (*Rosa rugosa*)	Fall, winter	Bluebird, brown thrasher, cardinal, cedar waxwing, evening grosbeak, goldfinch, junco, mockingbird, robin, song sparrow
Snowberry (*Symphoricarpos albus*)	Fall, winter	Bobwhite, cedar waxwing, grosbeak, robin, thrush, 20 other species; deer
Tatarian honeysuckle (*Lonicera tatarica*)	Midsummer–fall	Bluebird, cedar waxwing, hummingbird, mockingbird, purple finch, robin, yellow-bellied sapsucker; butterflies; bees

Attractions and Notes	Mature Height	Hardiness Zone
Heavy clusters of bright red, orange-red, orange, or yellow ⅓–½-inch berries; small white flower clusters in spring; oval 1–3-inch-long leaves; can be trained to a wall or fence; some cover, nesting	10–15 feet	6–7
Abundant bluish black fruit with a powdery bloom, much relished by birds as well as people; glossy 2–3-inch-long oval leaves turn yellow to a very striking red in fall; ⅓-inch white to pinkish urn-shaped flowers; a big favorite	8–12 feet	4
Bright red berries; ⅓-inch yellow flowers in spring; ½–1½-inch-long leaves turn brilliant scarlet in fall; makes a dense hedge; good cover, nesting; Atropurpurea and Crimson Pygmy have purple leaves, Aurea has yellow leaves	3–6 feet	4–8
Creamy white, highly fragrant, 1½-inch-wide flowers with showy yellow stamens, borne in 3–7 flowered terminal clusters in spring; 1½–4-inch-long oval leaves; dark brown, peeling bark; cover	To 10 feet	5
Exquisitely delicious black, red, or gold fruit, relished by birds as well as people; some cover; bees enjoy white flowers in spring; 3–5 ovate toothed leaflets with whitish undersides; canes are prickly	1–9 feet	3–4
Dense evergreen foliage; lance-shaped 1–6-inch-long leaves; showy, sometimes fragrant bell-shaped flowers in clusters 6–10 inches wide; lilac purple, pink, rosy purple, magenta, or white flowers in spring; big bushes make good cover	3–10 feet, depending on species and cultivar	4–6
Single or double 3½-inch-wide, red to white roses in summer; fragrant, continuous flowers; plentiful 1-inch-wide orange-red rose hips; interesting dark green wrinkled leaves turn red in fall; as hedge, provides good nesting, cover, and erosion control	4–6 feet	2
Attractive white berries like little mothballs, in small clusters; small pinkish flowers; oval 1–2-inch-long leaves	To 4 feet	3
White to pink ¾–1-inch-long fragrant flowers in spring; ornamental red berries an early source of food for birds; 1–2½-inch-long oblong leaves; arching habit provides nesting and cover	8–10 feet	4

Grapevine

Vines for the Naturalist's Garden

Species	Fruiting Season	Birds or Wildlife
Grape (*Vitis* spp.)	Fall	Blackbird, blue jay, cardinal, cedar waxwing, cuckoo, finch, game birds, grackle, oriole, tanager, thrush, vireo, warbler; deer, raccoon, other wildlife
Hall's honeysuckle (*Lonicera japonica* 'Halliana')	Summer, fall	Bluebird, brown thrasher, cedar waxwing, evening grosbeak, goldfinch, hummingbird, junco, mockingbird, robin, many others; bees; butterflies
Morning glory (*Ipomoea tricolor*)	N/A°	Hummingbirds; bees
Trumpet honeysuckle (*Lonicera sempervirens*)	Summer, fall	Hummingbirds; butterflies; bees
Trumpet vine (*Campsis radicans*)	N/A	Hummingbirds; butterflies; bees
Virginia creeper (*Parthenocissus quinquefolia*)	Late summer–winter	Catbird, chickadee, finch, flycatcher, mockingbird, scarlet tanager, tree swallow, vireo, warbler, white-breasted nuthatch, woodpecker, 25 other species

°Not applicable

Attractions and Notes	Mature Height	Hardiness Zone
4–8-inch-long, medium to blue-green, palmately lobed leaves; green, red, golden, blue-black, or purple grapes; fruit, cover, and nesting for wildlife; a favorite food	50–100 feet; usually pruned to 12–20 feet	3–5
Fragrant white 1–1½-inch-long flowers fade to yellow; 1–3-inch oval leaves; black berries; can be rampant; best for banks, fences, trellises, or railings	20–30 feet	5
Large, heart-shaped leaves; 4–5-inch, trumpet-shaped flowers in purplish blue, white, lavender, pink, or blue, from early summer to frost; this climber needs support	10–15 feet	8
2-inch-long trumpet-shaped flowers, orange or red outside, yellow inside, borne in terminal clusters in late spring through summer; orange to scarlet fruit; evergreen in mild climates	To 50 feet	4
3½-inch-long, 2-inch-wide orange-scarlet trumpet flowers borne in clusters in late summer; very showy; provides cover	To 30 feet	4
Blue-black berries; 5-leaflet clusters, 2–5 inches long, turn scarlet in fall; good cover and nesting	30–50 feet	4

Chapter 3

The Naturalist's Flower Garden

And time remembered is grief forgotten,
And frosts are slain and flowers begotten,
And in green underwood and cover
Blossom by blossom the spring begins.

Algernon Charles Swinburne,
"Atalanta in Calydon"

Trees and shrubs are only two facets of the naturalist's garden. For many people—and for butterflies, moths, bees, other insects, and hummingbirds—the focus of the yard is the flower garden. The shimmer of myriad colors and textures sets off the trees, shrubs, walls, and other architectural features of the landscape. The beauty and perfume of the flowers delight the senses. And the season-long supply of nectar and pollen sustains wildlife.

But how does one plan a beautiful flower border that will attract wildlife and bloom all season? This chapter will provide the essentials you need to plan, prepare, and plant your flower garden. Minimanuals for perennials, biennials, and annuals list reliable favorites with information on height, color, bloom time, regional and special characteristics, and attractions for wildlife.

Good planning takes many other factors into account besides plant choices, including soil building, siting, sun and shade, and plant placement. But the first consideration—at least if you are being logical and not just rushing for the catalogs—is your climate.

Climate in the Flower Garden

My own garden is in the Northeast, in lower New York State, where the last frost date is anywhere from the end of April to mid-May. It is important to ascertain the last frost date in your area, as this, plus a little bit more time for the earth to warm up, depending on local conditions, is your signal for the start of spring planting. Your country agricultural or cooperative Extension agent, the local weather bureau, newspapers, nursery staff, and seasoned gardeners are all sources for the last frost date in spring and the first in fall for all sections of the United States and part of Canada. You can also find maps showing freeze-free areas of the country in spring and fall that indicate when it is safe to plant.

There are also two maps that divide the entire country and lower Canada into hardiness zones according to average minimum winter temperatures. One map was compiled by the Arnold Arboretum, Harvard University, in 1967, and the other by the USDA (U.S. Department of Agriculture) and Agriculture Canada, in 1960. They differ slightly in the numbering and placement of climate zones. Most nurseries and references use the USDA Hardiness Zone Map. I use these maps but also rely on local sources to supply the information I need on temperature, forecast, and possibility of heavy rain or snow. Whatever map you use, bear in mind that actually there are no sharp demarcations between climate zones, and there is always some overlapping. Plants that flourish in the zone next to yours may do nicely in your garden as well.

Microclimates

Every garden has microclimates—small areas that differ in climate due to amounts of sun and shade they receive, protection from wind, and retention of water that may freeze in winter or create excessive humidity in summer. The slope of the land and the shelter of a wall both make a difference to plants. On the same plot of land, a plant may languish in a hot, dry spot but perform with gusto in another with filtered sunlight or part shade; a flower native to the South may surprise and delight the Yankee gardener in a sunny, protected spot with a southern exposure. Average temperatures and general climatic descriptions do not indicate effects of severe bouts of heat or cold, drought or rainfall, and other factors in your particular locality, but they do provide reasonable guidelines for planting.

Customized Climates

Gardeners in mild-winter climates have earlier springs, earlier spring planting dates, and longer periods of bloom for many species. They can also sow many seeds and plant seedlings in late summer or fall for late winter or early spring bloom. In cold climates, gardeners must wait until the ground has warmed up in spring and the danger of frost is well past.

Many plants classified as annuals perform as perennials in warm climates and don't lose their foliage. Occasionally in cold climates, an annual such as a snapdragon will survive a winter that is not too severe, provided it has been protected with mulch or branches, but this is rare. I leave snaps that are still alive and green in the ground, snugly blanketed. Some make it through the winter and bloom earlier next season than nursery seedlings. Gardeners in cold places and high elevations are happy enough to see their reliable perennials and bulbs return to bloom another year! Of special interest to gardeners everywhere are the desirable annuals, such as cleome, annual candytuft, sweet alyssum, bachelor's buttons, and garden balsam, that self-sow and reappear to flower again. Plants that retain some of their seed provide winter food for resident and migrant birds, as do shrubs and trees with fall and winter berries and seeds.

All plant material, of course, cannot do equally well in all parts of the country. Certain bulbs, perennials, and shrubs need cold winters and freezing or near-freezing temperatures in order to become dormant and set flowers and fruit. For example, a number of delightful spring-blooming bulbs, such as hyacinth, tulip, snowdrop, crocus, and lily-of-the-valley, need the chill of winter to induce bloom. In warm climates, the gardener buys these bulbs in autumn and stores them in the refrigerator for a month or more before planting, forcing them to bloom. Peonies, Oriental poppies, and lilacs bloom best in cold-weather areas. Conversely, some like it hot; for example, oleanders, bougainvilleas, and camellias are unlikely candidates for successful growing in northern regions, and gardenias, cymbidiums, and cinerarias exist only as pampered houseplants or greenhouse plants in cold climates.

Climate and Wildlife

Naturally, plants are not the only things that are affected by climate. If you live in the Deep South, you'll have chameleons in your shrubbery; in the mid-South, there will be black-, blue-, and cream-lined skinks; in the West, horned toads; but if you live as far north as Pennsylvania, you'll have no lizards at all. On the other hand, the northern states are hosts to pheasants and Canada geese that are only legends in the South, and northerners can watch the great hawk migrations that fill the autumn air with falcons, hawks, and eagles.

If you live in the North, the raucous scoldings in your treetops may be made by red squirrels rather than the gray and fox squirrels that predominate farther south. You may see a porcupine if you live near a forest, a beaver if you have water on your property, or a moose ambling confusedly through your field in summer. But you'll have to take a vacation in Florida to find the alligators and flamingos beloved of television producers. The woodchuck that raids your garden in the East gives pride of place to the marauding gopher in the West. Wherever you live, you're likely to find subspecies of birds and other animals adapted specifically to your area.

Enjoy your particular wildlife just as you do the plants that grow and bloom best in your yard.

The short summers of high-elevation regions, the early summers of hot desert areas, the cool summers and mild winters of coastal California, and the long, bitter New England winters, to name but a few of the widely and wildly diverse regions of this vast country, all bring their own special gardening challenges and pleasures. Find out about the topography, climate, seasonal changes, and best planting times for your particular area. Above all—and certainly below all— remember that no matter what you grow, it cannot do its best in poor soil. Providing nutrients and conditioners is the prerequisite for a productive garden that is also attractive to wildlife.

Designing the Flower Garden

If you are starting an herbaceous border or flowerbed from scratch, it would be wise to make a plan on paper, indicating the placement of the plants that you choose. First, of course, you will need to do some homework so that your choices will be the most pleasing to you and the creatures you wish to attract, and so that you can make certain that they have rich soil to grow in.

Since most plants like sun, the ideal location for the bed in cool-climate regions is one that faces south. In any case, the bed should get five to six hours of full sun a day and filtered sun (dappled shade) for the rest of the day. Where the climate is hot, more shade is desirable, but deep shade from big trees and competition from tree roots must be avoided everywhere.

Whether you are starting a new bed or adding to an established one, it's wise to visit nurseries, see neighbors' plantings or other local displays, and consult with your county agricultural agent, village naturalist, Department of Environmental Conservation, or other local specialists to find out what plants do best in your locality, how large they become when mature, which colors you prefer, and what is their appeal to the local wildlife.

Front, Center, and Rear

Perennials are particularly well displayed against a background of dark green evergreens such as yews, forming a low hedge; a wooden fence or brick or stone wall on which berry-bearing vines can clamber; or a mixture of flowering shrubs such as forsythia, viburnum, mockorange, deutzia, and lilac. This kind of background attracts many birds and other creatures seeking cover, safety, and food. If it is not available, you can create a bed where plants can be seen and tended from all sides. In such an island bed, the taller plants are placed in the middle. In all other beds, no matter what is in back of them, the tallest flowers are placed at the rear and the shortest in front.

High-rise flowers, like exclamation points, draw attention and lend dramatic accents. Among the tallest are the biennials hollyhock and foxglove; perennials including some of the lilies, daylilies, bee balm, solidago (garden goldenrod), and delphinium; and the annuals cosmos, cleome, tithonia, and sunflower.

Low front-of-the-border perennials include coral bells, whose slender stems rise from a low rosette of leaves; border pinks; creeping phlox; and primroses, which require some dampness and shade. The biennial (sometimes annual) pansy is an early bloomer. Annuals chiefly grace the border's edge and attract insects there. I like alyssum and ageratum because they reseed copiously from year to year. Others that self-sow are dwarf marigold and forget-me-not. Those I replace each year are verbena, creeping zinnia, and lantana. I love to see a potpourri of color spilling out of the border like a multicolored ribbon.

In the middle, between front and rear, are the vast majority of perennials. Some are most effective in groups of three of a kind, such as the narrow-spired blue sage, veronica, and liatris. Larger plants with wider leaves, such as gloriosa

An island bed is a delightful "island" of flowers in a "sea" of lawn. As it can be seen from all sides, its layout is different from that of a border, which is seen only from the front and sides. The tallest plants are at the center of an island bed, with progressively shorter flowers leading out to the edges.

daisy, those with immense flower heads like phlox, or any that flaunt an extremely vivid color, such as cardinal flower, may stand alone.

Spacing

The majority of perennials of intermediate size (1½ to 3 feet tall) are spaced about 1½ to 2 feet apart; the small ones (6 inches to 1 foot) at the front about 10 inches apart; and those that grow very large (3 to 6 feet), for example, hollyhock, loosestrife, Shasta daisy, gloriosa daisy, delphinium, and the annuals cosmos and giant marigold, 2 to 2½ feet apart. But don't let the spacing worry you. If perennials eventually become crowded, they can be dug up and divided. The divisions can be placed elsewhere in the garden or given away. Be sure to leave spaces for plenty of annuals, for they will give you more blooms and a longer season of bloom than most perennials, thus making more nectar, pollen, and seeds available to wildlife.

Informality Is the Keynote

The naturalist's garden is not a formal one. Clipped shrubs, geometrically straight edges, extreme neatness, coordination of colors, and special effects carefully arranged all take a lot of extra time and energy and do not contribute to the attractions for wildlife. I think all garden flowers are beautiful, as long as they are healthy! I don't follow a color scheme, but I do prefer pastels such as rose, pink, lavender, pale yellow, and blue, with some white. These are cool, tranquil shades that appear most charming and ethereal as the sun goes down. But I'm also fond of the bright, bold red, orange, salmon, and gold shades that add vivid accents to the border. A wide range of color draws in a wide range of butterflies, moths, bees, other insects, and hummingbirds.

What is most important about a flowerbed? Lush bloom on a diversity of vigorous plants in rich, healthy soil, with plenty of appeal for many kinds of wildlife. When you are designing, remember that you can always make changes. A garden need never be static. And it's fun to experiment.

Preparing the Flower Border

Hope is a necessary ingredient in gardening, for nature is often capricious, and our best efforts may be unsuccessful or need repeating. Hope, patience, and work—these are the Three Graces of spring. It is always an exciting time, full of renewal and anticipation, of warming earth, swelling buds, early blooms, and the bustle and song of nest-building birds.

On the first balmy day, overeager gardeners are tempted to rush to the nearest nursery, load up the car with seedlings, and plunk them into holes in the ground. Alas, if it

were only that simple. The garden season really begins in fall
with soil preparation.

Start with the Soil

Most authorities recommend that you test your soil to determine whether it is acid, alkaline, or blessedly neutral, and in
what elements it may be deficient. The gardener can buy a
kit for this purpose or send a soil sample to the state or county
agricultural agent or state university Extension office. The
test shows the pH of the soil. The pH scale ranges from 0 (extremely acid) to 14 (extremely alkaline). Neutral is 7, and
most annuals and perennials perform best in soil that tests
between 6.7 and 7 or slightly higher; most vegetables, too. To
counteract high acidity, add ground limestone. To reduce
alkalinity, add ground sulfur and organic materials of high
acid content, such as pine needles, peat, sawdust, and decomposed oak leaves.

On balance, I think it likely that if your garden is well
nourished and well conditioned, loaded with natural ingredients, replete with earthworms, lady bugs, and other beneficial insects, and if the organic input is constantly renewed,
you should be able to grow splendid flowers and vegetables.
Eleanor Perényi, a writer-gardener of vast experience and
author of *Green Thoughts: A Writer in the Garden* (Random House, 1983), concurs. She uses only compost, cow manure, bonemeal, and seaweed in her Connecticut coast garden
and has never felt the need for soil analysis. She says, "I
would rather assume that plants, like animals and people, are
hungry most of the time and need a balanced diet. I rely on
natural substances to supply that and leave it to the plants to
pick and choose what they want."

Feeding the Soil

Countless billions of microorganisms are at work in every
spadeful of soil, breaking down all matter so that plants can
take up nutrients they need. A soil fertilized with chemicals
and drenched with pesticides and herbicides is poor soil,

incapable of sustaining as many of these minute but essential organisms and earthworms as are present in organically enriched soil. All your efforts at gardening in worn-out soil without added organic matter will have poor to mediocre results. Why waste your gardening energy and enthusiasm on a disappointment?

You can't go wrong adding plentiful amounts of organic materials to your soil in any case, and as for compost, you can never have too much! If you haven't started a compost pile yet, it's high time. This marvelous brown stuff, cooked to a turn and blended into your flowerbed, will produce thrilling results. For specifics on composting and soil enrichment, see Chapter 10, The Stuff of Life.

Planting Time

Your last frost date, plus a few mild, sunny days, is the prelude to planting. But first, check your soil for readiness. Make a ball of earth and let it drop. If it holds together in a lump, it is still too wet. If it crumbles apart, you've got the green light. Planting too soon in cold, wet soil does not ensure you a head start; on the contrary. Seeds may rot or just lie about totally inert, waiting for the temperature to climb up out of the fifties. Seedlings will grow weak or spindly or be in a state of arrested development.

The flower border that was roughly dug in late fall and then organically mulched is the bed that is in the best shape the next spring. A rough surface over winter allows more penetration of oxygen and nutrients into the soil. In spring, turn under the mulch, and add more organic amendments to the soil. Soils are rarely perfect, and all of them benefit by generous helpings of humus (decomposed organic matter). As you turn these in when you fork or spade over the border, you will doubtless turn out an assortment of sticks, stones, weeds, grass, and earthworms. The worms, at least, are cause for rejoicing; their tunneling and castings make them invaluable assets to a well-aerated and fertile soil.

Keep a sharp lookout for self-sown plantlets from last year's flowers. Very likely, you will see some welcome volunteers, such as Johnny-jump-ups, hollyhocks, cleome, and annual candytuft, donated by nature's shed-and-spread propagation or from seed you sprinkled or sowed in the fall. (See the section on annuals later in this chapter.) Also be prepared for some disappointments—a cherished mum or delphinium may not have survived the winter. Perhaps next time, with thicker mulch and better protection, this won't happen.

In the spring, you may add a narrow ring of balanced organic fertilizer such as compost around old, established perennials. Scratch it lightly into the soil, then water well.

The organic material and conditioners have made your soil rich yet light, crumbly, and porous—in a word, friable. Break up any remaining lumps, rake the surface reasonably smooth and level, and take a breather. You've earned it! Now you're ready for planting.

Choosing and Using Perennials

Perennials are the backbone of the flower border. They live for years, some for decades, increasing in size and beauty and also in numbers, for they can be divided and replanted. Once well established, they need little care. Although many perennials have a shorter period of bloom than annuals, they can be chosen to give a succession of bloom from May into October, some even earlier and some later than that. By planting a spectrum of perennials, you will provide a continual source of nectar and pollen for butterflies, bees, other insects, and hummingbirds, and food plants for insect larvae. Most will tolerate partial shade, or less than full sun, all day.

Choosing perennials is an exhilarating experience for beginner and more experienced gardener alike. They are an important investment in color, fragrance, and places in the garden landscape for wildlife, as well as you, to enjoy for years to come. It is worth your while to do some homework before you buy.

Browsing through catalogs is fun and informative. But don't let yourself be carried away on a tidal wave of gorgeous photographs and glorious purple (and pink, red, blue, and yellow) flowery prose. It's educational and enjoyable to visit nurseries and garden centers, observe what flourishes in your locality, talk to some old hands at gardening, and bone up on what you need to know with well-illustrated garden manuals and a gardening encyclopedia. The naturalist/gardener will want to make many choices that will be attractive to birds, butterflies, moths, and bees. (See the Perennial, Biennial, and Annual Minimanuals for help in choosing flowers for wildlife.)

Make a sketch of your flower garden, showing where the perennials are situated or where you wish to put new ones, with notations as to sizes, colors, times of bloom, and attractions for wildlife. Note also those that should be divided and replanted this year (see the section, Perennials: Division and Multiplication, on page 41). A gardening friend or local garden club member may be happy to share or trade some extra divisions or seed with you; this is worth looking into as you make your plans. Leave space on the diagram for annuals, wildflowers, and vegetables if desired.

Change and Innovation

Don't be timid about making changes and trying something new. A garden is not sacrosanct. It is composed of living things subject to the vagaries of weather, to the welcome or unwelcome intrusions of insects and animals, and to our own ministrations. The flower border is in a constant state of growth and change. Its needs and responsiveness vary from one year to the next, from one season to another, even from one part of the garden to another.

A gardener should be flexible. If a perennial doesn't flourish where it is, or doesn't delight the eye, then move it to another place, offer it to a gardening friend, or add it to the compost pile, and replace it with something lovelier to look at. Nothing need be a constant if you don't love it. Off with its head—and out with its root. Don't be afraid to take a chance. That's part of the excitement of gardening!

Do you yearn for a bleeding heart, but feel that it would be impractical because the neighbor's bleeding heart stopped beating after the first season? Perhaps it was placed in a dry, sunny spot where it was doomed from the start. Were you warned that a flower you long for usually doesn't prosper in your climate? Try it for the fun of it. If it doesn't survive, it can be replaced with another perennial. For the pleasure it may bring and the slight expense involved, it is surely worth a try—and it just might be a triumph!

So introduce some new perennials, and cherish and propagate the solid, well-established clumps of handsome old favorites. The herbaceous border depends on the perennials' relative permanency and stunning accents.

Perennial Seasons

Few things mark the seasons as clearly as perennials. As I walk about my garden in early April, it is hard to say which gives me the biggest thrill—the sea of spring bulbs in bloom, the heavenly scent of hyacinths in the air, the foamy pink cloud of the weeping cherry, the pointed red noses of the peonies, or the volunteer columbines just beginning to show themselves. I think it has to be the peonies. They have greeted me each spring with huge, magnificent, fragrant blooms for more than a quarter of a century.

By the middle of June, the peonies have finished blooming and other perennials are taking over the succession of bloom. Although not many are as long lived, most hardy perennials will give you joy for a number of years and, with dividing and replanting and the proper nourishment, can be perpetuated almost indefinitely. That's why they're called perennials!

Of course, as with annuals and shrubs, the naturalist/ gardener will wish to invest most heavily with the space, resources, and time available in perennials that give pleasure not only to the people who see them but also to the birds, butterflies, bees, and other welcome garden residents or visitors who are seeking food and water, shelter, and safe places in which to bear their young.

Perennials:
Division and Multiplication

All perennials benefit by division every few years and will reward your efforts with more vigorous growth and more bountiful flowers. Spring is the time to divide and replant overgrown perennials that bloom in late summer and fall, such as phlox, chrysanthemum, and hardy aster. Those that bloom in spring and early summer, such as iris, primrose, and daylily, are candidates for division in late summer or fall.

Decide where you want to put divisions of the parent plant, and dig two or three ample holes. Mix the soil from the holes with some peat moss and a handful of bonemeal or compost, and add a little to the bottom of each hole. The large plant, carefully lifted, can be pulled, cut, or pried apart with two garden forks into two, three, or more sections, each with some strong roots, eyes (if appropriate), and stems. Use the original hole, properly prepared, for one of the pieces. Discard the unproductive or woody center part of the plant. Roots should have plenty of room to spread out in their new homes. Fill in with good soil, firm it snugly about roots, and water well. Make a slight earth "saucer" around the plant to help trap rain or water; later on this can be flattened out. And

Dividing a daylily. Lift the plant from the ground. Insert two garden forks back to back in the crown of the plant, and rock them until the root mass is pried apart. Continue until you have as many divisions as you want, but make sure each has a strong root system.

don't consider the job finished until you tuck an identifying label in the ground by each plant!

Divide and conquer—that's the motto for all rangy perennials, with the exception of Oriental poppies, bleeding heart, and baby's breath, which dislike being moved and live happily ever after in one spot.

Replanting

Dividing and replanting should never be undertaken in the middle of a hot, sunny day or in a strong wind; in fact, all plants brought into the garden or moved about at any time will recover from transplant shock much quicker under cloudy skies or in late afternoon. A nip of a liquid fertilizer like fish emulsion in their drinking water gives them a lift. Always have the planting hole prepared before removing the plant from its container or from one spot to another.

Sometimes a plant may have outgrown its container and become potbound, with roots twisting round and round. You will need to cautiously loosen up these roots and trim back any that are excessively long, broken, or damaged before planting. (For more on planting from containers, see the section on annuals later in the chapter.) Settle them into prepared planting holes as described. And remember, plants are tender living things whose roots will suffer if exposed, so remove them from their containers one at a time and water immediately after planting.

Continuing Care

Established plants as well as newcomers will benefit from regular feedings through the summer. Side-dress your flowers with aged manure or compost monthly, or water with fish emulsion, liquid seaweed, compost tea, or manure tea every three weeks. Stop feeding at summer's end, as plants must harden off to withstand the rigors of winter.

Once taller perennials such as New England asters, lupines, peonies, lilies, dahlias, delphiniums, and cardinal flowers are up, you may need to stake them to keep them upright through onslaughts of wind and rain. Tie tall plants to 4- to 6-foot-tall bamboo or wood stakes with soft twine. Tall annuals such as cosmos, giant marigolds, and zinnias may also need staking.

Making Minimanual Choices

I made a selection of perennials, biennials, and annuals for the Minimanual listings that follow out of hundreds of possible choices, based on their suitability to a variety of growing conditions and climates, their attractions for wildlife, and the pleasure their beauty, fragrance, and other qualities give to the gardener. The listings provide a guide to heights, colors, seasons of bloom, sun and shade preferences, and other characteristics. If specific wildlife are not listed with a flower, it is probably a draw for a variety of small insects and potential larval food for butterflies and moths.

PERENNIAL MINIMANUAL

Perennial Flowers

Astilbe (*Astilbe* ×*arendsii*): 2 to 4 feet tall. White, pink, red or lavender blooms. Blooms June and July. Tall, elegant plumy spires. Plants need moist, peaty soil and partial shade, especially in South or hot climates. Tends to spread. Zones 4–8.

Baby's Breath (*Gypsophila paniculata*): 2 to 3½ feet tall. Clouds of delicate, tiny white or pink flowers on slender stems add soft airiness to border. Blooms June and July. Full sun. Long lived; do not disturb. Zones 4–8.

Balloonflower (*Platycodon grandiflorus*): 1½ to 2 feet tall. White, violet-blue, lavender-blue (most common) or pink blooms. Unusual balloon-shaped buds open to star-shaped blossoms in July and August. Gray-green foliage. Shade- and drought-tolerant, especially in hot climates. Shoots come up late in spring; place label by plant to mark location. Zones 3–8. Bees, other insects will visit.

Bee Balm (*Monarda didyma*): 2 to 3 feet tall. Red, violet, purple, pink or white blooms. Blooms July and August. Foliage has pungent, minty scent. Full sun or light shade, moist soil. Bears watching, as it spreads aggressively. Zones 4–9. Clusters of tubular petals are one of the biggest attractions to hummingbirds in the garden and much favored by bees and butterflies. Also a wildflower.

Bleeding Heart (*Dicentra spectabilis*): 1½ to 3 feet tall. Deep rose, heart-shaped flowers with white protruding tips hang from gracefully curved stems. Alba has white flowers. Blooms April to June. Pretty, ferny foliage. Likes moist soil, light shade; not fond of very hot regions. Suitable for cold winters. Very long-lived in temperate zones, where every garden should have at least one. Zones 3–7.

Butterfly Weed (*Asclepias tuberosa*): 1 to 2 feet tall. Clusters of tiny brilliant orange or yellow-orange flowers in July and August. Happy in dry, sandy soil; drought-tolerant. Fragrant. Self-sows. Cut down spent stalks; plant blooms again in late summer. Prefers full sun. Zones 3–8. Irresistibly attractive to hummingbirds, and to most butterflies, bees and other insects. Also a wildflower.

Candytuft (*Iberis sempervirens*): 4 to 9 inches tall. Clusters of tiny white flowers in May and June. Low mounds of needlelike, glossy evergreen foliage. Full sun. Zones 3–9. Lovely, fragrant flowers attract butterflies, bees and other insects.

Cardinal Flower (*Lobelia cardinalis*): 2 to 4 feet tall. Fireengine red tubular flowers on tall spikes rising from a basal rosette of leaves. Blooms July to September. Partial shade to full sun and moist soil. Zones 4–8. Will lure hummingbirds down from the skies. Also a wildflower.

Chrysanthemum, Garden or **Hardy Mum** (*Chrysanthemum* ×*morifolium*): 14 inches to 2 feet tall. Single or double flowers in white, yellow, orchid-lavender, scarlet, red, purple, pink, orange or apricot. Plain and fancy petals. Pinch back tips several times during growing season for bushier plants, more blooms. Some species start to bloom in late August; most will flower September to frost, one of the last flowers in bloom; an autumn standby. Pungent scent. Full sun. Give winter protection in colder climates. Low cushion mums are nice for the front of the border. Plant annuals nearby for summer bloom. Zones 4–8.

Columbine (*Aquilegia* ×*hybrida*): 1½ to 2½ feet tall. Blooms are pink, yellow, red, blue, purple or combinations. Delicate spring charmer blooms in May and June. Moist soil and light shade are desirable. Self-sows freely. Suitable for cold winters. Zones 3–8. Unusual blossoms end in long "spurs," a great attraction to hummingbirds as well as bumblebees, butterflies and other long-tongued insects. Birds enjoy seeds. Also a wildflower (*A. canadensis*), with red-and-yellow flowers in April and May. Zones 2–8.

Coral Bells (*Heuchera sanguinea*): 1½ to 2 feet tall. Tall, thin stems bear clusters of tiny, bell-shaped white, pink, rose, chartreuse or red flowers. Blooms from the end of May through summer. Low, wide mound of glossy evergreen leaves. A charming border edging. Easy to divide and replant. Full sun but tolerates some shade. Suitable for cold winters. Zones 3–8. Lures hummingbirds; bees, small insects like it too.

Coreopsis (*Coreopsis grandiflora*): 9 inches to 3 feet tall. Bears bright yellow to yellow-orange, single to semidouble daisy-like flowers from June to August. Lancelike leaves. Also a wildflower. Full sun. Drought-tolerant. Zones 4–9. Attracts butterflies.

Daylily (*Hemerocallis* hybrids): 12 inches to 4 feet tall. Flowers are white, pink, lavender, red, coral, peach, mahogany, yellow or combinations. Funnel- or bell-shaped flowers on branched stalks over narrow strap-like leaves. Blooms May to September. Easy; little care. Clumps spread readily. Full sun to light shade. Drought-tolerant. Zones 3–8. Attracts butterflies, hummingbirds and bees.

Columbine

Bleeding Heart

Garden Phlox

Shasta Daisy

Perennials

Astilbe

Delphinium (*Delphinium elatum*): 2 to 6 feet tall. Flowers are white, blue, lavender, purple or lavender-pink, single or double, with white or dark eyes called bees. Blooms June and July. Tall, thick flower stalks must be staked; intermediate sizes are less prone to rain- and wind-damage. Keep flower stalks cut so more will arise later in season. Large leaves are deeply divided. A gorgeous but temperamental plant; likes full sun, but not long, hot summers; suitable for cool climate, cold winter, but mulching advised. May not be perennial in parts of South. Zones 3–7. Bees and hummingbirds go for it.

Dianthus, Border Carnation (*Dianthus caryophyllus*): 1 to 2 feet tall. White, yellow, pink or red blooms are single or double. Blooms June and July. Narrow grayish leaves. Resembles florist's carnation but is bushier and more compact. **Allwood Pink** (*D. ×allwoodii*) bears plentiful salmon or white flowers on mounds of grassy foliage. Spicy fragrance, fringed petals. Full sun. Perennial in temperate to warm climates, not in very hot areas. Zones 6–7.

Gerbera, African or **Transvaal Daisy** (*Gerbera jamesonii*): 1 to 1½ feet tall. White, scarlet, pink, orange or yellow single or double flowers. Blooms spring to fall. Needs full sun, moist, acidic soil and mild climate to be perennial. Usually treated as an annual.

Globe Thistle (*Echinops ritro*): 3 to 4 feet tall. Taplow Blue has deep blue, closely packed florets forming a round flower head. Blooms July to September. Sharp spines on leaves: handle with care. Full sun, tolerant of drought and dry soil. Easy, long-lived. Dramatic accent. Zones 3–9. Alluring to bees and butterflies. Many birds, especially finches and goldfinches, are wild about thistle seed. Beware of Russian and Canada thistles, deep-rooted, aggressive weeds that should never be planted in a garden.

Gloriosa Daisy (*Rudbeckia hirta* 'Gloriosa Daisy'): 2 to 3 feet tall. Yellow, orange, bronze or bicolored flowers with brown cone-shaped center. Blooms June to late fall. Bright, showy cultivar of the black-eyed Susan. Easy and tough; a sturdy, bushy plant. Spreads, self-sows. Prefers full sun. Drought-tolerant. Usually treated as an annual. Visited by butterflies and bees.

Goldenrod (*Solidago* spp.): 2½ to 3 feet tall. A cultivated variety of the wildflower (neither gives you hay fever; that's the unrelated ragweed), and very lovely, with graceful, vivid yellow plumes. Blooms August and September. Sun to partial shade. Easy and drought-tolerant. Zones 4–10. Extremely attractive to bees and many insects. If allowed to go to seed, will also bring in many birds.

Great or **Blue Lobelia, Blue Cardinal Flower** (*Lobelia siphilitica*): 2 to 4 feet tall. A many-spired, large, bushy plant with blue blooms in August and September. Self-sows freely. Prefers moist soil, some shade. Zones 4–8. It does not attract butterflies, but bees love it. Also a wildflower.

Iris (*Iris* spp.): Hundreds of varieties from 6 inches to 4 feet tall. 6-inch dwarfs bloom in April. Popular **Bearded Iris** blooms in May and June. Flowers are white, yellow, pink, brown, red, violet, purple, pale blue or bicolors; sweet scent. Full sun. Zones 4–8. **Japanese Iris** (*I. ensata*) is taller, blooming in June and July with lovely flat-topped white, blue, purple or red-violet blossoms. Prefers moist, acid soil. Zones 3–8. **Louisiana Iris** (*I.* בׂ'Louisiana') and **Yellow** (*I. pseudacorus*) and **Blue Flags** (*I. versicolor*) like wet feet; good for a water garden, by a stream or in very moist areas. Sun to partial shade. Zones 5–8. Blue and purple varieties very attractive to bees. A new bearded autumn-flowering form for the South is available.

Ligularia (*Ligularia stenocephala* 'The Rocket'): 5 to 6 feet tall. Small yellow flowers profusely borne in tall, black-stemmed clusters. Blooms from August to October. Mound of broad, toothed foliage. Prefers partial shade and rich, moist soil. Zones 4–8.

Lily (*Lilium* spp.): Bulbs, mostly hardy, are 2 to 7 feet tall. Flowers are white, red, salmon, gold, copper, orange or combinations, often freckled. Blooms from June to August. Blooms may be flat faced, trumpet shaped, pendent, upright or recurved. Most are fragrant. The tallest need staking. All are sun lovers but perform in light shade and well-drained soil. Zones 3–8. Visited by bees, hummingbirds.

Marguerite Daisy (*Chrysanthemum frutescens*): 2 to 3 feet tall. Abundant, daisylike, 1½- to 2½-inch-wide flowers in white, pale yellow or pink. Summer bloom. A bushy plant with ferny, divided dark green foliage. Self-sows freely. Highly ornamental. Full sun. Annual north of Zone 9. Attractive to butterflies.

Mealy-Cup Sage (*Salvia farinacea*): 1½ to 3 feet tall. Shades of blue or lavender flowers from July to frost. A tender perennial that seldom survives cold northern winters. Bears spikes of small blossoms on narrow stems. Full sun to partial shade. Zone 8. Attractive to bees and hummingbirds, many small insects.

New England Aster, Michaelmas Daisy (*Aster novae-angliae*): 4 to 5 feet tall. White, lavender-blue (most common), red or pink blooms. Many clusters of small, gold-centered, daisylike flowers from September to November; in the South, from August to November. In growing season, must be cut back 2 or 3 times to make a bushy plant; tends to sprawl and spread. Prefers full sun. Zones 4–9. Relished by bees; enjoyed by butterflies, particularly monarchs. Also a common wildflower.

Oriental Poppy (*Papaver orientale*): 2 to 4 feet tall. Flowers are red, scarlet, orange, salmon pink, rose pink or white. Single or double, huge, spectacular, crinkly blooms in June. Coarse, toothed foliage dies down after bloom (use labels), returns in late summer and remains over winter. Prefers full sun. At its best in cool climate with cold winters. A dazzling and long-lived favorite. Zones 3–8.

Penstemon (*Penstemon gloxinioides*): 1½ to 3 feet tall. White, red, pink, blue or lavender flowers from June to August. Long spikes of small, trumpet-shaped blooms. Full sun or light shade. Drought-tolerant. At best in warm climates; not hardy where winters are cold. Zones 7–10. High on the hummingbird's menu. Also a wildflower.

Peony (*Paeonia lactiflora*): 2 to 4 feet tall. White, red or pink single, semidouble or double flowers in May and June. Enormous flowers on large plants; give them space—at least 2-foot centers. Heavenly scent. Likes sun but tolerates light shade. Needs cool climate, cold winters. Prefers not to be disturbed or divided. Very long-lived. Zones 3–8.

Phlox (*Phlox paniculata*): Garden or summer phlox. 2 to 4 feet tall. Pink, rose, red, blue or purple flowers in July and August. Large clusters of tightly packed flowers, very showy and highly perfumed. Deadhead flowers and side shoots will bloom. Full sun to partial shade. Drought-tolerant. Zones 3–8. A mainstay of temperate-zone gardens and popular with hummingbirds and butterflies too.

Pitcher's Salvia, Blue Sage (*Salvia azurea* var. *grandiflora*): 4 to 5 feet tall. Bears spikes of small sky blue, violet or white flowers in August and September. Tolerant of drought, poor soil; needs full sun. Zone 6. Attractive to bees and hummingbirds, many small insects.

Polyanthus Primrose (*Primula* ×*polyantha*): 6 to 10 inches tall. Blooms in May. Large clusters of flowers in every color of the rainbow or combinations. Moist, acidic soil and partial shade. They like it cool. Zones 3–10. Early blooms attract butterflies and bees.

Rose (*Rosa* spp.): Probably the most popular and beloved of all summer garden flowers, with new types introduced every year, roses present a bewildering choice of thousands of varieties in a vast range of sizes, shapes, colors and uses. Some varieties are in bloom from early summer to frost. They grow in almost all parts of the country, but in cold-winter areas need considerable protection to survive. Full sun. Beneficial insects will come to feast on the aphids and other harmful bugs. Rose hips attract birds and wildlife to rambling, climbing and shrub roses.

Shasta Daisy (*Leucanthemum maximum*): 1 to 3 feet tall. Big, white, single or double daisylike flowers with yellow centers. Blooms June through August. A member of the vast chrysanthemum family, Shasta daisies deserve special mention for their ruggedness, heat tolerance and dependability. A garden classic. Full sun to partial shade. Zones 4–9. Many insects, including butterflies, visit.

Showy Stonecrop (*Sedum spectabile*): 1 to 2 feet tall. Pink, rose, red, coppery rose, mahogany or white flowers. Blooms August to frost. Tiny star-shaped flowers make fluffy cluster of bloom. Autumn Joy is a showy bright pink to rusty red variety. Fleshy oval leaves. A maintenance-free plant for full sun or light shade. Zones 3–9. Masses of bloom attract hordes of butterflies and bees.

Spike Gayfeather (*Liatris spicata*): 18 inches to 6 feet tall. Rosy lavender, purple or white flowers. Blooms July to September. Hundreds of tiny flowers clustered fluffily on spikes resembling bottlebrushes. An arresting accent in the flower border. Kobold is a compact variety. Prefers full sun and moist soil. Zones 3–8. Butterflies, bees and small insects are attracted.

Sweet Rocket, Dame's Rocket (*Hesperis matronalis*): 2 to 3 feet tall. Flowers are mauve, white, pink or purple. Phloxlike clusters of extremely fragrant blossoms. Blooms June to August. Full sun to partial shade. Zones 3–8. Attractive to bees and many other insects. Also a wildflower.

Perennial Ornamental Grasses

Grass seed is an important source of food from summer through winter for birds, mice and other mammals, and numerous insects. A small selection of ornamental grasses for various conditions follows. Grasses are important accents in a lawn, provide vital cover at the water's edge, and add pleasing contrast to the perennial border.

Blue Fescue (*Festuca caesia* var. *glauca*): Silver-blue foliage 8 to 12 inches tall. Forms delicate clumps of slender evergreen foliage. Grown for beautiful foliage but also bears ornamental flower spikes with alternating panicles from June through midsummer. Clumps multiply and spread. Full sun. Zone 4.

Fountain Grass (*Pennisetum alopecuroides*): 2 to 3 feet tall. Beautiful fountains of slender, bright green arching leaves.

Delicate plumes of silvery purplish or rosy flowers from August through early fall. Foliage lasts into late winter. Full sun. Zone 5.

Japanese Silver Grass (*Miscanthus sinensis*): 4 to 8 feet tall. Many varieties, including Gracillimus (**Maiden Grass**), a fine-textured arching grass, with buff fall color and handsome rosy plumes from September through early winter; Variegatus (**Variegated Silver Grass**), with creamy stripes on its wide leaves; and Zebrinus (**Zebra Grass**), with horizontal yellow zebra stripes. Good as specimen plants or for screening. Foliage lasts into late winter. Full sun, moist soil. Zone 5.

Manna Grass, Sweet Grass (*Glyceria maxima* 'Variegata'): To 2½ feet tall. Daylily-like 20-inch-long pointed leaves are striped with creamy yellow or white. Seeds are borne in branching panicles. Full sun. Good for the water's edge or in shallow water but will also grow in regular garden soil. Zone 5.

Pampas Grass (*Cortaderia selloana*): 8 to 12 feet tall. High mounds of narrow leaves. Female plants bear extremely showy, ostrich-feather–like silvery to pale pink, 1- to 3-foot-tall spikes. Full sun. Zone 8.

Plume Grass, Ravenna Grass (*Erianthus ravennae*): To 14 feet tall. Narrow leaves to 3 feet long borne on tall stems. Silvery branching flowering plume to 2 feet long turns beige in fall. Plumes last from August to late fall; foliage persists into midwinter. Fall foliage is chestnut brown. Full sun. Zone 6.

Biennials

Biennials are a small group of plants that display some of the characteristics of perennials and some of annuals. As their name suggests, they normally live for two years, developing leafy growth from seed the first year and flowering the second. But some tender perennials, such as hollyhocks and Iceland poppies, are usually treated as biennials. New breeding programs are making annuals of some biennials, such as the Foxy foxglove, that bloom the first season from seed.

Biennials contribute some of the loveliest and most spectacular flowers to the garden. Seeds sown in early summer will produce big, sturdy plants by late summer or early fall, but they will not flower until the following year. After they flower, they set seed.

Cutting down spent flower spikes on most biennials will stimulate them to send up a second set later in the season. If a few stalks are allowed to ripen, the seed will produce plantlets that usually survive the winter, with some protection in colder climates. Tuck mulch around the plants, not over their crowns. The parent plant, which may survive too, never flowers again, so pull it out and use the empty space for something else. Biennials purchased from a nursery are ready to bloom and should be set in place early in the season. Most will tolerate some shade.

BIENNIAL MINIMANUAL

Canterbury Bells (*Campanula medium*): 2 to 4 feet tall. Chunky spires of white, violet, blue or pink bell-shaped flowers. June bloom. The charming double variety (*C. medium* var. *calycanthema*), called cup and saucer, has a bell within a bell. Birds enjoy the seeds. Bees go for the nectar.

English Daisy (*Bellis perennis*): 6 inches tall. White, pink or red daisy flowers. Spring or early summer bloom. Double and semidouble cultivars as well as the singles, which have yellow centers. Will bloom in winter in mild climates. Prefers full sun and moist soil.

Forget-Me-Not (*Myosotis sylvatica*): 6 to 18 inches tall. Dainty little sprays of blue, white or pink. Plants form a low border. Spring to summer bloom. Prefers some shade and moist soil. Self sows and blooms on new plants later in the season, if birds don't get to the seed first. Usually grown as a hardy annual.

Foxglove (*Digitalis purpurea*): 2 to 4 feet tall. Flowers white, yellow, pink, apricot, purple or rust, with speckled throats. June and July bloom. Dramatic spikes of bell-shaped elongated flowers, closely packed. An annual cultivar, Foxy, has been developed that takes 5 months from seed to flower. In hot, dry climates, foxglove needs light to medium shade. Thrives in Northeast and Northwest areas near the coasts. Attractive to hummingbirds and bees; birds eat the seeds.

Hollyhock (*Althaea rosea*): 4 to 8 feet tall. Single and double large flowers, white, cream, yellow, apricot, pink, rose, red or maroon. July to August bloom. Needs sun. A striking background accent often regarded as delightfully old-fashioned. Hummingbirds regard its nectar as delightful, too. Tall varieties may need staking.

Honesty, Silver Dollar (*Lunaria annua*): 1½ to 3 feet tall. Purple or white. Blooms May and June. Prized for seedpods, round green disks that dry brown. When outer layer is peeled off, "silver dollar" is revealed. As a dried flower, honesty lasts for years. My grandma called them "dust catchers."

Iceland Poppy (*Papaver nudicaule*): 1 to 2 feet tall. White, salmon, yellow, orange, scarlet, red, pink or bicolor. Early spring bloom. Cup-shaped flowers with silky petals. Some are double. Many blooms per plant. Full sun. Extremely hardy; withstands coldest winters. In mild climates, sow seed in fall for late winter/early spring bloom. Usually grown as a hardy annual.

Larkspur Rocket (*Consolida ambigua*): 3 to 5 feet tall. Dwarf cultivar 1 to 2 feet tall. White, pink, rose, lavender or purple. Late spring to summer bloom. Spikes of delicate flowers. Blooms early in cool climates; prefers sunny, cool weather. In warm regions, sow in fall. Self-sows. A tempting entrée for hummingbirds and butterflies. Usually grown as a hardy annual.

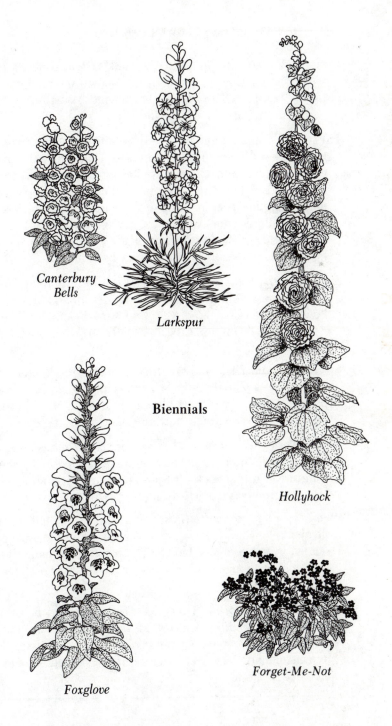

Canterbury
Bells

Larkspur

Biennials

Hollyhock

Foxglove

Forget-Me-Not

Mullein (*Verbascum* spp.): 3 to 6 feet tall. Yellow, white, tawny red or purple flowers borne on tall, showy spikes. Summer bloom. Basal rosettes of huge, showy whitish or silvery green hairy leaves. Full sun. Also a wildflower.

Pansy (*Viola* spp.): 4 to 9 inches tall. White and every color of the rainbow (except green), many with "faces" in a different color. Spring bloom. Giants have flowers 2 to 4 inches across. There are smaller standard varieties, also the tiny purple, lavender or yellow **Johnny-jump-up** (*V. tricolor*), which reseeds very readily. Distinctive sweet scent, velvety petals. Prefers cool weather; provide afternoon shade in warm climates for longer bloom. Usually grown as a hardy annual.

Stock (*Matthiola incana*): 1 to 2½ feet tall. White, blue, pink, red, creamy yellow or purple, usually double fragrant flowers in stocky spikes. May and June bloom. Full sun. Also called Brompton stock. Usually grown as a hardy annual.

Sweet William (*Dianthus barbatus*): 6 inches to 1½ feet tall. Clusters of small close-set flowers, white, pink, red, rose-purple or bicolors. June bloom. Full sun. Nice border plant; self-sows. Attracts butterflies and small insects.

Wallflower (*Cheiranthus cheiri*): 2½ feet tall. Yellow, orange, red-brown, red or purple flowers in spikes. Spring bloom. Fragrant. Prefers cool weather, full sun to partial shade. Usually grown as a hardy annual.

Weld, Dyer's Mignonette (*Roseda luteola*): 5 feet tall. Long, slender yellow flower spikes rise over a basal rosette of lance-shaped leaves. Summer bloom. The plant yields lemon yellow, gold or orange dyes. Prefers partial shade and alkaline soil.

Woad (*Isatis tinctoria*): 3 feet tall. Yellow blooms borne in lovely large cloudlike panicles. May and June bloom. Basal rosette of foot-long, blue-green leaves. Flowers are followed by ornamental clusters of black berries. The leaves yield a blue dye. Full sun.

Annuals

Annuals grow, bloom, and die in one season, unlike perennials, which arise from their roots each year and have a relatively short season of bloom. But they will be back to bloom again next year! Annuals must perpetuate themselves by growing fast and blooming prodigiously for as long as possible in order to make a great deal of seed. The more flowers you cut, the more buds the plant will produce.

Annuals come in a dazzling range of species and varieties, colors and sizes, and can be planted in a great number of places. Most love sun, but impatiens and coleus are shade lovers. They are quite tough and adaptable. A lingering cold, wet spell in spring may dampen their ardor for a while, but they will catch up with bloom in summer and put on a smashing fall display as well, if flowers are kept picked. A hot, dry spell will not discourage them, provided that they are well watered.

Care of Annuals

Since their roots are not as deep as those of perennials, young annuals can be carefully transplanted to fill in bare spots. For bushier plants that produce more flowers, pinch back the tip of the central stem above the top pair of leaves when the plant is 4 or 5 inches tall. Side branches will grow, and some of these can be pinched too. Unpinched, many annuals will produce far fewer flowers. At the nursery, you may find seedlings that have already been properly pinched and are getting bushy. So much the better.

Because of their relatively short life, annuals are not often seriously damaged by pests or diseases. One of their worst enemies is the cutworm, a fat, grayish caterpillar that chews its way across the stem of a young plant, killing it. This despicable grub can often be found in the ground next to the toppled plant, digesting its meal no doubt, where you will see to it that it will never have another. Gluttonous slugs can strip plants of leaves if not detected and controlled. (See Chapter

11, Battling Bugs and Diseases . . . Naturally, for controls.) Mildew on leaves affects some annuals, notably zinnias, late in the season and occasionally in damp, cool weather. Keep picking the flowers, remove affected leaves, and when the plant has finished blooming, pull it up and discard it; do not add it to the compost pile.

Using Annuals

Versatile, exuberantly blooming annuals can be used in a multitude of places and ways. The smaller or dwarf varieties are ideal as colorful edgings for the front of the flower border, along a driveway, or in rock gardens. Bees and other insects will visit. Others, planted around spring-flowering bulbs such as tulips, daffodils, and hyacinths, help to mask the dying bulb foliage, which should be left on the plants until it has completely yellowed to nourish the bulbs for their next season. Annuals can fill in spaces between perennials or be set in groups of three, five, or more for bursts of color, the tallest toward the back of the border. Interspersed between vegetables, annuals serve as a natural barrier to the spread of diseases in certain crops. Others work for their living in another way: They are natural repellents to insect pests that usually attack target vegetables. These bright and pungent flowers, and a number of herbs as well, add a unique and lively touch to the vegetable patch. (See Chapter 6, On Growing Vegetables.)

Annuals in Containers

Many of the most popular annuals are used in container planting. In window boxes and hanging baskets, in pots, tubs, and planters of every size and description, annuals brighten up the outdoor living area with masses of color, and draw butterflies and hummingbirds where you can enjoy seeing them up close. Familiar favorites that thrive in a mixture of sun and shade include impatiens, wax begonia, geranium, petunia, lobelia, lantana, and the gaily patterned coleus. Container-grown plants need rich soil, frequent liquid feedings, and liberal amounts of water, once a day for some. You can be highly imaginative with these container-grown plants on terrace, patio, steps, or elsewhere and create spectacular displays with different combinations.

In early fall, potted plants and cuttings taken from those too large to move indoors will provide you with a winter garden that will flourish in sunny windows and supply you with still more cuttings to root. In this way, many annuals keep getting a new lease on life—an almost perennial lease! Impatiens, coleus, wax begonia, and geranium are among those that lend themselves most willingly to this form of propagation.

Flower Volunteers

The ability of annuals to self-sow, or reseed themselves, is part of nature's regeneration program, assisted by winds that blow seeds about and birds and small animals that eat and redeposit them. The gardener can assist, too. As with plants grown from cuttings, it's cost-free, easy, and fun. Here's how:

Let some favorite flowers ripen their seed on the stem. Leave some there for seed-eating songbirds and migrating birds. Collect others when they look dry; then spread them out on paper and let them dry until seed heads or loose seeds look and feel very dry and pods feel papery and rattle when shaken. At this stage, seeds may be loose and fall out, so shake them over paper so you won't lose any. Place the seeds in labeled, airtight glass bottles, plastic bags, or metal containers, and store over winter in the refrigerator or a dry, cool place for planting next spring. In a warm climate, sow in fall for winter or early spring bloom. When collecting seed, make certain that it is from a healthy plant and that you have plenty, to allow for some sterile seeds, whether from your own plant or a seed packet. With a little bit of luck, you will have more plantlets than space; they will need to be thinned out or transplanted, and you can even give some away!

I can rely on mounds of white sweet alyssum, pink, white, and rose candytuft, lavender-blue ageratum, dwarf marigold, sky blue forget-me-not, and the winsome tiny purple, white, and yellow Johnny-jump-up to return along the front edge of the border. Farther back, there will be self-sown white nicotiana (flowering tobacco) that opens at night and perfumes the air; bushy balsam, a cousin of impatiens, loaded with blossoms of every conceivable hue that pop up abundantly; and sturdy, vivid golden gloriosa daisy.

Saving Seed

Among the seeds that I collect in autumn and plant the following spring, I'm very successful with zinnias of all sizes and colors, giant marigolds, pink and lavender cleome (the spider flower), and pink, rose, and white cosmos for tall background plants. All these flowers, with the exceptions of balsam and forget-me-not, keep blooming until nipped by heavy frost—a real plus! And some of them, including again the vigorous alyssum, nicotiana, Johnny-jump-up, and cleome, in addition to certain wildflowers, such as coreopsis and black-eyed Susan, self-sow and bloom again in the same season. I have had 6-inch cosmos seedlings, from 6-foot parents, that burst into bloom in a mild autumn as late as the end of October!

Some authorities do not advocate growing garden plants from their own seed on the grounds that they are not always true to the parent or that the seed doesn't germinate as plentifully as freshly bought seed. This is often true, as many flowers today are hybrids, pedigreed plants carefully bred from identical parents by growers. But whereas your own seedlings will not necessarily resemble the parent in all ways or germinate as abundantly as fresh seed, that needn't be of primary importance. I sow plenty of seed so that I don't have to worry about the percentage of germination, and buy new seed or seedlings after the old strains appear to be less colorful and pleasing in a few years. Of course, I also want to try new and different varieties, but it's a lot of fun to see what comes up from your own seed, whether the seedlings are volunteers or sown by hand; and the butterflies, bees, and other insects aren't in the least particular about where the flowers come from!

Plants that self-sow will be indicated in the Minimanual that follows. Seed planted or self-sown in fall will not germinate until spring except in warm climates, where it will bloom in late winter or early spring. Hummingbirds migrating northward are well aware of the progression of bloom and wing it along with the flowers that bloom in the spring— and the summer.

Planting Annuals

Starting seed indoors is a tricky procedure. Cultural requirements include sterile potting soil; warm temperatures and high humidity; proper ventilation but no drafts; very judicious watering; bright sunshine or fluorescent light when seedlings appear; thinning; transplanting at the right stage to individual containers; continued careful regulation of water, light, and temperature; and hardening off a few hours daily outdoors for a few days before finally transplanting into the garden.

There, a late frost may nip them or hot sun scald them before they are toughened up. Then there is the possibility that they may not ever get that far. One of the worst hazards a tender baby seedling can encounter is a fearsome fungal disease called damping off, which may destroy an entire flat or container of seedlings overnight. Nonetheless, if you have plenty of time, patience, space, and sunny windows (without displacing your houseplants), and start off on a small scale, you may find that growing seed indoors is an interesting experience that brings good results.

I, however, prefer to set seeds and plants directly in the garden where they are to bloom. I've found that direct-seeded plants usually progress better and bloom sooner and more abundantly than those started indoors and transplanted. By the time spring arrives and the soil feels light, warm, and crumbly, my fingers are itching to start planting.

For optimum results with direct seeding, add a bit of packaged potting soil to the garden furrows to speed germination. Barely cover tiny seed with soil; cover larger seed with about a quarter-inch of soil. Press down firmly, and water gently with a fine spray from hose or watering can. Don't forget the labels! From now on, seeds need to be kept moist. If plantlets come up cheek by jowl, they must thinned out so that they have room to grow. This will hurt you more than it will hurt them. Some, if carefully dug with soil around sufficiently developed roots, can be transplanted or given away to gardening friends.

Transplants

The easiest, least troublesome, most expensive, but also most successful method of starting annuals is to buy the seedlings from a reliable nursery and plant them where you want them to grow. Before buying, examine plants closely for any signs of ill health. Avoid tall and skinny or dry and wilted transplants or those already in full bloom. Seedlings in plastic four- to six-packs or in individual pots are usually well rooted, hardened off, and easily pushed up from the bottom. Those grown together in a flat or market pack must be gently pulled apart with the least damage possible to intertwined roots or sliced into cubes with a sharp knife and quickly planted. Liquid fertilizer—compost or manure tea, fish emulsion, or liquid seaweed—lessens transplant shock for these seedlings and, in fact, is a quick pick-me-up for all young plants and transplants. Plants in peat pots will come along better if the bottom and the rim around the top are removed and the sides pierced or loosened before planting. Peat pot edges that stick up above the soil surface act as wicks to pull water away from the roots.

ANNUAL MINIMANUAL

Annuals are beloved for their cheerful, sturdy good looks, their easy care, bright colors and long bloom season. Because a summerlong bloom season is typical of annuals, flowering time won't be specified for each flower unless it differs from the normal pattern.

Ageratum (*Ageratum houstonianum*): 6 inches to 1 foot tall. Blue, pinkish blue, violet-blue, or occasionally white flowers in fluffy clusters. Good border edging plant. Full sun to partial shade. Self-sows. May be invasive. Need not be pinched back. Bees and butterflies visit.

Alyssum, Sweet Alyssum (*Lobularia maritima*): 12 inches tall. White, deep rose or violet. Low mounds of blossoms, excellent for edging the border. Sweet-scented. Cut back spent blossoms, will bloom later in summer and up to frost. Full sun to partial shade. Reseeds freely. Bees and butterflies visit.

Balsam (*Impatiens balsamina*): 10 inches to 2 feet tall. Many shades of rose, red, lavender, yellow or salmon. This charming old favorite bears a multitude of small, camellia-shaped blooms. Grows almost everywhere. Self-sows freely. A favorite of bees and butterflies.

Begonia, Wax Begonia (*Begonia semperflorens*): 6 inches to 1 foot tall. White, pink or red waxy single or double flowers. Compact masses of bloom. Foliage green, mahogany or variegated green and white. One of the most popular plants for container planting and border edging. Easy, adaptable, happy in shade or sun.

Browallia (*Browallia speciosa*): 12 to 16 inches tall. Blue with white throat, purple or white. Tends to trail or hang; good for edging or containers. Blooms until frost. Cousin of the petunia. Full sun to partial shade. Nectar lines on petals attract bees and other insects.

Calendula (*Calendula officinalis*): 1 to 1½ feet tall. Bright gold, orange, apricot, lemon or combinations. Single or double. Late bloomer in cool climates. Does not thrive in extreme heat but will bloom abundantly in fall up to frost. In warm areas, sow seed in late summer or early fall for winter or spring bloom. Sturdy; many flowers. Pungent leaves. Repels insects. Self-sows. Edible.

California Poppy (*Eschscholzia californica*): 1 foot tall. Orange most common; also white, yellow, scarlet or bronze. Cup-shaped silky flowers, single or double. Full sun. May be perennial in warm climates. Commonly included in wild-flower seed packets. State flower of California, where it grows wild. Self-sows freely. Birds enjoy seeds.

Carnation (*Dianthus caryophyllus*): 1 to 2 feet tall. White, pink, yellow, red or combinations. Spicy cinnamon-and-clove scent. Performs as biennial or perennial in warm climates. Full sun. Nectar interests hummingbirds; seeds appeal to birds.

Cleome, Spider Flower (*Cleome hasslerana*): 3 to 6 feet tall. White, pink, rose or lavender. Large, showy clusters of fragrant flowers, bushy palmlike foliage. Narrow seedpods like spider legs emerge from flowers. Easy. Full sun to partial shade. Prefers dry soil. Self-sows. Nectar favored by hummingbirds and bees.

Coreopsis (*Coreopsis tinctoria*): 1 to 3 feet tall. Vivid yellow, brown or purple-red notched petals with brown or maroon centers. Very vigorous bloomer and self-sower; flowers almost continuously until frost. Easy. Drought-tolerant. Full sun. All insects visit. Also a wildflower.

Cornflower, Bachelor's Button (*Centaurea cyanus*): 1 to 3 feet tall. White, blue (most common), purple, pink or red. Profuse blooms. Easy. Prefers full sun. Self-sows. Seeds attract butterflies and birds, especially finches. Also sold as a wildflower.

Cosmos (*Cosmos bipinnatus; C. sulphureus*): 3 to 6 feet tall. White, pink, rose, magenta, red, yellow or orange, with yellow centers; some double varieties. Long period of bloom. Lovely background flower. Tall, with wide side branches; needs staking. Dwarf cultivar Sunny Red is 2 feet tall with vibrant orange-red flowers. Birds eat seeds; a major goldfinch attraction! Also attracts hummingbirds, bees, butterflies and many other insects. A favorite roost of mantids seeking prey.

Dianthus, China Pink (*Dianthus chinensis*): 6 inches to 1 foot tall. White, pink, red or bicolors. Nice border edging plant. Frilled or "pinked" petals. Fragrant. Full sun.

Four-O'Clock, Marvel-of-Peru (*Mirabilis jalapa*): 1½ to 3 feet tall. Inch-wide, fragrant, trumpet-shaped flowers in white,

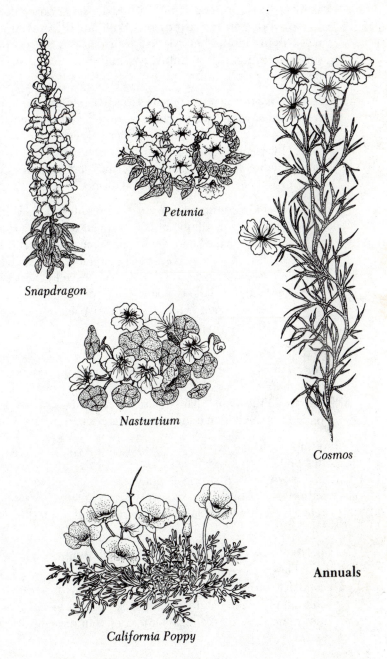

Snapdragon

Petunia

Nasturtium

Cosmos

California Poppy

Annuals

yellow, pink or red, some with stripes or variegations. Blooms open in the afternoon. Full sun. Blooms attract night-flying moths; before the flowers close in the morning sun, hummingbirds, bumblebees, and other long-tongued insects may stop for breakfast.

Gazania (*Gazania rigens*): 6 inches to 1 foot tall. Bright yellow, red, orange, gold, bronze, pink, cream or multicolors; daisy-like petals. A splendid front-of-the-border plant. Perennial in parts of California and the Southwest, where they will flower in later winter and early spring. Full sun. Most have dark centers or rings of contrasting color that attract insects.

Geranium (*Pelargonium hortorum*): 1 to 2 feet tall. White, scarlet, pink, coral, salmon or bicolors. Cultivars have leaves with different shapes and markings; some are delightfully scented. This old reliable is easy and adaptable. Likes full sun but tolerates some shade and dry soil. Ivy-leaved varieties are nice for hanging baskets. Considered perennial in warm regions. Pest-repellent; white most effective against Japanese beetles. Attractive to hummingbirds.

Impatiens (*Impatiens wallerana*): 6 inches to 1 foot tall. Every color but blue and purple. Popular favorite for low border, containers. Cut back for bushy plants, masses of bloom. Easy, requires little care, shade-tolerant. Perennial in frost-free regions. Attractive to hummingbirds and small insects.

Lantana (*Lantana camara*): 1 to 3 feet tall. Yellow, red, lavender-pink, or combinations. Clusters of tiny flowers. Leaves and flowers have strong lemony scent. Attractive trailing variety for planters, baskets. In warm climates, stems may reach 6 feet, and the plants may be perennial. Butterflies and bees visit.

Lobelia (*Lobelia erinus*): 6 to 12 inches tall. White, bright blue, pale blue, wine red or reddish purple, with white eye. Low, compact form for border edging; trailing form cascades charmingly over containers. Cut back for later bloom. Tolerates some shade. Attracts butterflies, hummingbirds and bees.

Marigold (*Tagetes* spp.): 6 inches to 3 feet tall. **African Marigold** (*T. erecta*): yellow, cream, orange or lemon. Large double flowers, big sturdy plant. **French Marigold** (*T. patula*): yellow, orange, dark red, maroon or combinations; single or double. Bushy petites great for edging; prolific bloom. Self-sow. All are dependable garden standbys, good insect-repellents. Pungent scent. Full sun. Attract butterflies and bees. Birds eat seeds.

Nasturtium (*Tropaeolum majus*): 8 inches to 1 foot tall. White, red, pink, yellow, orange, mahogany and coral. Single or double. Pungent scent. Some varieties are low, compact; some climb high, with support; some trail. Full sun. Easy, thrives on neglect. Pretty saucer-shaped foliage. Young leaves tasty in salad, snappy like watercress. Insect-repellent. In frost-free areas, sow in early fall for winter bloom; may be perennial. A hummingbird, butterfly and bumblebee appetizer.

Nicotiana, Flowering Tobacco (*Nicotiana alata*): 1 to 2 feet tall. White, pink, yellow, chartreuse, maroon or dark red. Easy. Self-sows and spreads freely. Fast-maturing new plants may bloom until frost. Do not plant near tomatoes; may carry tobacco mosaic virus harmful to them. Older white variety opens at night, releasing delicious fragrance; attractive to many gorgeous moths, also to tobacco hornworm moth. Others visited in daytime by butterflies, bees and hummingbirds.

Petunia (*Petunia hybrida*): 1 foot tall. Every color of the rainbow (except green) and combinations. Single or double, large or small, rippled, fringed or ruffled petals, many with nectar lines. Thrives in full sun but tolerates some shade. Good for border, path, driveway, edging; blooms prodigiously if pinched and cut back. Petals may be damaged by heavy rain. Cascade forms are fine for hanging baskets. Fragrance lures moths at night; a favorite of the sphinx or hummingbird moth. Bees and hummingbirds will visit.

Salpiglossis, Painted Tongue (*Salpiglossis sinuata*): 2 to 3 feet tall. Glowing orange, red, purple, gold, pink or maroon, velvety, trumpet-shaped blossoms. Cousin of the petunia. Very showy. Prefers full sun and cool weather. Fine contrasting lines on petals guide bees, other insects to nectar and pollen.

Schizanthus, Butterfly Flower (*Schizanthus* spp.): 1 to 2 feet tall. Bicolored flowers in combinations of pink, rose, red, violet, purple or white. Blossom is split into many segments; clusters of bloom give light, airy effect. Cool, moist situation in full sun or partial shade preferred. Gold veins serve as nectar guides for butterflies and other insects.

Shirley Poppy (*Papaver rhoeas*): 1½ to 2 feet tall. Red, orange and pink with white. Single or double. Fragrant. Self-sows. Annual poppies in frost-free regions can be sown in fall, and like full sun. A cultivated variety of the scarlet wild corn poppy.

Snapdragon (*Antirrhinum majus*): 6 inches to 3 feet tall. White, yellow, bronze, rose, pink, red or scarlet. Bushy petites good for edging the border. Intermediate and giant forms have tall, thick flower spikes. Pinch back center tip and some side shoots of young plant for bushiness and more bloom. Keep flowers and spent blooms cut for later flowering. Full sun. Perennial in mild climates; may survive mild northern winters if mulched. A handsome, vigorous garden favorite; bees fancy it too.

Sunflower (*Helianthus annuus*): 6 to 12 feet tall. Yellow or gold with large brown centers. Very showy giant daisy flowers may be a foot or more across. Some double varieties. Easy, thrives in any soil, but may need staking. Full sun. A background plant. Bushy 2-foot dwarf Teddy Bear has huge golden flowers. Attractive to bees. Seeds are a feast for the birds and will lure goldfinches. Save a few for next season's sowing. Also a wildflower.

Tithonia, Mexican Sunflower (*Tithonia rotundifolia*): 3 to 4 feet tall. Blazing orange-red. Blooms August to September with 3- to 4-inch blooms. A striking background plant. Needs full sun. Thrives in hot, dry climates.

Verbena (*Verbena hybrida*): 6 to 10 inches tall. White, pink, rose, red or lavender-blue. Jewel-like clusters of tiny flowers, most with white "eyes." Low border plant of trailing habit. Easy. Needs full sun. Perennial in warm regions. Attractive to bees, butterflies, and small insects.

Zinnia (*Zinnia elegans*): 6 inches to 3 feet tall. What would we do without it? Every color but blue; many combinations. Single, double, plain, ruffled or cactus-flowered. Dwarfs studded with tiny blossoms, pretty for the edge of the border. Flowers on intermediate and giant forms may be 3 to 4 inches across. One of the easiest, most vigorous and prolific annuals. Leaves may be subject to mildew late in the season or in damp weather; water at ground level if possible. Full sun. A favorite nectar source of butterflies, which especially love the red and orange colors, and bees. Birds eat the seeds.

The Moonlit Garden

As the sun goes down, the nectar-sated butterflies, sleepy birds, and hardworking bees disappear to take their rest. Gardeners put their tools away and go into the house. Day is done.

Or is it?

At sundown, in your garden as in the jungle or in a tropical forest, a whole new dimension of life begins to unfold. There are strange and fascinating sights and sounds as nocturnal creatures and plants rouse themselves. Those flowers whose petals were shut tight all day will open at dusk and waft seductive perfumes into the night air. White and pale pastels emerge vividly in the moonlight, even in starlight on a clear night, because they are visible to human eyes that are ill equipped to distinguish colors in the absence of light.

The special enchantment of a moonlit garden can be yours with night-blooming, sweetly scented flowering plants and white, cream, pale pink, and yellow varieties of day bloomers. You can blend these plants into your existing garden or, if you have the space, create a separate moonlit garden that's magically white and bright. A flagstone path can bring you close to its fragrances. Simple low-voltage lighting (use the bulbs that don't attract flying insects) will provide soft illumination on moonless nights. It is practical to illuminate pathways, and dramatic to highlight points of interest such as a statue, fountain, or gazebo. And by all means, have container plantings on terrace or patio, where flowers and fragrances are right under your eyes and nose.

Tropical Beauties

The exceptionally beautiful and fragrant blooms, all white or creamy white, are native to tropical countries. These exotic plants can flourish only in a consistently warm climate and, in temperate zones, are grown in large pots that winter over in a greenhouse. Among them are angel's trumpet (datura), a shrubby plant with blue-green leaves and huge white trumpets, and the vining, night-blooming jessamine, with yellow flowers that exude a delicious fragrance. There are also various species of night-blooming cereus. Their gorgeous blossoms open very slowly one a night and last for that night only. You can watch it happening—it's a marvelous show!

For your pond or pool, there are the richly colored and heavily scented night-blooming tropical waterlilies and the smaller, lightly scented white, pink, or yellow hardies that stay open in daylight. Most spectacular of water plants is the enormous lotus. Some species are night blooming; all are intensely fragrant. (See Chapter 5, Pools and Water Gardens.)

Not exotic, but equally striking, are a number of true lilies with stems 4 to 7 feet tall that are royalty among scented flowers. Queens among the trumpet-flowered lilies are white Madonna and Regale, pale yellow Moonlight, white-and-rose Black Dragon, and Pink Perfection. Staked, they also do well in pots on the terrace. Magnificent day or night, the blossoms have a heady fragrance.

More Choice Night Bloomers

Night-blooming daylilies—a contradiction in terms that doesn't in the least concern the sphinx moths and other nocturnal moths that visit them—open pale yellow or peach-colored trumpets that seem to glow in the dark. Before these flowers fade in the morning sun, hummingbirds eagerly seek their nectar. Night-blooming varieties include Lemon Lace, Pink Tangerine, Golden Trinkets, and ivory yellow Ida Miles. Two other delicately perfumed night bloomers are the yellow or white evening primrose and the white evening campion, or catchfly.

That old-time favorite, white flowering tobacco (nicotiana), an annual, opens at dusk. By day the straggly plant with droopy, closed blossoms has little charm. At night it is transformed. Flowers gleam like bright stars and release delicious perfume. Moths love nicotiana. Newer, colorful varieties are day blooming but have no scent, so plant white varieties such as Grandiflora Alata for the moonlit garden.

Another highly fragrant night bloomer is the four-o'clock, or marvel-of-Peru. True to its name, it opens around four o'clock, sensing a slight drop in temperature as the sun goes down. In white and a variety of colors, four-o'clock is very showy as a terrace pot plant as well as in the garden.

Garden phlox is a perennial with surpassingly sweet fragrance. Its huge flower heads in white or pale pink are standouts in the moonlight. Roses of many kinds are a must for scent, but beware of some newer varieties that have little if any fragrance. Many older white varieties have the sweetest perfume. Sweet rocket, which may be annual, perennial, or biennial, has rose or mauve spikes that smell sweet by day and sweeter at night.

Placing Night-Blooming Plants

Some tall perennials stand out well in the dark. Among these are the white-spired varieties of liatris (gayfeather), veronica (speedwell), astilbe, Russell hybrid lupine, and delphinium. Canterbury bells and foxglove are tall, handsome biennials. Large, bushy marguerite, not always hardy but a self-sower, is studded with daisylike blooms and makes an excellent patio plant. For a spectacular background plant, choose white hibiscus (rose mallow), which grows up to 7 feet tall, with blooms 6 to 10 inches across.

For the front of the moonlit garden, to edge a patio, or to feature in pots on the terrace, try annuals such as white sweet alyssum with its honeylike fragrance; delicately scented verbena, petunias, and the biennial sweet william; pungent lantana; peppery nasturtiums, some of which will trail or climb if given support; and impatiens, which becomes a solid mound of bloom if kept properly pinched back. All except lantana have white or creamy white varieties.

Herbs such as lavender, thyme, rosemary, basil, and the mints are either sweetly, pungently, or spicily scented and are well suited for the front of the border, as are Silver Mound artemisia (*Artemisia schmidtiana*), a sun-loving perennial hardy in zones 4 to 8, which forms foot-tall mounds of fine silver foliage about 18 inches wide, and dusty miller, because their silvery gray foliage shows up well at night. By day, they make a cool contrast to more colorful neighbors.

Vines (and More) for Moonlight

Surely no garden is complete without a fragrant honeysuckle bush or vine. I grow mine on a trellis on the garage and by the terrace steps, where the delectable perfume greets me coming and going and permeates the air on a still summer night. Its flowers are much favored by hummingbirds, butterflies, and other long-tongued insects, and the berries that follow are a bonus for birds.

Two unusual vines can add charm and grace to the moonlit garden or terrace, with a trellis or other support to grow on. The white moonflower vine or moonvine, perennial in the South, can grow 10 to 20 feet. Early in the evening, its long buds slowly unfurl into large morning glory–like, sweet-smelling flowers. The bottle gourd vine offers twofold bounty. Numerous delicate and lightly scented blossoms open at night. The gourds that will develop can be made into bird-houses or used as decorative objects when dry and hard.

Yucca, thought of by many northerners and easterners as a southern or desert plant, is in fact hardy in temperate, even cold climates, and is often grown there. It is impressive for its imposing size, up to 5 feet tall, its 2-foot-long, sharply pointed lancelike leaves, and its tall central stalk topped by a large cluster of ivory, bell-shaped flowers that are extremely fragrant to entice pollinating moths. Yucca is a particularly exciting addition to the northern landscape. Tender species can be pot-grown and taken indoors in winter.

Adding Flowering Shrubs

Landscaping for a moonlit garden should include shrubbery with scented white blossoms. Butterfly bush (buddleia) is a splendid choice in white, and purple, too, for its rich, honeyed scent and attraction for butterflies in daytime. Mock-orange has a profusion of orange-blossom-scented white-and-yellow flowers, and viburnums may be chosen in pink and white fragrant varieties. Small trees might include flowering cherry, crabapple, apple, and the mimosa, which bears abundant clusters of heavily scented cotton-candy blossoms irresistible to butterflies, bees, and hummingbirds. My favorite ornamental tree is the kousa dogwood, which bears incredibly profuse, brilliant white (but unscented) flowers that blanket the tree for weeks, a blaze of light under the moon.

The flowers that stay open all day are far more numerous than night-blooming species and are the chief attraction for many insects, birds, butterflies, and bees, while the night bloomers draw nocturnal moths.

Night Life in the Garden

Night-flying moths are by no means the only creatures abroad in the garden after the sun goes down. Many other residents and visitors are nocturnal.

It's not unlikely that you'll see a raccoon, skunk, or opossum ambling about in search of fruit and berries or a tasty bug, worm, grasshopper, mouse, or other small creature. At night they forage for food and are not at all particular about what they eat. One night sound you would rather not hear is the clanging of garbage pail lids—all too likely if they're not tightly secured.

You might catch a glimpse of a frog plopping into your pond or a toad hopping into dense grass or undergrowth in search of insects. Perhaps you'll hear them call. The hoot of an owl may be heard from a thick stand of conifers. A bat may flit overhead in its nocturnal quest for flying insects.

The chirp, buzz, or trill of crickets, depending on the species, is usually present on a summer night. The sound, made only by the male, means many things to other crickets: "Get out of my bailiwick" or "Try to stop me" to other males; and to a female, "We could make beautiful music together"! Cicadas buzz loudly, and katydids are fun to hear as they shrill "Katy *did*, Katy *didn't*" from the treetops.

On a midsummer's eve there's a glittering spectacle of fireflies. Different species make different signals with their flashing lights that blink on and off, from ground level to the tops of trees. But they are all the language of love, and both males and females use them to attract mates.

Their twinkling lights make a lively aerial show for your viewing as you sit relaxed on your terrace or by the back door, with the scent of honeysuckle and nicotiana heavy in the air and white flowers emerging out of the darkness, mysteriously beautiful in the moonlight.

Chapter 4

Wildflowers in the Garden

By chance (seeds deposited by birds and other creatures or blown in by the wind) or by design (yours), wildflowers may appear in your garden. And by all means, short of illegal digging, have them. They add beautiful and novel touches to the naturalist's garden and greatly increase its attractions to wildlife.

A bulldozer put this thought into my head over 30 years ago. Basking in the sun on a rock near the site where our new home was being built, I saw one of the mechanical monsters chew up a patch of daisies and black-eyed Susans farther off in the big meadow where other homesites were being laid out. I suddenly realized that pretty soon there wouldn't be any more meadow, or wildflowers, or butterflies and bees, or birds in the trees that would soon be destroyed, and it made me very sad.

Although at the time I knew very little about flowers

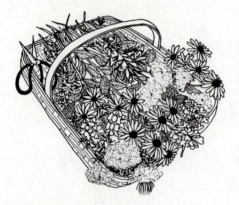

Many wildflowers make lovely cut flowers as well. When you grow your own wildflower garden, you'll have baskets full of cheerful flowers all season.

and plants of field and forest, I knew a wildflower when I saw one, and I was determined to rescue at least some of them before they were bulldozed out of existence. That summer, and the following spring, while there was still some empty land, I roamed about with basket and trowel digging up the Susans and the Queen Anne's lace, daisies, butter-and-eggs, jewelweed, mullein, and some unfamiliar but interesting-looking clumps. As I nibbled on sweet wild blackberries, I thought why not?, and at the price of a few nasty scratches I brought some blackberry bushes into my backyard, too.

In the moist shade, violets, trilliums, wild geraniums, columbines, ferns, Dutchman's-breeches, a splendid jack-in-the-pulpit, and several other woodland plants flourished under the trees. Obviously, they weren't going to be happy out in the hot sunshine with the field flowers in my backyard. After a couple of hours of hasty research in the library, I chose the spot for a small woodland garden on the northeast side of the house near some white pines and an oak. This was the best place for shade, moisture, and the gradual accumulation of oak leaves and pine needles as a mulch.

Over the years, my fascination with wildflowers grew. Although the wild meadow did indeed disappear, some of it lived on in my garden and became so vigorous I had to pull some up or give it away. With trusty trowel and basket always in the car, I stopped at construction sites and landscape renovations and asked permission to snoop for wildflowers. No one ever refused it, although some people thought I was a little crazy. I planted a separate patch of wildflower seed given to me by our village naturalist. From a local nursery I obtained some dazzling cultivated varieties of perennial wildflowers such as bee balm, butterfly weed, cardinal flower, and gloriosa daisy. With enormous satisfaction, I watched the hummingbirds, butterflies, honeybees, bumblebees, and all sorts of other insects and birds flock in for the nectar, pollen, and seed.

As for the little woodland garden, I replaced a few tender and finicky plants that didn't survive with fragrant, fast-spreading lilies-of-the-valley; pink and blue spring-blooming scilla; dainty yellow trout lilies with freckled leaves; tiny pastel windflowers; white bloodroot; and Christmas, lady, and cinnamon ferns. The star performer is the old faithful jack-in-the-pulpit. Its maroon snoots pushing through the leafy mulch greet me each spring, and it has produced several offspring, welcome additions to the woodland garden.

Digging in the Wild

The best advice is don't, unless you are certain that the plant you have your eye on is not on the endangered or protected plant list. You can find this out from your county agricultural agent or State Department of Environmental Conservation. Roadside plantings should not be touched in any case, as they are there for everyone to enjoy.

There *are* a few permissible ways to obtain wild plants. Sites that are scheduled for construction of buildings or roads, that are under construction, or that are undergoing landscaping changes are good bets. If you can keep a step ahead of the bulldozers, you may be able to find and save some treasures to add to your collection. Be sure you are not trespassing on private property or a public park. Get permission from the owner or person in charge, if that's possible.

The backyard of a friend or neighbor may not be very wild, but it just might harbor an interesting wildling that you can obtain as a gift or in a trade. The best source of all is often a catalog. Seeds and plants of many wildflowers can be pur-

chased by mail order from reputable seed houses and dealers. See Resources at the back of the book.

The Wild Garden

If you can spare the space, set aside an area to become a wild garden. This is not at all on the wild side. It's very easy, inexpensive, lots of fun, and richly rewarding to you and the birds, insects, and other creatures. The prime requisite is sunshine. Soil need not be a concern, unless it is extremely poor (very sandy or very heavy and clayey). If it is, add a little peat moss, compost, or other organic matter, and turn it in. Wildflowers do not need rich soil.

Wildflower seed is very fine, and growers recommend that you mix it with either sand or grass seed (sheep fescue or tournament fescue) so that too much seed will not fall in the same spot. (These grasses look good in a wild garden and don't form dense, spreading mats.) Sow very shallowly, barely covering the seed, and water in. Keep the soil moist, but don't soak it. Germination takes from two to four weeks; in warm weather, some seedlings may appear sooner. In the North or cool climates, sow seed in late fall or early spring, preferably the latter. In the South, California, and other warm climates, sow seed in fall. Keep a small amount in reserve to fill in any bare spots.

One of the charms of a wild garden is that it requires practically no maintenance. Of course, if you can tell a weed from a wildflower (and sometimes it isn't easy), pull the weed—unless its flower appeals to you. Water only in a prolonged dry spell when all the other plants have had their share. Remember, these wildflowers are native to fields, meadows, pastures, and roadsides where no one pampers them. Most are highly adaptable and will manage to survive.

Some of the loveliest wildflowers prefer shade, like the trillium, lady's slipper, and jack-in-the-pulpit shown here. Ferns are the perfect complement for the woodland wildflower garden.

SEVEN WILDFLOWER COMMANDMENTS

1. Don't use fertilizers. Artificial feeding—even with organic supplements—is not needed or desirable: It only encourages the growth of weeds at the expense of flowers.

2. Don't use pesticides on or near wildflowers. Beneficial insects will die. Herbicides kill wildflowers; if your neighbors use them, site your garden out of reach of herbicide drift.

3. Don't try to grow open field and meadow sun lovers in the shade or woodland plants in the sun.

4. Don't expect success in growing a plant from a region totally different from your own. A groundcover such as bunchberry, native to northern woods, cannot endure a warm southern climate any more than a camellia can live through northern winters.

5. Don't tug or pull plants from the wild. Dig them with as much soil around the roots as possible, and cut entanglements with other roots carefully.

6. Don't delay transporting and transplanting. If this is unavoidable, try to keep plant roots and soil moist and shaded, best accomplished in a plastic bag with wet peat or other material. After planting, water well, protect from hot sun if necessary for at least a day, and add mulch to keep roots cool.

7. Don't let the field flowers bully you! Many of them (black-eyed Susans, daisies, and loosestrife, for example) reseed very freely and grow rampantly almost anywhere. They can crowd desirable garden flowers and invade lawn and shrub areas. Remove the aggressors' seedpods, and don't hesitate to thin unwanted seedlings. Confine the roots of particularly invasive species by sinking lawn edging around them—the deeper the better, up to 12 inches.

Mow or cut them down in fall after seed ripens (that is, seed-pods or seed heads turn brown and dry), or leave stalks standing; the seed will provide fall and winter food for birds in either case, and the annuals will reseed themselves. If some of your favorites fail to reappear, just sow fresh seed as you would in the annual border.

If you don't have the space for a separate wild garden, wildflowers may be combined very attractively with garden flowers, vegetables, and herbs. Have a care when sowing the seed, for prolific specimens may pop up where you would rather not have them in competition with less vigorous cultivated flowers. Single wildflower plants that you buy or beg can be placed where you wish. The next season, if they have grown too large or reseeded too freely, you can make corrections by thinning out or transplanting.

The Wild Meadow

Do you have a sunny, dry strip or patch of lawn where the grass does poorly, is weedy, and has bare spots? And you don't want to go through the tedious, expensive routine of trying to turn it into an elegant greensward (an expanse of weedless turf)? Then turn it into a wildsward! Pull the large weeds. Scratch the empty spaces, and add a bit of soil to any holes, then drop in wildflower seeds.

This kind of meadow cannot be mowed along with the rest of the lawn and may look messy to some people. Neighbors tend to regard such a project as less than picturesque. To avoid friction or a possible clash with a local ordinance on lawn height, locate this wilder wild garden to the rear or side of your property, if possible. The biggest burst of bloom is in spring and early to midsummer; but some wildflowers, such as black-eyed Susan, golden coreopsis, red-and-yellow gaillardia, and blue or purple cornflowers, continue blooming until frost—at least in my garden. Thus, insects, birds, and small mammals may continue to find food and habitat in the wildflower patch, with or without grasses.

Speaking of grass, if yours is spattered with patches of white Dutch clover, rejoice. It is a tough, pretty, weed-resistant spreader, and honeybees adore the blossoms. When clover is in bloom, don't go barefoot on the grass! Red clover blossoms are adapted to the long-tongued bumblebees, but the plants are too rangy for mowed lawns.

Buying Seed and Plants

The growing interest in wildflowers has encouraged nurseries to grow more of them and offer more varieties of seed. It is possible to choose mixtures or separate varieties that are determined by the growers to be suitable for your area. There are nurseries that specialize in wildflower plants and seeds and mail-order catalogs that list them according to geographic regions. These generally are Canada and the Northeast, the Southeast, the Midwest, the East, the West, California and the Pacific Coast, and the Southwest. There are also "all-purpose" mixes of wildflowers that have been found in many different regions of the country and are quite common. Most mixtures include annual, perennial, and biennial seed.

Most cultivated varieties of wildflowers are obtainable in small seed packets at garden centers, hardware stores, and grocery stores. Follow directions on the packet, or refer to one of the wildflower guides listed in the bibliography at the back of the book.

Sometimes perennial wildflowers are available at nurseries as plants. If you have never seen or grown butterfly weed, lupine, penstemon, bee balm, or coneflower, to name a few, buying some of these large, well-rooted perennials and settling them in your sunny flower border will give you the chance to see what they can do. Most will self-sow. If you don't want to grow your flowers from seed, and know that choice specimens are not legally available in the wild, this is the way to go.

Wildflower Programs, Public and Private

Here in Scarsdale in lower New York State, our village naturalist sows a wildflower seed mixture called Tapestry in early
April on roadside areas and other public places. Bare spots
are reseeded a few weeks later. Reactions of the public are as
mixed as the mixture. Some people think the wildflower
strips are an eyesore and should be grassed over. Others pick
the flowers—something they would never dream of doing to
a neat public plot of tulips or begonias! But most people view
the colorful patches of wildflowers with delight and treat
them with respect.

The advantages of such a program are becoming more
and more apparent to highway and park departments, large
corporations with extensive grounds, and landscape archi-
tects: bright and lively additions to the scenery, low cost and
maintenance, and little if any need for watering.

For the naturalist/gardener, there is the pleasure of
helping to perpetuate the existence of plants that have lived
for thousands of years, only to face endangerment, and in
some cases extinction, in modern times. Wildflowers as well
as native trees and shrubs are part of our national heritage.
And with them go the added attractions of their nectar, pollen, and seeds for the birds, insects, and other wildlife in the
backyard.

Choosing Wildflowers

Regarding the selections of sunloving and woodland wildflowers that follow: Out of thousands of species, I have
chosen only those few that have some value for wildlife and
that are commonly known in most regions or available from
seed houses or nurseries. Where wildlife attractions are not
specified, it may be assumed that small insects are drawn to

the plant or flower, or that moth and butterfly caterpillars dine on the leaves, and that the flower is a pretty and an unusual one for the gardener to enjoy.

PERENNIAL WILDFLOWERS FOR SUNNY SITES MINIMANUAL

Bee Balm, Oswego Tea (*Monarda didyma*): 2 to 3 feet tall. Scarlet tubular flowers in July and August, pungent minty scent. Prefers moist places in partial shade to full sun. Great favorite of hummingbirds, butterflies and bees. Garden variety is red, white, pink or purple. Zones 4–9.°

Black-Eyed or **Brown-Eyed Susan** (*Rudbeckia hirta*): 2 feet. Orange-yellow petals, dark central cone, daisylike. Blooms in summer. Tough, persistent, widespread. Full sun. Drought-tolerant. Common in wildflower seed mixtures. Bees, butterflies and other insects visit. Garden variety, gloriosa daisy, has large flowers, is usually grown as an annual. Zones 3–7.°

Butterfly Weed (*Asclepias tuberosa*): 1 to 2 feet tall. Gorgeous bright orange flower clusters in July and August. Dry places, drought-tolerant. Root may grow 2 to 3 feet into ground. Full sun. Zones 3–8.° Butterflies, bees and many other insects flock to it. Protected in wild.

Cardinal Flower (*Lobelia cardinalis*): 3 to 4 feet tall. Spikes of flaming red tubular flowers shout "Look at me!" from July to September. Hummingbirds do, and drink deep; also bumblebees and other long-tongued insects. Likes moist soil, partial shade. Protected in the wild. Zones 4–8.° Garden variety very showy.

Gaillardia, Blanket Flower, Indian Blanket (*Gaillardia aristata*): 2 to 4 feet tall. Cheerful red, yellow, red-tipped or maroon-red daisylike blooms from June to frost. Toothed petals. Drought-tolerant, prolific bloomer. Full sun. Self-sows freely. Zones 2–8.° Bees, butterflies and other insects visit. Common in wildflower mixtures. Fine garden variety.

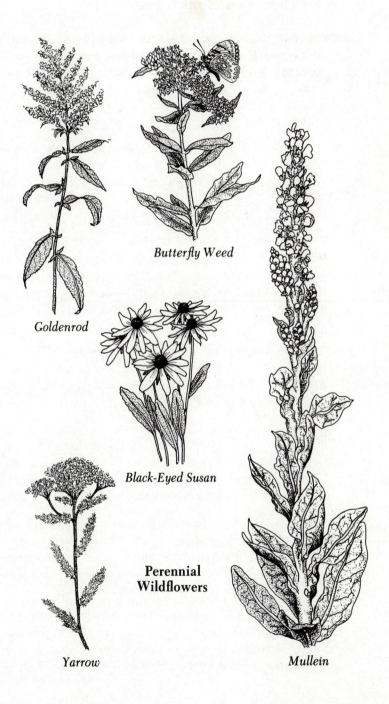

Goldenrod

Butterfly Weed

Black-Eyed Susan

Yarrow

Perennial Wildflowers

Mullein

Goldenrod (*Solidago* spp.): 1 to 7 feet. Many species. Large yellow plumed flower heads in August and September. Does not cause hay fever; ragweed does. Full sun. Zones 4–10.° Enormous appeal to butterflies, bees and most other insects, as nectar and pollen are easily reached. Birds enjoy seed. Lovely garden flowers.

Great or **Blue Lobelia, Blue Cardinal Flower** (*Lobelia siphilitica*): 3 to 4 feet tall. Cousin of cardinal flower. Light or sapphire-blue flowers in August and September. Partial shade to full sun, moist soil. Zones 4–8.° Attracts bumblebees, honeybees, small insects. Lovely many-spired garden plant.

Liatris, Blazing Star, Gayfeather (*Liatris pychnostachya*): 1 to 5 feet tall. Tall, narrow, rosy purple, lavender or white showy spikes that bloom, contrariwise, from the top down from midsummer to fall. Full sun. Drought-resistant. Zones 3–9. Big attraction for butterflies. Also a garden variety.

Mullein (*Verbascum thapsus*): A biennial. 5 to 6 feet tall or more. Strong, stout stem, tall striking spikes of yellow flowers from June to September, fuzzy leaves. Full sun. Widespread. Zones 4–8. Plentiful seeds attract birds, especially goldfinches. Also a garden variety.

New England Aster (*Aster novae-angliae*): 3 to 4 feet tall or more. Blue, purplish blue or pink flowers from August to October. Found throughout eastern United States, Southern Canada, except hot areas. Full sun. Zones 4–9.° Beloved by honeybees, butterflies, many insects. Also a garden variety.

Ox-Eye Daisy (*Chrysanthemum leucanthemum*): 1½ to 3 feet tall. Common wild daisy found nearly everywhere. A bright, cheery mass of white and yellow bloom in the garden in June and July. Full sun. A vigorous spreader. Zones 4–8. Attracts butterflies and many other insects.

Penstemon (*Penstemon gloxinioides*): 1 to 3 feet tall. Many bright colors, including red, violet, blue or pink, from June to August. Native to California and West; traveled to central and northeast areas. Tolerates hot, dry climate. Full sun.

Zones 7–10.° Tubular flowers invite hummingbirds, butter-flies and other long-tongued insects. Also a garden variety.

Purple Coneflower (*Echinacea purpurea*): 2 to 3 feet tall. Red-dish purple daisylike flowers with recurved petals from July to September. Drought-tolerant. Full sun. Found throughout Midwest, South. Zones 3–9. Favored by bees, butterflies and many small insects.

Purple Loosestrife (*Lythrum salicaria*): 3 to 6 feet tall. Magenta spires from June to August on a big, bushy plant. Common field and roadside resident; thrives also in damp places and almost anywhere in garden. Partial shade to full sun. Striking but very invasive. Zones 3–8. A great favorite of butterflies and bees, other insects.

Rugosa Rose (*Rosa rugosa*): Shrub rose; may grow to 6 feet if not pruned. Native to New England coast but will grow well elsewhere in temperate zone. Can be grown as a hedge. Blooms June to fall. Zones 2–5. Very fragrant magenta-pink flowers draw bees. Large orange-red rose hips (fruit) favored by birds.

Swamp Milkweed (*Asclepias incarnata*): 3 to 4 feet tall. Related to butterfly weed. Clusters of pink, purplish pink, or rose-purple flowers in July. Succulent leaves. Prefers full sun and moist to wet soil. Wide range in southern Canada and northeastern and central United States. Zones 3–8. Attracts butterflies, bees. Monarch lays eggs on leaves, also on com-mon milkweed; milkweeds are the sole food of its larvae.

Swamp Rose Mallow (*Hibiscus moscheutos*): 3 to 5 feet tall. Related to hibiscus. Large rose, pink or white flowers from July to October. Prefers marsh or wet places but does quite well in garden soil. Full sun to partial shade. Suitable for cold winters. Zones 5–9.

Yarrow (*Achillea millefolium*): 2 feet tall. White or pink flower clusters from June to September. Pungent ferny foliage. Very common in temperate zone. Full sun. Drought-resistant. Zones 2–8. Bees and butterflies visit.

°See Perennial Minimanual, page 43.

ANNUAL WILDFLOWERS
*FOR SUNNY SITES MINIMANUAL**

Butter-and-Eggs, Toadflax (*Linaria vulgaris*): 1 to 3 feet tall. Yellow-orange flowers look like tiny snapdragons. Orange on lower "lip" is a sure lure to bumblebees, butterflies, other long-tongued insects. A related flower is **Blue Toadflax** (*L. canadensis*). Both have nectar in spurs. Very widespread.

Catchfly, Silene, Campion, Fire Pink (*Silene* spp.): 1 to 2 feet tall. Pink to red single flowers with toothed petals from spring to midsummer. Pairs of dark green spear-shaped leaves. Light shade to partial sun. Widespread in United States. Often in wildflower mixtures. **Sweet William Catchfly** (*S. armeria*), 18 inches tall, bears light to rose-pink, ½-inch, 5-petaled flowers in clusters from midsummer to fall. Full sun. **Rose Campion** (*S. coronaria*) and other garden varieties are biennials or perennials.

Clarkia, Farewell-to-Spring (*Clarkia amoena*): 18 inches tall. Pink or red delicate divided petals. Blooms in summer. A showy westerner, often used in gardens. Full sun. Attracts bees.

Coreopsis (*Coreopsis tinctoria*): 18 inches to 3 feet tall. Flowers yellow, some with maroon; daisylike. Blooms summer to fall. Perennial form east of Rockies. Full sun to partial shade. Common in wildflower seed mixtures. Also a garden variety.

Cornflower, Bachelor's Button (*Centaurea cyanus*): 2 to 3 feet tall. Blue, purple or red ragged blooms. Blooms spring and summer. Prefers cool climates. Found throughout United States. Drought-tolerant. Full sun to partial shade. Seeds attractive to birds. Often in wildflower mixtures. Also a garden variety.

Evening Primrose, Sundrops (*Oenothera* spp.): Many species. **Common Evening Primrose** (*O. biennis*) is 2 to 4 feet tall. 4-petaled yellow blooms open in late afternoon, luring moths

°Season-long bloom unless otherwise indicated.

Butter-and-Eggs

Queen Anne's Lace

Cornflower

Annual Wildflowers

Coreopsis

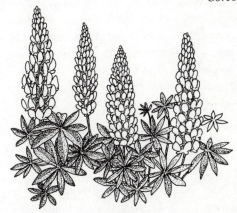

Lupine

in evening. Full sun. Drought-tolerant. Found throughout United States. **Sundrops** (*O. fructicosa*), perennial in Northeast to South, 1½ to 2 feet tall, is day-blooming. Large dayglow yellow flowers. Bright spot in garden in early summer but a rapacious spreader. Butterflies, bees, many other insects visit.

Jewelweed, Touch-Me-Not (*Impatiens capensis*): 2 to 4 feet tall. Pendent yellow-orange flower has nectar in spur prized by hummingbirds, bumblebees, sphinx moths, other long-tongued insects. Ripe seeds pop out of pods at touch.

Lacy Phacelia (*Phacelia tenacetifolia*): 2 to 3 feet tall. Pale blue flowers in crooked 3- to 5-inch cluster in early summer. Delicate tansylike foliage. Full sun. Drought-tolerant. Sturdy and aggressive. Bees, small insects visit.

Lupine (*Lupinus* spp.): 2 to 4 feet tall. Many colors, including gold and blue, several varieties. Pretty palmate 5-lobed leaves. Native to California, West Coast. Blooms spring or summer. Full sun. Drought-tolerant. Perennial species in New England, Midwest; suitable for cold winters; very handsome in the garden. **Bluebonnet** (*L. subcarnosa*), an annual species, is the state flower of Texas. Attractive to bees, other insects.

Poppies (Annual) (*Papaver* spp.): 1 to 3 feet tall. Native to California, West, Canada, but found in many other regions. Predominantly orange; also yellow or white. **Shirley** or **Corn Poppy** (*P. rhoeas*) is red. Cup-shaped blooms in spring and summer. Full sun to partial shade. **California Poppy** is *Eschscholzia californica* (see Annual Minimanual, page 62). Adaptable, prolific. Bees, other insects are attracted. Common in wildflower mixtures.

Queen Anne's Lace, Wild Carrot, Bishop's Flower (*Daucus carota*): A biennial. 3 feet tall. White, lacy flower clusters with strong scent in summer. Full sun. Big magnet for butterflies, bees, wasps, beetles, many other insects; nectar is easily reached. Found throughout United States and in wildflower seed mixtures. Also a blue garden variety.

Siberian Wallflower (*Cheiranthus allionii*): 1 to 1½ feet tall. Tiny bright orange flowers in clusters in spring and summer. Dark green lance-shaped leaves. Widespread in northern United States and Canada. Full sun. Often in wildflower mixes.

Sunflower (*Helianthus* spp.): 6 to 10 feet tall. Many varieties. **Common Sunflower** (*H. annuus*) is a plant with large coarse leaves and big flower heads to over 12 inches across with dark center disk and many seeds. State flower of Kansas. Widespread, prairie, roadside. Full sun. Bees go for flowers; birds, squirrels and other wildlife extremely fond of seeds. (People too.) Also a garden variety (see Annual Minimanual, page 62). Some butterflies choose leaves for their eggs.

The Woodland Garden

In general, woodland plants are more fragile, less likely to appreciate being transplanted into a new environment, and more likely to be rare or endangered than field and roadside flowers, which often seem to require little more than a sunny spot in order to thrive. Fortunately, many of these woodland beauties are available from wildflower nurseries; a well-stocked nursery near you may have some. By creating your own woodland garden, you can help to perpetuate these delicate—but lovely and desirable—plants.

Your woodland garden may be small, but it has some very specific requirements. It should be located on the north or northeastern side of the house, where the house itself will give some shade and shelter. It should get shade from other directions as well. The soil should be light but rich in organic matter; heavy clay soil or very sandy soil just will not do. You may have to incorporate considerable amounts of peat moss, compost (even partially decomposed), leaf mold, and/or some good sterile (weed-free) topsoil into the soil.

If oaks and pines grow nearby and drop their leaves and needles there, let them remain. They will act as a slightly acid mulch while decomposing and improve the soil further, just as they do in the forest or wood's edge where the plants grow naturally. Or bring these leaves and needles from another part of the property or another source and spread them around the woodland plants. Mulching also discourages weeds and keeps roots cool and moist, and moisture is a requirement of most woodland plants.

Even if you have created perfect woodland conditions, you may find that some plants are unable to adapt to an environment that is not truly native. They may hang on for a season or two and then disappear. They have their own mysterious reasons. Instead of attempting to replace the vanished wildflower with another of its kind, try another species, or fill in bare spots with some others that you know will not disappoint you. Add more ferns and some small bulbs that will delight you with blue, pink, yellow, or white blossoms in early spring. If there are three or four hours of indirect sun or even dappled shade, they will do well. Even in dense shade, many will survive, among them crocus, scilla, snowdrops, winter aconite, and lily-of-the-valley. Violets will perform under almost any conditions.

The Trouble with Violets

The trouble with violets is that nobody can have just one. In spring, the purple and white blossoms are so enchanting that you can even forgive those that sprinkle the lawn and the flowerbed. But when the blooms disappear, there you are, faced with countless deeply rooted plants and tiny plantlets to get rid of. Allow a few white ones into your woodland patch (they are not so aggressive), and *try* to keep the purple ones by the kitchen door and under the shrubs.

A few plants—Dutchman's-breeches, gentians, and mayapples, for example—don't need or like acid soil. Your woodland is probably neutral to acid, and they may do well. If not, they may do better in another shady spot, where the soil is more neutral.

WOODLAND WILDFLOWERS
MINIMANUAL

Bloodroot (*Sanguinaria canadensis*)*: White flower bud arises first; tightly curled, pale green, 4- to 8-inch-wide lobed leaves open later. Daisylike, 8-petaled flowers close at night. Blooms early to midspring before trees leaf out. Prefers full sun to partial shade and a humus-rich, neutral to slightly acidic soil. Self-sows and spreads freely. Perennial, Zones 3–8.

Canada Lily (*Lilium canadense*)*: To 4 feet tall. Lovely, pendent, yellow or orange speckled flowers in June. Moist meadows in full sun. Perennial, to Zone 4. Honeybees love it.

Dutchman's-Breeches (*Dicentra cucullaria*): White fragrant flowers like upside-down pantaloons borne in groups of 4 to 10 on 3- to 8-inch stalks in midspring. Related to bleeding heart, with similar ferny gray-green foliage that dies back in late spring or early summer. Does not enjoy acid soil. Perennial, Zones 3–7.

Forget-Me-Not (*Myosotis sylvatica*): To 2 feet tall. Delicate, tiny blue flowers to ¼ inch wide. Likes moist shade. Biennial. Birds like seeds. Also a garden flower.

Gentian (*Gentiana* spp.)*: Several species. Shades of blue or purple. Moist, neutral to acid soil, woods or wood borders. Various species bloom spring, summer or fall. **Closed Gentian** (*G. andrewsii*) is 1 to 2 feet tall, with clusters of 2 to 5 flowers and pairs of 2- to 4-inch leaves. **Fringed Gentian,** with 4 delicately fringed petals, is biennial and must reseed to reappear. Blooms in fall. Does not like acid soil. Others are perennial. Zones 3–6.

Hepatica (*Hepatica* spp.): Several species. Violet-blue, blue, pink or white delicate single flowers in early spring. Leathery, brownish green leaves are 3-lobed, 4 inches wide. Prefers light shade. Perennial, Zones 3–7.

Dutchman's-Breeches

Mayapple

Woodland Wildflowers

Trout Lily

Hepatica

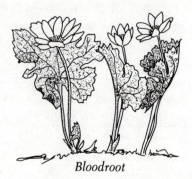

Bloodroot

Jack-in-the-Pulpit (*Arisaema triphyllum*)°: 1 to 3 feet tall. A novel flower, greenish or brownish trumpetlike spadix, usually with dark stripes, very striking; blooms spring to early summer. Chunky spike of green berries turns bright red in late summer and reseeds if not eaten by wildlife. Sharply divided 3-lobed leaves. Prefers full shade and moist, acidic soil. Perennial, Zones 3–8.

Marsh Marigold, Cowslip (*Caltha palustris*): To 2 feet tall. Bright golden yellow 2-inch flowers in late April. Requires very moist or wet soil, nice for pond or pool area. Full sun to light shade. Likes cool climate. Perennial, to Zone 4.

Mayapple, Mandrake (*Podophyllum peltatum*): Fragrant, 2-inch, white nodding flower in midspring under large, 6-lobed, umbrella-like leaves. A fine groundcover but taller than most (12 to 18 inches) and requires more space. Does not need acid soil but likes it damp and partly shaded. Large, yellow, lemonlike fruit, in late spring, is enjoyed by wildlife. Perennial, Zones 3–8.

Trillium (*Trillium* spp.)°: Many species. **Large White Trillium** (*T. grandiflorum*) is showy, with 2- to 3-inch 3-petaled flowers; spreads readily. Red or maroon species (*T. erectum*) is called **Purple Trillium** or **Wakerobin**. Both are 6 to 18 inches tall, with 3-lobed leaves. Trilliums need rich, moist soil with spring sun and partial shade in summer. White trillium blooms in mid- to late spring and is a perennial hardy in Zones 3–8; purple trillium, also perennial, blooms in late spring to early summer in Zones 2–8.

Trout Lily, Dogtooth Violet, Adder's Tongue (*Erythronium americanum*): Yellow or pink 1- to 1½-inch nodding flowers like tiny lilies in early to midspring. Beautifully mottled 3- to 6-inch-long green-and-brown leaves. Prefers sun. Goes dormant in late spring. Takes a few years to settle in before blooming. Perennial, Zones 4–7.

Turk's Cap Lily (*Lilium superbum*)°: Deep orange, speckled, upturned petals in July; very striking. Many flowers on one stalk. Tall, may grow 4 to 8 feet. Likes damp habitat but performs well in garden soil. Light shade. Perennial, to Zone 5.

Violet (*Viola* spp.): Numerous species, very widespread. Blue, purple, white or yellow flowers in May. Common blue violet can be extremely invasive. Chosen larval fare for great spangled fritillary butterfly. **Bird-Foot Violet** (*V. pedata*)° is blue, with a pretty pansy face in May; unusual trilobed leaves. All prefer shade to light shade (except bird-foot violet, which likes sun) and moist, acidic soil. Perennial, to Zone 5. All species have purple veins on petals as nectar guides to insects, small bees, butterflies.

Virginia Bluebell, Virginia Cowslip (*Mertensia virginica*)°: 1 to 2 feet tall. Pink buds open to blue trumpet-shaped flowers in midspring. Oval, 3-inch, pale gray-green leaves. Plant goes dormant in midsummer. Moist soil, full sun to partial shade. Perennial, Zones 3–9. Bumblebees and other insects visit.

Wild Bleeding Heart (*Dicentra eximia*): To 1 foot tall. Pink flowers from May to September, similar to garden variety but smaller. Intricately cut leaves. Prefers moist, acidic soil in full shade. Perennial, to Zone 4; not in hot regions.

Wild Columbine, Eastern Columbine (*Aquilegia canadensis*): Pretty, 2-inch, red-and-yellow nodding blooms in midspring to early summer. Plants to 2 feet tall with gray-green 3-lobed leaves. Adaptable, will take some sun. Self-sows. Perennial, Zones 3–8. Blooms and seeds lure hummers, butterflies, bumblebees, other long-tongued insects to nectar in spurs, as in garden columbine. Blue-and-white **Rocky Mountain** or **Colorado Columbine** (*A. caerulea*) is state flower of Colorado. Nodding 2- to 3-inch flowers are borne late spring to midsummer. Needs neutral, moist soil in full sun to partial shade. Perennial, Zones 2–7.

Wild Geranium, Crane's Bill (*Geranium maculatum*): 1 foot tall. Lilac pink to rosy purple flowers in May and June. Delicate, deeply cut palmate leaves. Moist, acidic soil in light shade. Seed explodes from case. Goes dormant in late summer. Perennial, to Zone 5. Bees and other small insects.

°Protected species. Do not dig or pick. Buy only from a reliable nursery that propagates its plants on the premises. For wild perennials for wet or moist places, see Perennials for Difficult Sites, page 234, and Chapter 5, Pools and Water Gardens.

WOODLAND EVERGREEN GROUNDCOVERS MINIMANUAL

Low evergreen groundcovers with berries are native to woodsy areas in Canada and the northern United States. They are perennials and like varying degrees of shade, moisture and soil acidity, unless otherwise stated. Their fruit is relished in fall and winter by birds, including game birds, and by deer and many kinds of wildlife. Hot, dry climates do not suit them. Meet their needs, and they will do well in your garden. Do not take them from the wild unless you first ascertain that they are not on a protected plants list.

Some of my favorites are:

Baneberry (*Actaea* spp.): 1 to 2 feet tall. Bushy plant. Small white flowers in terminal clusters. Large, toothed compound leaves. Red baneberry has crimson berries. White baneberry has white berries with a black dot, called doll's-eyes; it lives deeper in the woods, fruit ripens later in summer. Both are poisonous to people. Partial shade. Canada, northern and Midwest areas of United States, over to Oregon.

Bearberry, Kinnikinnick (*Arctostaphylos uva-ursi*): To 1 foot tall and 6 feet long. Tiny pink bell-shaped flowers in spring. A trailing shrub with evergreen foliage. Light shade to full sun, sandy or rocky places. Withstands heat and cold well. Zone 3. Red berries enjoyed by game birds and all wildlife; an important winter food.

Bunchberry (*Cornus canadensis*): To 6 inches tall. Pretty white flowers tinged with purple in late spring; bright red berries. Handsome oval, deeply ribbed leaves, 2 inches long. Dwarf relative of the dogwood tree. Must have cool or cold climate, rich acid soil. Tolerates shade. Zone 2.

Creeping Snowberry (*Gaultheria hispidula*): Creeping evergreen groundcover often found mantling fallen conifers. Oval leaves to ¾ inch long. Tiny white flowers in late spring. Acid soil, cold climate. Zone 4. White fruit for wildlife.

**Woodland
Groundcovers**

Wintergreen

Partridgeberry

Bunchberry

Snowberry

Bearberry

Partridgeberry (*Mitchella repens*): To 2 inches tall and 15 inches long. A good creeper for deep shade. Rounded ¾-inch-wide evergreen foliage. Fragrant, white, funnel-shaped, ½-inch-long blooms in early summer. Zone 4. Showy red berries a great favorite of birds, including game birds.

Wintergreen, Checkerberry, Teaberry (*Gaultheria procumbens*): To 4 inches tall. Fragrant white or pink flowers in late spring to early summer. Pea-sized red berries with wintergreen flavor savored by game birds, some wildlife. Shiny evergreen 2-inch-long leaves turn purple in fall and winter. Needs acid soil; tolerates shade. Zone 5.

Protected Native Plants

Every state has its rare and endangered plants that cannot by law be picked or removed. You can obtain the list for your state from the State Department of Environmental Conservation, county agricultural agent (both should be listed in your telephone directory's blue pages), botanical garden, or horticultural society. These lists are periodically updated and expanded. Learn to recognize and identify protected plants and flowers, and help to conserve them. Many are fast disappearing from the land where they once flourished in vast numbers because of overcollecting and habitat destruction.

Quantities of native (mostly woodland) plants are dug by nurseries or wholesalers from the wild, since germination of seed is slow and propagation by other means often difficult. Because they need a special combination of conditions, many cannot survive transplanting from the wild; thus, the species are hastened on their way to extinction. If it is possible, purchase rare wild native plants only when they have been propagated on the nursery premises. This may be difficult to ascertain, unless you have faith in the integrity of your nursery staff. Another way is to contact the New England Wild Flower Society (see Resources). They have a list of nearly 200 nurseries that state the percentage of wild plants for sale that were propagated by them, taken from the wild, or bought from wholesalers. It costs $4.50 postpaid. They also offer a leaflet, "Endangered Plants," for 85¢ postpaid.

Nurseries often breed wildflowers to enhance or introduce certain qualities to make them more attractive to home gardeners. In the process, the plant is altered genetically and is not exactly the same as its wild ancestor. However, "tamed" wildflowers are a lot better than illegal ones, or none at all, and add distinction to the garden while luring bees, butterflies, other insects, and hummingbirds.

The New York State Protected Plants Law lists a number of plants that are also native to much of the northeastern, north central, and Great Lakes areas and southward into Missouri, Kentucky, and Virginia, overlapping other states as well. Among them is the Turk's cap lily. It is sad to reflect that, according to wildflower guides—and memories—dating back a few decades, this gorgeous lily bloomed so prolifically that it carpeted the fields in orange and was as common as daisies; yet now it is a rare wild plant, along with most other native lilies.

Collecting seed and flowers in small quantities from large stands of common meadow and field flowers such as daisy, Queen Anne's lace, black-eyed Susan, and lythrum, or digging a few plants, will not endanger their populations.

Chapter 5

Pools and Water Gardens

Water, contained in almost any shape or form, adds a new dimension to the garden, at times dramatic, at times serene, always of interest. With plants in and around it, and the addition of fish and possibly amphibians, a water feature becomes a charming focus of attention and an attraction to birds, butterflies, dragonflies, and other creatures as well.

The Pool

Your pool can be as simple as a fiberglass, wood, plastic, or galvanized aluminum tub about 20 inches deep and 2 or more feet wide, which can accommodate waterlilies or other pond plants. Another simple method is to dig a hole, remove rocks with sharp edges, and line it with polyvinyl chloride (PVC), a synthetic liner, which can be anchored around the rim with overhanging flat stones. This may last five to ten years before it must be replaced. Prefabricated fiberglass pools, although more expensive, are easier to install and come in many shapes and sizes.

More elaborate pools with water pipes, pumps, and filters are best constructed by experts and are usually made of concrete, in any size that space permits. A shallow ledge about 2 inches deep around the edge will invite birds to drink and bathe. A jet of water from the supply pipe will make a simple fountain, adding a delightful sparkle and tinkling sound to a summer day. The larger pools can accommodate more intricate sprays, fountains, and sculpture.

Waterfalls

Water can be used in combination with elements of architecture and landscaping in many ways. It can be piped to the

With loosestrife framing one side and yellow flag iris, waterlilies, and other water plants blooming in the water, this pool is a delightful focus for wildlife and visitors to your yard.

CREATING A POOL

You can create your own water garden with a hose and a sheet of PVC liner. Site the new pool carefully—waterlilies need at least four to six hours of direct sunlight. A wildlife pond should be informally shaped, with soft, irregular lines and an edge that looks natural (formed by bog plants, sod, fieldstone, or a combination). It's the opposite of the formal rectangular brick-edged cement pool with a lion's head fountain at one end. Plan your pool to be big enough for all the plants you want to put in it. Waterlilies need space, and a crowded planting is always unattractive, whether in a garden bed or a garden pool.

Shape the pool by laying a garden hose or a length of twine on the ground until you have the design you want. Measure the basic length and width, then decide on the depth. In areas where the ground freezes, 18 to 24 inches is best if you wish to leave hardy lilies in the pool over winter. Plan for "shelves" around the sides of the pool to hold edge plants like cattails. These shelves should be at least a foot wide—wider if you want a massed planting—and about 12 inches deep.

To determine the size liner to order, add the length and width of the pool to twice the depth, plus 2 feet for edging. Use a level when you dig to make sure that surfaces are even. Remove all rocks, and line the pool bottom with ½ inch of sand to cushion the PVC liner. Line the sides with wet newspaper for cushioning. Install the liner, weighting the edges with bricks. If you must step on the liner, wear rubber-soled shoes. Fill the pool, making adjustments to the anchoring bricks as needed so the liner fits snugly. Trim the excess liner, leaving a 6-inch edge. Edge the pool with sod or stone, then empty the pool and refill. Allow a couple of days for the chlorine to evaporate before adding plants.

top of an artfully heaped pile of rocks or to an ornamental spout set into a stone or brick wall. From there the water will flow down to a basin and can then cascade down to a second basin or to a pool at or near ground level, through clefts in the rock or concrete. A recirculating pump will take the water back up again. Around these basins and in holes and crevices in the rocks, pockets of soil can be tucked to hold small wild-flowers, grasses, ferns, or herbs. Try to avoid placing water plants, especially waterlilies, in close proximity to waterfalls and fountains—these plants like still water. Fish, however, enjoy the motion.

But fish come later. First, the water plants you grow will oxygenate the pool. Soon, insects will appear, among them caddis flies and certain beetles whose larvae feast on the plants. But never fear, beneficial insects are on the way: big, beautiful dragonflies, damselflies, and golden mayflies. Their favorite foods, and those of their larvae (naiads), are larval and adult mosquitoes, water bugs, and beetles. If you introduce pond snails, they will help keep the pool clean by feeding on the green algae that inevitably appear.

The Plants

Waterlilies (*Nymphaea* spp.)—those glamorous, exotic flow-ers—can they grow in your backyard? Indeed they can! And once established, they need little care. In a natural pond the tubers (thick underground stems with buds called eyes) can be pressed down into the mucky bottom. For a pool, it's best to pot up the lilies instead of planting them directly in the pool bottom. Plant them shallowly in wood, clay, or plastic containers in rich garden soil with added bonemeal and/or rotted manure. Put a layer of pea gravel or pebbles over the soil to hold it in place. The surface of the soil should be 12 to 18 inches below the surface of the water. Waterlilies bloom best in full sun and are heavy feeders.

Most native lilies are hardy and can survive cold win-ters, provided that the tubers are below ice and don't freeze. Small, deep pools can be covered with boards topped with branches and leaves for extra winter protection. If your pool

PLANTING A WATERLILY

Detailed instructions for planting and maintaining waterlilies and other aquatics are given in most water garden catalogs. Here is a summary:

• Plant waterlilies in individual pots. These may be tubs, pans, pails, or English baskets. Obviously, drainage is not a concern here.

• Use a rich, heavy topsoil (clay is best), mixed 3:1 with well-rotted cow manure. Do not use potting soil.

• Half fill container, add lily, and tamp in soil until it reaches—but does *not* cover—the crown of the plant.

• Cover the soil with ½ to 1 inch of clean pea gravel to keep it from washing into the pool. Don't cover the crown of the waterlily.

• Saturate the soil with water, then set the pot in the pool so the plant is covered with 6 to 18 inches of water. If the water is too deep, put bricks or stable rocks under the pot.

• Don't set out tropicals unless the pool's water temperature is 70°F or over; they won't break dormancy in cooler water.

• Repot hardy lilies each spring in fresh, manure-enriched soil.

is too shallow to leave hardies outdoors, bring them into a cool basement (40 to 50°F) after light fall frosts have browned the foliage. Drain the pots, cover them with damp peat moss, and see that they stay moist. Flower colors are white, pink, apricot, yellow, and red. All hardy lilies sit on the surface of the water. Dwarf varieties can flourish in pools as small as 3 or 4 feet in diameter.

The spectacular tropical varieties, some of which open at night and have a heavenly fragrance, are not hardy and will succumb to cold weather. Treat them as annuals unless you live in Zone 10 or have a greenhouse pool where they can be kept over winter. Tropicals are larger and produce more blooms than hardies and bear the blooms on stems a few inches above the water.

There are many waterlily varieties suited to pool culture (write for one of the catalogs in the Resources section—there are an amazing number to choose from!). Some notable hardy lilies include the dwarf pink Joann Pring; the canary yellow *Nymphaea ×helvola*, which has mottled leaves; the sweet-scented, lemon-white sweet waterlily (*N. odorata* 'Sulphurea grandiflora'); and the white waterlily (*N. alba*), with 4- to 5-inch-wide, cup-shaped flowers from spring to fall. The best tropical waterlily for a small pool is the pygmy waterlily (*N. colorata*), with fragrant wisteria-blue flowers from May to frost.

Lotuses

The most stunning flowering water plant is the Egyptian or East Indian lotus (*Nelumbium speciosum*), also grown in a container of rich soil. It is a very large plant with heavily scented flowers up to a foot wide. The enormous leaves rise 3

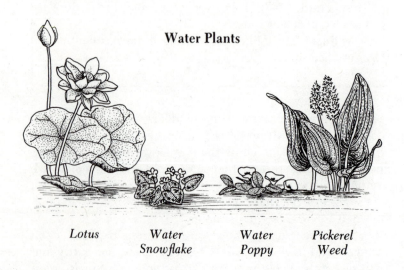

Water Plants

Lotus   Water   Water   Pickerel
         Snowflake   Poppy   Weed

to 6 feet above the surface of the water. It's not a plant for the pint-sized pool!

A better choice for the backyard pool is the hardy native yellow lotus (*Nelumbo lutea*), which blooms in summer. It has beautiful lemon-yellow flowers and handsome seedpods borne above 2-foot-wide, saucer-shaped leaves, which rise out of the water. Hybrids include the double carmine Momo Botan and double rose-pink Mrs. Perry D. Slocum. Both are hardy.

More Water Plants

Other water plants can be set on rocks or stones in the pool, and some will thrive on the shallow ledge around the edge of the pool, where they will keep their feet wet in 2 or 3 inches of water. Among these are Egyptian paper plant (papyrus), which has graceful, curving stems and grows up to 10 feet tall; horsetail (*Equisetum hyemale*), also tall; cattail (*Typha latifolia*), with 6-foot brown-topped tails; a dwarf variety (*T. minima*), which grows only about a foot tall; water poppy (*Hydrocleys nymphoides*), which has yellow flowers and 2- to 3-inch-wide leaves, and resembles a miniature waterlily;

Poolside Plants

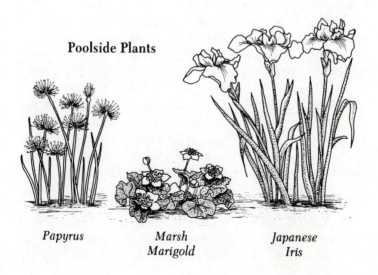

Papyrus   Marsh   Japanese
                 Marigold   Iris

water plantain (*Alisma natans*) and water snowflake (*Nymphoides indicum*), both small plants with pretty white flowers, nice for small pools.

Perhaps the most elegant flower to grow in moist soil beside a pool, or in any truly moist spot, is the Japanese iris (*Iris ensata*), which produces large, flat-topped blooms, to a foot wide, of white, vivid blue, purple, or rose on spikes to 4 feet tall in June and July. Siberian iris (*I. sibirica*) has extremely handsome, straplike foliage and a similar color range with smaller blossoms. The wild yellow flag (*I. pseudacorus*), another iris, has small, rich yellow flowers on 3-foot stalks. It needs full sun and wet soil to flourish. These iris can also be grown in pots set on the ledge in an inch or two of water. Blue flag, *I. versicolor*, has gorgeous purplish blue flowers borne in spring on 2-foot stalks and grows best with its root crown just under water. The same applies to the marsh marigold (*Caltha palustris*), whose bright yellow blooms open in early spring above clumps of glossy, heart-shaped foliage. Pickerel weed (*Pontederia cordata*) is another plant that flourishes in several inches of water. It bears spikes of lovely blue flowers. A very popular water plant is arrowhead (*Sagittaria latifolia*), with handsome arrow-shaped foliage and small white flowers. It grows in a few inches of water or very wet soil.

Oxygenating plants absorb carbon dioxide and supply oxygen to goldfish and other water residents. Waterlilies; some of the arrowheads; eel or tape grass (*Vallisneria spiralis*), with leaves like long, twisted ribbons; water violets (*Hottonia palustris*), with delicate leaves below the surface and white or lavender flowers on stems 6 to 12 inches above; elodea; and floating water lettuce (*Pistia stratiotes*) are some attractive oxygenating plants. Some can be obtained from local aquarium shops. Others can be purchased from suppliers of aquatics, pools, tubs, and water equipment.

If the soil around the pool or pond is damp or woodsy and partly shaded, many woodland wildflowers will flourish there. A woodland wildflower garden can be created close to the edge of the pool with violets, lily-of-the-valley, marsh marigold, ostrich, cinnamon and interrupted ferns, trout lily,

A shaded pool provides a picture of contrast with violets, lily-of-the-valley, swamp milkweed, and ferns.

forget-me-not, and the swamp milkweed (*Asclepias incarnata*) beloved by butterflies, especially the monarch, which lays its eggs there.

Many perennials, including bee balm, wild aster, the great or blue lobelia, scarlet cardinal flower, primrose, tall magenta loosestrife, and orange-yellow jewelweed, perform very well in moist poolside areas. These wildflowers are discussed in detail in the Perennial Wildflower Minimanual in Chapter 4, Wildflowers in the Garden. See Moisture—Too Much of a Good Thing? in Chapter 12, Weather or Not, for more moisture-loving plants. This group is particularly alluring to butterflies, moths, bees, and hummingbirds. It begins to look as though the water garden area could be the center of attraction in the backyard!

The Animals

But there's more. Once your pool has become a properly balanced habitat with well-established water plants, insects and their larvae, and snails to keep after the algae, you may wish to enjoy the further pleasure of seeing the color and lively movement of goldfish. They will do very well there, dining on insects, eggs, and larvae, and especially mosquitoes. The water must be at least 18 to 20 inches deep for goldfish, which will live under ice if winters are not too severe. They will merely become very torpid and will stop eating.

If your property is near, or borders on, a stream or lake, a marsh or damp woodland, it is very possible that your artificial pool or pond will be visited by amphibians. Frogs, toads, newts, salamanders, and painted turtles may wander over, or you could try catching your own. Frogs, which breed in streams, prefer to remain in swamps and wooded places, although they do go about in search of insects. You would have better luck with a toad. A toad might live happily in your garden, especially in a patch of seldom-mowed wildflowers or grass and weeds where insects abound, with sheltering shrubbery nearby, and a watering hole, preferably equipped with lily pads. A better slug- and insect-eater than a toad cannot be found.

If your water garden is thriving and you find some frog or toad eggs floating in a nearby creek, bring some back in a pail in spring and watch them hatch in your own pond or pool. Tadpoles are great pool scavengers.

Visiting Wildlife

Naturally, some backyard wildlife will become interested in this source of water. If the opossum or skunk feasts on some odious grubs, is it not entitled to a drink to wash them down? Do we tell the animals that this water is strictly for the birds to drink and for people to look at and admire? The pool is there because of the intrinsic beauty of water and because it completes what a natural habitat, with all its diversity of plant and animal life, ought to be. Enjoy your mammalian visitors as well as the birds and water wildlife.

A cat will sit motionless by the side of a pool for hours, eyes intent on flashing gleams of gold below. I have never heard of a goldfish in a pool having a nervous breakdown because of a cat's gaze, or of a cat taking a dive after a gold-fish. On the other hand, raccoons, which view snails and goldfish as delectable hors d'oeuvres, do not hesitate to take action. There may be casualties. Try adding more rocks and other objects for piscine hiding places.

Beware of Spray

Fish, butterflies, bees, other insects, and small creatures will almost certainly sicken or die if pesticides, including the botanical, rotenone, or other chemical sprays, float over the pool area. The warning bears repeating: *Chemical sprays are hazardous, and some are lethal to fish.* Other forms of plant and animal life can be seriously damaged by poison sprays and contaminated water. If your neighbors spray, site your pool behind sheltering shrubbery and put a wall (or your house) between the pool and the neighboring property.

A well-established water garden doesn't need much maintenance. Excessive algae may mean that there aren't enough oxygenating plants or pond snails or that there is a great deal of sunshine, which stimulates growth. Several hours of direct sunlight, however, are needed by the flower-ing plants. A cleanup of algae by hand or rake may occasion-ally be necessary. Fallen leaves, twigs, and other debris should be removed before they decompose.

Otherwise, your aquatic realm will maintain its own natural balance and look after itself, while giving you the pleasurable diversion of another form of gardening. Warn-ing: Pond watching may be addictive! Better get your chores done before you relax in a comfortable chair and abandon yourself to gazing at the aquatic world.

Chapter 6

On Growing Vegetables

*Short rows of different vegetables
interspersed with herbs and flowers . . .
not only do they limit the spread
of a blight, they discourage
methodical attack by insects.*

Eleanor Perényi,
*Green Thoughts: A Writer
in the Garden*

Seeing those little seeds you sowed spring up from the earth and become the makings of a crisp salad or steaming vegetable platter is very gratifying. It's a fine feeling knowing that you and your family are getting full flavor and high vitamin content from produce that was on the bush or vine just minutes before. And you've gotten plenty of sunshine, fresh air, and exercise along the way. But how does the vegetable garden fit into the naturalist's garden?

The main purpose of the naturalist's garden is to create an attractive and varied landscape that is inviting to many forms of wildlife and includes many kinds of edibles for them. A vegetable garden, on the other hand, is composed of edibles for *you*. If you want to grow your own produce while inviting wildlife to other parts of your yard, you must take precautions to ensure that the vegetable plot is off-limits to hungry herbivores. Fortunately, ingenious organic gardeners have devised effective ways to safeguard vegetables.

If you're an ardent vegetable gardener and think you've seen more wildlife in your plot the last few years than you can remember being there before, you might be right. As their natural habitat is encroached upon, polluted, or destroyed, many forms of wildlife move closer to suburbia, or houses anywhere, in search of food and shelter. Garden goodies are a magnet for wildlife if your property is near or borders on woodland, parkland, open fields, or land undergoing construction. Companion planting, fencing, and other protective devices may be needed to discourage hungry visitors.

Companion Planting

More and more, home gardeners are viewing a vegetable patch as an extension of the flower border. A healthy mixture of flowers, vegetables, and herbs looks attractive and offers favorable conditions for pollinators and natural enemies of pests. There's no necessity to grow vegetables in perfect rows, with each crop isolated and bare soil between the rows. Such techniques invite pests, diseases, and erosion.

Flowers growing among vegetables look delightful and also serve as companion plants, repelling or confusing injurious insects. Among these are marigold, nasturtium, geranium, petunia, and calendula. Herbs, including parsley, rosemary, thyme, tarragon, oregano, sage, summer savory, and the mints, also tend to repel insects. Onions, chives, and garlic seem to have a similar effect. Bees, butterflies, and other beneficial insects attracted to garden flowers pollinate vegetables like cucumbers and squash. Without them, these crops would set no fruit.

Some companion plants work by acting as "trap crops" for pests, attracting them away from the plants you want to harvest. For example, French marigolds attract nematodes, radishes attract maggots, nasturtiums attract aphids, and larkspur and borage attract Japanese beetles. Others work by

Interplanting vegetables, herbs, and flowers creates a beautiful, dynamic garden. Interplanting helps confuse pests and reduce disease damage.

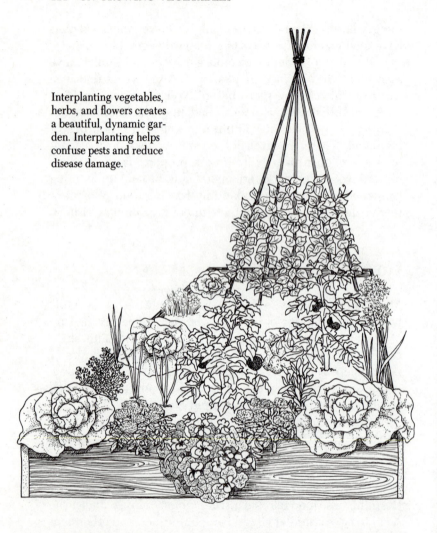

confusing pests that smell their suppers: Onions planted with carrots keep the carrot fly from finding the crop; garlic keeps aphids from roses. Many companion plants are simply said to repel certain pests: Onions repel cutworms; sage repels ants; mint, sage, and mustard repel cabbage pests; savory, cosmos, and asters repel bean beetles; radishes repel squash borers; horseradish, flax, marigolds, and garlic work for Colorado potato beetles; and green beans and potatoes repel each other's pests. Little research has been done on companion planting; try your own experiments, see what works in your garden, and keep a record of your results.

Certain species of fly, ladybug, and wasp, after enjoying a drink of nectar, go in search of destructive worms, aphids, leaf rollers, beetles, and other harmful insects on vegetables. These either get eaten on the spot, are parasitized and die, or are brought back to the nest as food for the hunter's young. Beneficials are particularly attracted to wildflowers such as Queen Anne's lace, yarrow, daisies, black-eyed Susans, cornflowers, and goldenrod, in addition to a variety of colorful annuals such as zinnias, cosmos, petunias, and marigolds.

Fencing Pests Out

For the larger pests—animals—a sturdy fence is the best defense. If deer are not a problem in your area, but rabbits and woodchucks are, a 1-inch-mesh chicken wire fence that extends 6 or more inches below ground and 3 to 3½ feet aboveground should keep your invaders out. Space slender wooden posts 8 feet apart and bury them 1½ feet deep. Till the ground around the garden to make it easy to sink the wire, or bend the bottom foot outward to make it harder for animals to burrow under. Tie the fence to the posts at ground level and again a foot from the top, so it will flop back to throw a daring 'chuck who tries to climb over. An electric fence wire run 6 to 8 inches above the ground and a foot outside the chicken wire fence will provide an extra barrier for raccoons.

Dealing with Deer

To keep out deer, a stronger, taller, and more expensive fence is needed. The standard is an 8-foot-high fence of 6-by-12-inch wire mesh, with barbed wire running an additional 2 feet to bring the total fence height to 10 feet. Less expensive, but also highly effective, is electric fencing. The best design slopes outward from the garden, with seven wires spaced at 12-inch intervals for a total height of 4 feet and depth of 6 feet.

An alternative is a vertical fence with six or seven wires spaced at 8- to 10-inch intervals, with an additional wire set 15 inches aboveground and 38 inches outside the fence. Use bipolar, low-impedance fence energizers, and electrify the fences as soon as they're up so the deer will respect them. Keep the ground under electric fencing mowed to avoid shorting the fence. Naturally, you don't want to hurt the animals, so don't use a charge that's stronger than that used for livestock. (The clerks that sell you the electric fence can advise you.)

Additional Protection

In garden centers and catalogs you will find various protective devices designed to repel, trap, or terrorize unwanted garden guzzlers or visitors. They range all the way from Havahart traps for small animals and not-so-humane mole traps to grotesque giant inflatable scarecrows that might send a toddler screaming back to the house.

Unfortunately, the scarecrows are unlikely to have the same effect on wildlife—they are more decorative than useful. More functional but still far from foolproof devices include black metal cats with glittering eyes, realistic inflatable vinyl great horned owls and curvy snakes with staring eyes, and poles with mirrored disks that whirl in a breeze. All are meant to scare off birds and small animals. To be effective, these "predators" must move around like their live counterparts. Attach the plastic owls firmly to stakes, and change their location every few days. Move snakes to different areas to "bask in the sun." Unlike all these devices, the best of them—a helium-filled Cooper's hawk balloon, which "flies" above the garden on a 30-to 100-foot tether—carries a steep price tag.

The best place for birds and mammals is outside the vegetable patch and orchard. The plastic great horned owl, plastic snake, heavy-duty electric deer fence, and groundhog-proofed chickenwire fence will all deter invaders.

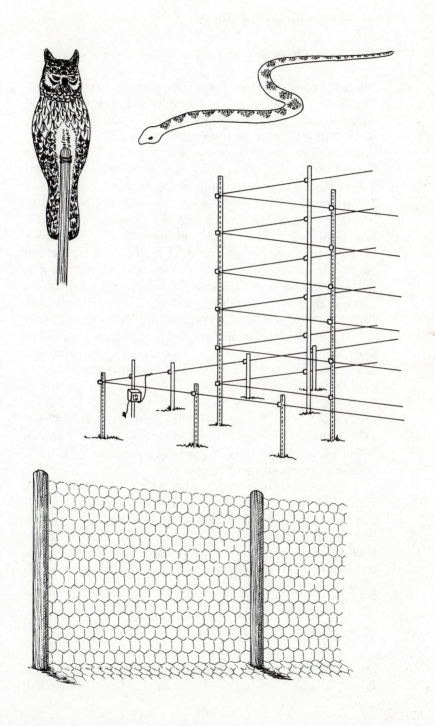

Effective Alternatives

There are plenty of other reasonably priced (or free) options. Tests in Louisiana found that a spray of 18 eggs in 5 gallons of water would protect an entire acre of soybeans from deer, which disliked the smell (mercifully too diluted to be objectionable to people). Experiments in Alabama revealed that bags of human hair (1 ounce per bag; try barbershops and beauty parlors for a supply) placed 2 feet above the ground at 5-, 10-, or 15-foot intervals along the outside of a field protected sweet potatoes, melons, and cowpeas from deer. Black polypropylene or white nylon netting draped on low stakes over a strawberry bed and secured with boards around the edges of the bed will keep birds from the fruit, as long as there are no holes in the netting. If you're not sure what is vandalizing your vegetables, sift flour around the area to reveal the paw prints or hoofprints of the guilty party.

The powerful aroma of mothballs is often a deterrent to scavenging mammals such as raccoons, skunks, squirrels, mice, and burrowing moles. Only mothballs made from naphthalene, a coal derivative, and not from camphor, a chemical that may have toxic effects, can be considered for use in the garden. Scattering mothballs in and around your corn is an effective repellent for raccoons, which are drawn to the garden by the smell of ripening ears. Spread the mothballs as the corn silks start to appear.

Scent-Off, HiLo, and other dusts and sprays are intended to keep dogs and cats away from certain areas. Thiram is an effective taste repellent for deer and rabbits. Hinder works as an odor repellent for the same animals. These products must be reapplied after each rain. Some contain chemicals; read the labels carefully, and wash your hands after using.

Avoiding Disease

Start with humus-rich soil in a sunny, well-drained area. Good soil leads to strong plants that are less likely to succumb to disease. The preparation of soil for vegetables is much the same as for flowers. (See Preparing the Flower Border in Chapter 3, The Naturalist's Flower Garden, and Chapter 10, The Stuff of Life.) Vegetables are heavier feeders than flowers and need more nutrients during the growing season. Compost is the best all-purpose fertilizer and soil builder. Leafy vegetables like a high-nitrogen fertilizer, such as guano, bloodmeal, fish meal, or cottonseed meal. Crops with pods or fruit like more phosphorus, supplied by colloidal phosphate, rock phosphate, bonemeal, and some guanos; root crops like more potassium, available from kelp meal, langbeinite, greensand, and granite dust. A liquid fertilizer like fish emulsion, liquid seaweed, or compost or manure tea is ideal for quick assimilation and as a starter solution for newly set vegetable seedlings, as with flowers.

Where possible, choose varieties of seed or plants that are labeled or described as disease-resistant or at least disease-tolerant. Two such designations are VF (verticillium and fusarium wilt–resistant) and PM (powdery mildew-resistant or –tolerant).

Resistant Varieties

Seed catalogs always call out disease resistance in vegetables, and the list of resistant and tolerant varieties grows yearly. For example, a review of recent tomato introductions turns up Sweet Chelsea, tolerant of tobacco mosaic virus, verticillium and fusarium wilts, leaf mold, leaf spot, and nematodes; Summer Delight, resistant to verticillium and fusarium wilts; the Summer Flavor series, resistant to verticillium and fusarium races 1 and 2; and Stokesdale, resistant to fusarium race 1 and tolerant of blossom-end rot, cracking, and catfacing.

A look at new cucumbers shows County Fair '83, which is resistant to scab, anthracnose, cucumber mosaic, angular leaf spot, and fusarium and bacterial wilts, and is unappetizing to cucumber beetles; Burpee's Picklebush is tolerant of, and Levina is resistant to, cucumber mosaic and powdery mildew. Golden Gopher muskmelon is resistant to field rot and fusarium wilt; Summer Sweet Charlie I Hybrid water-

melon is tolerant of fusarium and anthracnose; Prime Choice
Y.R. Hybrid cabbage is tolerant of tipburn and yellows.
There are many others. If you know a certain disease is prev-
alent in your area, make your selections accordingly.

When purchasing seedlings and other plant material,
examine them carefully to make sure they are healthy, vigorous, and free of pests and diseases. Don't buy a transplant if it
looks weak and spindly, has wilted leaves and dried-out soil,
is infested, shows pest damage such as shotholing (tiny holes
in the leaves), or has leaves that are yellow or mottled.

Of particular importance to vegetables is crop rotation.
Despite all your precautions, soilborne diseases or pests may
affect certain plants and may remain in the soil for years.
Make it harder for them to become entrenched by not setting
the same crops—or their relatives—where they are planted
the previous year.

Weeding and Feeding

Although they are a source of nectar and seeds for birds and
many other creatures, weeds, if allowed to grow unchecked,
usurp nutrients and moisture from edibles and can crowd
and shade them out. Pull weeds when they're small—they
will resist less if the soil is wet. Remove flowers or seeds, if
any, and toss the offending plants into the compost or back to
the earth, rootless. Keep your soil mulched or lightly cultivated. And remember, a few weeds are not a calamity. Every
garden has them.

The same may be said for insect pests. Although their
numbers are low, their damage tends to be superficial—more
a blow to the gardener's ego than to the garden's productivi-
ty. But if careful monitoring shows that pests are gaining a
foothold, it's time to plan a control strategy. You might be
willing to share some parsley or a few carrot tops with swallowtail butterfly larvae, which are fat, black-, gold-, and
green-striped caterpillars, but be understandably unwilling
to have your cabbage, Brussels sprouts, and other crucifers
devoured by the cabbageworm. After all, the parsleyworm

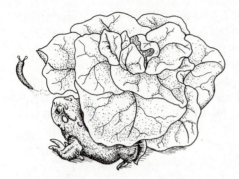

The pest-eating toad is
your garden's best friend.

will become a gorgeous swallowtail, whereas cabbageworms
are larvae of the nondescript, all-too-prolific cabbage butterfly, which seems to be around all summer long, laying
appalling numbers of eggs. This destructive insect must be
given no quarter.

Handpicking the slender, 1- to 1½-inch-long green
worms helps to some extent, but you will probably need to
use Bt, the bacterial control sold under various trade names
(see Chapter 11, Battling Bugs and Diseases . . . Naturally) if
you have a severe infestation. This spray is toxic only to leaf-
eating caterpillars—including tomato hornworms—and does
not leave a residue harmful to humans, so it is safe to use right
up to harvest. However, it will affect other butterfly larvae if
they are nearby. Other safe sprays such as Safer's Insecticidal
Soap or a homemade spray using Ivory Flakes or vinegar, a
teaspoon to a gallon of water, will help control pests such as
aphids, mites, whiteflies, and mealybugs.

Making Choices

Even if you have favorite varieties that do well for you, I sug-
gest a yearly browsing through some seed and plant catalogs,
which are fun to read, informative, and up-to-the-minute
with new varieties. The color photographs are guaranteed to
make your mouth water. The catalogs give detailed descriptions of vegetables, herbs, and fruits, plus their flavors and
uses. Helpful advice on pests and diseases, where, when, and

how to plant and harvest, and more, is provided. Seed packets also usually have information on when to plant, spacing, thinning of seedlings, space needed by mature plants, and time from planting to harvest.

Some guides for planting vegetables give instructions based on staggering figures—for example, 50 or 100 feet of row of this seed, an average yield of 120 pounds per 100 feet of that. And a packet of carrot seed may contain 1,000 to 1,500 seeds, enough for 40 feet of row; a packet of radish seed, enough for 20 feet; lettuce, for 30 feet. Don't be intimidated! Your entire space for vegetables may be 10 by 15 feet or less. Use only as much of the seed as you want, sow more later in the season if desired, and/or store the remainder in a cool, dry place, as with flower seed. It will remain viable for a year or two, often longer. What would you do with 20 feet of radishes anyway?

Vegetable Variety

Almost every vegetable is offered in a stunning variety of types, sizes, shapes, colors, and even times to maturity. Grow what you and your family like, but by all means, experiment with something new. Have you tried the purple-podded beans that grow from beautiful amethyst-colored flowers? They turn green when cooked and are extremely tender. What about yellow beets, white eggplant, and yellow-and-white tricolor corn? Decorative mounded basils form tiny hills of aromatic, bright green foliage. Purple Ruffles basil has fringed leaves and, with its sibling Green Ruffles, is highly ornamental in the front of the border. There are red lettuces that are most decorative in a salad and dwarf varieties of lettuce whose mature heads are each just right for one portion. Some vegetables grown as ornamentals can be useful to the naturalist/gardener. Trellis-grown gourds can be dried, hollowed out, and used as birdhouses!

Many kinds of veggies are available in dwarf or mini-sizes. A midget tomato can be grown in a 3- or 4-inch pot on a patio or sunny windowsill and bear a crop of small cherry tomatoes. It's fun to watch them grow! Dwarf watermelons will bear cantaloupe-sized fruit 6 to 8 inches around. At the other extreme, and fun to grow, too, are pumpkins, which need a lot of space to ramble about in. But if space is limited, stay away from large vegetables, which often have large leaves, such as squash, melons, Brussels sprouts, cabbage, spinach (a lot of spinach cooks down to very little in the pot), and potatoes, with vines that flop around for some length on top of the ground.

Perennial Vegetables

Among my favorite perennial vegetables are rhubarb and asparagus. Set them in places where they will not be disturbed, nourish them well, and they will produce bountifully for many years. Rhubarb leaves are very decorative in the garden; they are very poisonous as well. Chives are also perennial. Those that are not cut down bear pretty lavender flowers. Garlic chives, another perennial herb, has an interesting mild garlic flavor and bears starry white, rose-scented flowers that attract many nectar-seekers, especially bees. Thyme and the mints are more perennial herbs with insect-attracting blooms. And don't forget that wonderful bee draw, strawberries, often grown in the perennial section of the vegetable plot.

Crops in Season

Like flowers, vegetables produce well at certain times of year. Take these preferences into account when you plan your vegetable garden. Most vegetables can be divided into cool- or warm-season crops. Cool-season crops include asparagus, rhubarb, garden peas, cole crops, carrots, radishes, lettuce, beets, parsley, onions, garlic, chives, spinach, potatoes, turnips, and parsnips. Cool-season crops may be planted even before the last expected frost date in your area, and most will continue to grow until a light fall frost, some even later. When the early peas, lettuce, and radishes are finished, fill in with beans and quick-maturing or heat-tolerant lettuce. Compost the pea vines. By succession-planting every two weeks except in midsummer heat, beans and lettuce can be kept producing into fall.

The soil must be rich and friable for carrots, beets, parsnips, turnips, and other root crops. They don't thrive in extreme heat and should be planted very early in the season. A second planting of carrots and beets made in early summer provides a fall harvest. Other cool-season crops can be replanted in mid-August as nights turn cool; in the South and mild-winter areas, replant in late summer or fall for enjoyment all winter.

Warm-season crops include beans, corn, cucumbers, peppers, tomatoes, squash, melons, and southern peas. Eggplant, lima beans, and sweet potatoes need four months or more of warm growing weather and thus are not common in northern gardens. Northerners who determine to grow their own should choose fast-maturing varieties, grow healthy transplants, and set them out in black plastic under hotcaps or other frost protection. Warm-season crops can be severely injured or killed by a late frost and should not be planted until the ground has thoroughly warmed up.

Filling in Spaces

Between plants that grow slowly and take longer to mature, such as peppers, tomatoes, cabbages, parsnips, potatoes, and onions, you can plant fast-growing vegetables such as lettuce, beans, radishes, and spinach. Harvest these quick-maturing crops while their slower neighbors are still growing.

Where you pull up a root vegetable or a head of lettuce, you will have a hole. Drop in a couple of radish or lettuce seeds. Or have fast-growing, low annuals such as alyssum, nasturtium, and lobelia nearby. They tend to spread or sprawl and fill in bare spots. Many-colored garden balsam and blue ageratum that self-sowed the year before are delightful taller fillers. Many nurseries carry pots or packs of annuals for sale well into midsummer. Cut them back if leggy, give them a boost with a splash of liquid fertilizer, and they will come along nicely, filling in empty spots here and there.

Busy naturalist/gardeners dedicated to other matters may choose to buy a small selection of sturdy young vegetable plants from a garden center or nursery rather than grow them from seed, thus eliminating a certain amount of labor and care. And if you don't have time for a whole vegetable garden, or don't trust your wildlife to keep out of it, you still don't have to give up homegrown vegetables altogether. One option is to move the vegetables close to the house by growing them in containers—pots, tubs, barrels, baskets, or boxes—on patio, deck, steps, against a wall, or up a trellis. When they're near at hand, it's easier to keep an eye on them. The bibliography for this chapter (found at the back of the book) will provide you with informative reading matter on home food growing.

Part Two

THE GARDEN AS BACKYARD NATURE CENTER

Chapter 7

Birds in the Backyard

If birds could describe their vision of a perfect suburban garden, it would include plenty of big trees; a clump of berry-laden shrubs; fruit trees; many kinds of flowers, clovers, and grasses; weeds allowed to go to seed; a running brook or a pond; and feeders well stocked for much of the year. This avian paradise would exclude cats, dogs, snakes, and other predators, lawn mowers, leaf blowers, and all kinds of chemical sprays and dusts.

Wishful thinking on a bird's part? Not necessarily! The naturalist/gardener can fulfill many of these wishes one way or another. After all, most birds are lovely to look at, delightful to know, and practical to have around. They are the biggest gun in nature's arsenal for insect pests, especially grubs and caterpillars. So even *without* a babbling brook, and even *with* a pet on the premises, it's a good idea to make the property attractive to birds. Such a habitat appeals to many other creatures as well, so that when you plan for birds you will also

129

attract bees, butterflies, and moths, as well as other insects, squirrels, and chipmunks.

Cover

Cover is shelter, cover is safety, cover is a place to hide, breed, cool off, warm up, and dry out. Cover is a stand of dense evergreens, a hedge, a clump of shrubs, a big leafy tree, or a briar patch; thick vines on a wall; or an unmowed strip of grasses and wildflowers for ground-nesting birds, pheasants, and other game birds, and millions of insects. Cover should not be far from food and water sources so that birds and other creatures can make quick forays and quick getaways, even if the only predator in sight is a fat, sleepy old cat, too lazy to chase anything (the birds don't know that and are always nervous anyway).

One form of cover that's fast and easy to construct is the brush pile. A brush pile is made with a base of rocks and stones or logs with spaces in between, topped with branches, twigs, and sticks to a height of 3 or 4 feet or more. A discarded Christmas tree would be a fine addition here or elsewhere in the rear of the property. Brush piles attract many small mammals and some birds.

Nesting

Some birds nest high up, some close to the ground, others in between, on branches, in holes, or in your bird house. To attract different species, you need diversity—it cannot be stressed too often—in the varieties, sizes, and densities of trees and shrubs on your property. Birds look for concealment and protection in their choice of places to breed and care for their young.

A varied setting draws many species of birds that build different nests in different places. Some, such as the meadowlark, are ground-nesters. The average suburban property is not likely to have this kind of bird, for their natural habitat is fields and pastures, but if you establish a wildflower meadow, you may be rewarded with a meadowlark. Others, including woodpeckers, are hole-nesters. Unless there is a dead tree or tree trunk on the property, you are not likely to have them either. Sadly, that includes the bluebird, whose numbers are fast diminishing, especially in the East. Can you live with a dead tree? If so, a bluebird family might be able to live with you. If not, try putting up a nest box on a fence, post, or tree trunk about 4 or 5 feet above the ground in a fairly open area. See Bringing Back the Bluebird in this chapter for full details and a nest box diagram.

The tree-nesters constitute by far the greatest number of birds. They prefer thick clumps of evergreens—pine, fir, hemlock, spruce, and cedar—or any fairly large tree, such as an oak or beech, near some dense shrubbery for additional

The beloved bluebird enjoys living near open meadows. A nest box on a fence post might draw a pair of them to your garden.

Sweet gum seeds are choice goldfinch food. Many highly ornamental trees and shrubs are also "natural bird feeders."

shelter. Birds look for nesting places in the spring. They don't live in the nests all year round, but they do need cover at all times and shelter in windy or stormy weather.

Birds in Your Yard

Birds commonly seen in the Northeast, mid-Atlantic, and Midwest regions include the cardinal, grackle, purple martin, catbird, brown thrasher, Carolina and black-capped chickadees (the latter also in Canada and up into Alaska), tufted titmouse, starling, house wren (also in the West), Carolina wren, brown-headed cowbird (also in the South), barn and tree swallows (also in Canada and up into Alaska), red-winged blackbird, American goldfinch, purple finch, house finch, and the sparrows. Most of them stay for the winter, especially if they are fed. Winter also marks the arrival of the dark-eyed junco nationwide. The redwing blackbird arrives early in spring from the South and soon departs for Canada, where it has its breeding grounds. The mockingbird, a true southerner, can often be seen (and heard) as far north as New York and lower New England.

One of the most intriguing of all birds is the owl. The sound of an owl may be awesome and even frightening to some people, but if one lives near you, consider yourself fortunate. The tiny screech owl, robin-sized, feeds on insects, grubs, moths, and mice. It might take up residence in a hollow tree or a bird's nest box and from there conduct its search for prey. The barn owl, which lives in buildings and steeples as well as barns, is a world-class mouser. Larger owls prefer woodlands; if you live near them, you may see these big predatory birds on the wing looking for rodents, rabbits, small mammals, and small birds.

Two much-loved birds, the bluebird and the hummingbird, deserve special mention. See Bringing Back the Bluebird, and Hummingbird: The Sprightly Mite, in this chapter.

Nature's Menu

Mainly, birds love berries! Some of the berry-bearing shrubs that birds are most partial to include viburnum, bush honeysuckle, cotoneaster, barberry, pyracantha (firethorn), spicebush, elderberry, mulberry, and almost anything else that ends in -berry. Your raspberry, blackberry, and blueberry bushes will be very tempting. But given enough alternative food sources, birds will not deprive you of more than a few nips, especially if you cover the plants with cages or netting before the fruit ripens.

Favorite trees are flowering crabapple, dogwood, wild cherry and other cherries, hackberry, hawthorn, Russian and autumn olives, holly, red cedar, elder, mountain ash, sassafras, and juniper. Birds also enjoy the fruits of such vines as Virginia creeper, bittersweet, and wild grape.

A wide variety of flowers, including wildflowers, is sure to attract birds as well as butterflies, moths, bees, and insects. Food choices for birds differ according to the species and shape of the bill. The seed eaters, mostly with short, stubby bills, go for seeds from weeds, flowers, and grasses. A flock of noisy starlings on the lawn is good for something; watch them vacuum up crabgrass seeds. Some of the common annuals, among them California poppy, marigold, calendula, cosmos, cornflower, and zinnia, and perennials such as New England or wild aster, garden phlox, and coreopsis, offer fine pickings

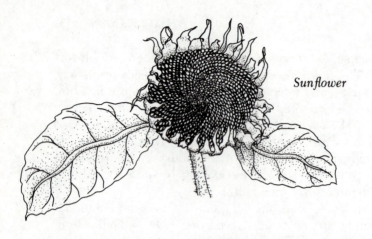

Sunflower

Dogwood

Virginia Creeper

You can choose from a diversity of trees, shrubs, vines, and flowers when planting a garden to attract birds. Here are some of their favorites.

to seed-eating songbirds, including cardinals, finches, grosbeaks, sparrows, thrashers, towhees, chickadees, nuthatches, and titmice, if some flowers are allowed to go to seed on the stem. At fall cleanup time, I always leave some seedy clumps of aster, cornflower, and marigold standing over the winter for birds to nibble.

Sunflower seeds are ambrosia for most birds. Grow your own sunflowers at the back of the border from seed you bought to feed the birds. One sunflower has hundreds of seeds. Let some ripen on the stalk, and the birds will have a banquet. Save a few of the seeds to plant next spring.

To find out more about suitable plantings and regional wildlife in your area, consult local sources such as your county agricultural agent, state university Extension office or soil conservation office, Audubon Society, nature center, knowledgeable nursery staff, and experienced gardeners. Helpful information is often provided in local newspaper and magazine articles about gardening and nature, in national publications, and in mail-order catalogs. In addition, the National Wildlife Federation offers very useful and inspiring information on creating a backyard nature sanctuary and maintaining it properly (see Resources).

Insect Eaters

For much of the year, most birds subsist largely on insects in larval and adult stages, though they eat seeds and berries as well. Woodpeckers, creepers, and nuthatches climb up, down, and around tree trunks (the nuthatch goes down head first) in search of insects and their eggs in cracks and crevices of tree bark. Sapsuckers and woodpeckers drill holes in the trunks; if the sap is running, certain insects will come for a free meal. Blue jays are omnivorous and gobble almost anything in sight, including caterpillars, beetles, seeds, acorns, insects, and even an occasional egg or baby bird of another species. Robins are prodigious insect eaters, as anyone knows who has seen them on the lawn lunging for earthworms and grubs. But in winter, when insects are dead or hibernating, birds need a helping hand.

Food for the Birds in Winter

The birds that remain all winter usually manage—though often with great difficulty—to endure the cold and scrounge up enough weed seeds, berries, hibernating insects, insect eggs, and pupae to survive. Giving them a helping handout has become a national pastime. Not only is it entertaining to watch birds at the feeder as you sit by a window on a cold or snowy day, but it is rewarding to know that you are helping them survive the winter and "make it" in a world where their existence is threatened by pollution, pesticides, and loss of habitat. They will thank you by devouring emerging insects and grubs in spring and "cleaning up" latecomers all season.

Seeds, crumbs, nuts, apple cores, bits of bread, and raisins tossed out under a tree will draw a flock of sparrows, juncos, starlings, mourning doves, blue jays, and possibly, alas, pigeons. Cardinals are also ground feeders, but they often like to dine late, arriving at dusk, after the bourgeoisie has left. Save some supper for them.

Fixing Up a Feeder

Most of the other birds prefer their pie in the sky. Feeders should be placed on a pole, attached to a tree trunk, or hung firmly from a branch near some cover such as evergreen shrubbery, if possible. If this is not possible, or you prefer a window-ledge feeder, many birds will undoubtedly be hungry and interested enough to come anyway.

All-purpose commercial packages of birdseed found in supermarkets usually contain substantial amounts of inexpensive milo, wheat, oats or groats, and cracked corn, which don't have much taste appeal. Garden supply and hardware stores, seed and feed stores, and nature centers stock preferred seeds and mixes, as do specialty catalogs (see Resources). Sunflower seed seems to be the great favorite of most wild birds. The smaller black oil sunflower seed is generally preferred over the black-striped variety, according to studies conducted in various parts of the country. Most birds

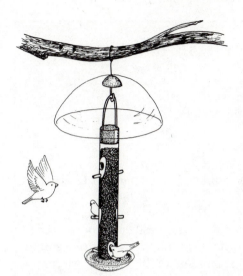

Bird feeders are an integral part of the naturalist's garden in winter. The domed baffle keeps squirrels from vandalizing the feeder. Once you put out a feeder in winter, keep it filled until bugs appear in the spring garden—your birds will be counting on it.

that like sunflower seed in the shell also like it hulled. (A word of caution on sunflower seed hulls discarded by the birds: Rake them up from time to time and discard them. They have a toxic effect on grass and plants and should not be left to pile up or added to garden beds or compost.) Other favorite foods are white, red, and golden millet and thistle seed.

Feeding Tips

Aelred D. Geis, wildlife specialist with the U.S. Fish and Wildlife Service, collects data on the feeding habits of wild birds. Geis advises that you avoid packaged seed mixtures and supply seed that is preferred by your local bird population. Feeding should not end abruptly when spring arrives, since seeds and other bird foods found in nature are still scarce. (For more information, see Resources.)

If you do buy packaged mixes, add more of the goodies most prized by your backyard birds (see the chart Favorite Foods of Some Common Wild Birds in this chapter). Many of them are also not at all averse to broken nutmeats, cookies, and crackers, if squirrels, chipmunks, or other wildlife don't gobble these delicacies before they do.

A BLIZZARD IN BIRDLAND

Bird watching in winter, from the comfort of an inside seat by the window, is a delightful pastime. When snow is on the ground, it can become an obsession! The day after an unusually heavy blizzard dumps 10 inches of snow in our area, I watch, mesmerized by the increased activity in the backyard. At the hub of it all is the big sugar maple near the back door.

This tree does everything that a large leafy tree can be expected to do. It shades and cools the terrace and the back of the house in summer, and its blazing foliage is a gorgeous sight in fall. In winter its strong, graceful limbs are revealed, and on them I hang bird feeders. Beneath the tree I scatter food for the ground-feeding birds.

The heavy snowfall and bitter cold bring many more birds than usual to the backyard looking for a handout. For just such "emergencies" I stockpile ample supplies of several kinds of birdseed (especially sunflower seed, which is the greatest favorite), peanuts, day-old store bread, popcorn, nuts, dried-up raisins, stale and broken bits of crackers, cookies, cake, candy, and every uneaten crumb from the table.

Finches, Cardinals, and Flickers

The purple finches (why they are called "purple" I can't imagine, as the male's breast and head are rosy red) and the little olive-drab goldfinches with white-and-black-striped wings are mobbing the feeders, almost knocking each other off the perches in their feeding frenzy. Thistle seed is what they're after. The bright yellow finery of the male goldfinches is muted in winter, and they are barely distinguishable from the females. Gray-tufted titmice with perky crests arrive and joust in the air for places on perches. Back and forth dart tiny chickadees, tossing out rejected seeds from the feeders, selecting a sunflower seed, and speeding off. All the shaking the feeders get adds more seeds to the snow and attracts more ground feeders to "come and get it." These diners are juncos, sparrows, mourning doves, blue jays, crows and, of course, the voracious squirrels.

A red cardinal on the white snow—is there a prettier sight? Yet perhaps his mate, elegantly feathered in taupe and light brown with touches of red, is just as lovely.

Suddenly, a large bird I have never seen in my yard before appears on the tree. It's a yellow-shafted flicker, a sleek woodpecker with spotted breast, brownish back, a red band at the back of its head, and a black breast band. I hope it will stay, but the big handsome bird soon moves on.

More Woodpeckers

The downy woodpecker who has taken it upon herself (I know she's a female because she doesn't have the male's red head patch) to keep the maple free of insect eggs and larvae has also discovered the feeder. Maybe she thinks it is just an extension of "her" tree—with different goodies. At any rate, it's easy pickings for a change. I don't begrudge her a free lunch, but when the jays get the same idea, I don't feel nearly as charitable. A blue jay brigade is constantly on the alert, especially for the sound of peanuts hitting the ground. They are too big to sit on a perch and feed comfortably. But, not to be thwarted, they dart close, hang on for a split second, snatch a sunflower seed, and make off. Leave it to the ingenious jays to figure an angle!

(continued)

A BLIZZARD IN BIRDLAND—*Continued*

A small patch of red appears on a branch, and as the rest of a bird comes into view I catch my breath in excitement. Another "first" for my birdland! This one is a red-bellied woodpecker, one of the ladder-backs, with a pale beige breast, white-and-black-barred wings, and red cap and nape. It taps awhile at the tree, then settles down in a sturdy fork in the trunk and seems to take a birdnap. Then it, too, flies away.

I go out to replenish air and ground supplies and notice robins on the hawthorn tree, no doubt gleaning the last of the remaining berries. They are a welcome if unusual sight in January. Soon, having no use for my handouts, they take flight. But I know they'll be back in early spring. For now, I have hungry customers to tide through these bleak winter days until food in nature is plentiful once more. It's a wise bird that escapes, or survives, January blizzards.

Still, for the gardener, snow has two really good things going for it. It's the quintessential mulch, and the price is right.

Suet

Suet balls made from beef fat (at the butcher's) or homemade balls of cooking fat can be coated or mixed with seeds or grains and are considered highly delectable fare by almost all birds. They can be hung from a branch in a mesh or string bag (the kind onions and citrus fruits come in) or put inside a piece of screening or wire mesh attached to a tree trunk.

Peanut butter is a great favorite too. It can be stuffed into pine cones, which can be tucked into shrubbery or tied to twigs, pushed into holes bored in a piece of wood or a log, or even smeared directly on a branch or tree trunk. These items will win your avian cuisine its fourth star.

A pinecone stuffed with peanut butter makes a nourishing winter treat for birds like this tufted titmouse.

Squelching the Squirrels

Don't let the squirrels drive you nuts. They are insatiable marauders and doubtless will find a way to get at that feeder no matter how cleverly it was designed to keep them out. Try throwing peanuts, bread, and stale baked goods a distance away, along with acorns or any other nuts you gathered in autumn that they didn't find first. This will assuage their hunger, for a while. But it does seem that country squirrels, like cockroaches everywhere, cannot be discouraged, much less excluded, wherever a smidgen of food is to be found.

Look at it this way. They have to eat. And they are fun to watch, as they chase each other, chatter away, scold the cat, scramble and scurry, and otherwise enliven the backyard with acrobatic feats and frolics. They are also part of nature's scheme when they bury those acorns all over the place. From forgotten acorn stashes, big oaks grow.

A final word about feeding the birds. Once you start, they will depend on it and may go hungry if you forget or go away. So don't forget! And if you go away, or cannot go outside because of illness, try to have a substitute do the job at least once a day. Keep plenty of supplies on hand. Then if the weather is severe, you and the birds will not run short.

Favorite Foods of Some Common Wild Birds

Kind of Bird	Oil (Black) Sunflower	Black-Striped Sunflower	White Proso Millet	Red Proso Millet	Golden Millet	Niger Thistle	Cracked Corn	Peanut Kernels
American goldfinch	■					■		
Blue jay	■	■						■
Brown-headed cowbird			■	■	■			
Cardinal	■	■						
Chickadee	■	■						■
Common grackle	■	■					■	
Downy, hairy, and red-bellied woodpeckers	beef suet—see page 140							
House finch	■					■		
Junco			■	■			■	
Mourning dove	■		■	■	■		■	
Pine siskin	■	■				■		
Purple finch	■					■		
Red-winged blackbird			■	■	■			
Rose-breasted and evening grosbeaks	■	■						
Rufous-sided towhee			■					
Tufted titmouse	■	■						■

Kind of Bird	Oil (Black) Sunflower	Black-Striped Sunflower	White Proso Millet	Red Proso Millet	Golden Millet	Niger Thistle	Cracked Corn	Peanut Kernels
White-breasted nuthatch	■	■						
White-crowned and white-throated sparrows	■	■	■	■			■	
All sparrows			■	■				

Water

Birds need water for drinking and bathing all year round. Sometimes water is hard for them to come by. If you are near a pond or stream, or better yet, have one of your own, the birds that come to your backyard will have no drinking problem. Otherwise, water can be offered in as simple a container as a large, shallow pan or bowl, or a large flowerpot saucer, not deeper than 2 to 3 inches. To help keep the water from freezing in winter, raise the container off the ground on boards, flowerpots, or other objects. Waterproof aquarium or birdbath heaters can be purchased in pet shops or from garden centers and catalogs. Make certain the extension cord from the house is weatherproof. A concrete or cement birdbath on a column is more likely to frustrate cats or other interested four-footed parties, but concrete may crack in freezing weather. Any container of water should be placed close to a shrub or flower border so that birds can take cover quickly.

These small amounts of water must be replenished often, and the containers kept clean and free of debris. A large stone in the center makes a good perch for the birds. If ice should form, break it up and add hot water. Do *not* add anything else. Antifreeze or alcohol will make birds sick or kill them.

More Ways with Water

There are ways and means to provide more substantial watering holes. A child's sturdy plastic swimming pool is one. A fiberglass pool, precast in one piece, can be sunk in the ground. You can dig a hole and line it with heavy plastic anchored around the top edge with rocks. Your local Audubon Society or nature center can help with instructions.

A more unique and durable birdbath is an old sink, wash basin, or tub, obtainable from a junkyard, salvage company (they advertise), or possibly from your plumber or sanitation department. Fill this with enough stones so that birds hopping in don't drown but do have a place to stand, drink, and preen their feathers. You might add some water plants in pots. (For more information on this, see Chapter 5, Pools and Water Gardens.)

In warm weather, many birds enjoy flying through a sprinkler, or squatting and flapping blissfully about in puddles it may make, getting all their feathers wet. They also love it when you're watering plants and let the hose trickle out slowly to make a puddle or little stream. This attracts butterflies too. They love mud puddling.

Birdhouses and Nest Boxes

Some properties don't have enough kinds and sizes or densities of trees and shrubs to attract a variety of birds looking for nesting sites in early spring. To remedy this, or merely for your own enjoyment, you can build or buy nest boxes. Just as no one kind of food, whether natural or supplied as a handout, can satisfy all birds, no one kind of birdhouse can suit them all.

For the little ones, among them chickadees, nuthatches, downy woodpeckers, wrens, and titmice, the entrance hole should be no larger than 1¼ inches in diameter in order to keep out the bigger birds. For a bluebird, the hole should be 1½ inches, and for larger birds such as a house finch, red-headed woodpecker, and purple martin, 2 inches is about right. The boxes should be made of wood with brass screws and nails, which won't rust, and firmly attached to a tree or post rather than swinging in the wind.

Not only is the size of the entrance important, but the inner dimensions are a matter of concern to house-hunting birds—even as they are to you and me. (See the chart Dimensions for Birdhouses in this chapter.) The smaller birds prefer a 6- to 8-inch inside height and a floor space about 4 inches deep by 4 or 5 inches wide. Larger birds look for somewhat more ample accommodations. Some species like to breed 10 feet above the ground; others are quite content to be a mere 5 or 6 feet up in the air. Then again, many get nervous if they're not near thick cover, whereas others like the wide open spaces. Few like nests very close together, but the purple martin really prefers communal housing. Their nest boxes are like small apartment houses, with two or three stories and six to eight rooms to a floor. (These can be purchased, if you're not up to the job!)

Suburban Swallows

At nesting time one spring I was confronted with a sad and frustrating situation. A pair of barn swallows, which look for beams in barns or similar structures on which to nest, flew into my garage one day and exhibited great interest in the beam that went from side to side. They flew out and back several times, apparently sizing up the possibilities. What they didn't realize, of course, was that the garage had no outlet other than a door that went up and down. When the birds were inside, they swooped out in a panic as the door went

Dimensions for Birdhouses

Kind of Bird	Size of Floor (inches)	Depth of Bird Box (inches)	Height of Entrance above Floor (inches)	Diameter of Entrance Hole (inches)	Height to Fasten above Ground (feet)
American kestrel	8 × 8	12–15	9–12	3	10–30
Barn owl	10 × 18	15–18	4	6	12–18
Bluebird	5 × 5	8	6	1½	5–10
Carolina wren	4 × 4	6–8	4–6	1½	6–10
Chickadee	4 × 4	8–10	6–8	1⅛	6–15
Crested flycatcher	6 × 6	8–10	6–8	2	8–20
Downy woodpecker	4 × 4	8–10	6–8	1¼	6–20
Flicker	7 × 7	16–18	14–16	2½	6–20
Golden-fronted woodpecker and red-headed woodpecker	6 × 6	12–15	9–12	2	12–20
Hairy woodpecker	6 × 6	12–15	9–12	1½	12–20
House finch	6 × 6	6	4	2	8–12
House wren and Bewick's wren	4 × 4	6–8	4–6	1–1¼	6–10
Nuthatch	4 × 4	8–10	6–8	1¼	12–20
Purple martin	6 × 6	6	1	2½	15–20
Saw-whet owl	6 × 6	10–12	8–10	2½	12–20
Screech owl	8 × 8	12–15	9–12	3	10–30
Starling	6 × 6	16–18	14–16	2	10–25
Titmouse	4 × 4	8–10	6–8	1¼	6–15
Violet-green swallow and Tree swallow	5 × 5	6	1–5	1½	10–15
Wood duck	10 × 18	10–24	12–16	4	10–20

SOURCE: *Homes for Birds*, Conservation Bulletin 14, U.S. Department of the Interior, Washington, DC.

down. When the door was up, they were back, flying in circles, perching on the beam, and obviously hoping to call it home. One even brought grasses in its beak. These futile sorties went on for several days, until the birds finally became discouraged and left for good.

Perhaps the swallows learned that suburban garages are not barns, and therefore cannot be trusted. They surely had to go farther afield to find a suitable nesting place. Fortunately, there are many other species that are easier to satisfy. Your local Audubon Society or nature center can advise you on nest boxes and their placement for the birds in your area that you most want to attract.

Most birds do not want or need man-made nests. But come spring, all are on the lookout for nesting materials, even for the birdhouses. A few short pieces of string and ribbon and bits of dog or cat fur or cotton left on the lawn or hung on a bush or rope will be seized upon as welcome additions to what nature provides. Some birds incorporate the most extraordinary materials into their nests. Sticking out from behind my shutters where sparrows nest each spring are, besides the usual grasses, twigs and stems, scraps of paper, fabric, and foil, feathers, hairnets, price tags with string, plastic wrap, spent balloons, and a number of unidentified objects. A veritable junk heap, but admittedly imaginative.

To Feed or Not to Feed

Providing generously for food and nesting is a policy not all naturalists wholly embrace. Some believe that it encourages dependency on humans; that the bolder, pushier birds get the lion's share; and that it can be a chore to bundle up in winter to go out and fill the feeders once or twice a day.

My feeling is that it's better for birds to be a little dependent on us than to starve. Filling a feeder doesn't seem too much to ask to help the birds get through winters when food in nature is scarce. As you watch them feast on your bounty in bitter cold or snowy weather, and later build nests or occupy your nest boxes and hatch out their broods, that's entertainment!

In spring, taper off the feeding gradually. The winter visitors, the migrants that go elsewhere to breed, will depart. The "locals" will get busy with the available natural food supply and will readily learn not to depend upon a perpetually well-stocked feeder. And when their nestlings arrive, they will clamor for bugs and grubs, not birdseed!

The birds' worst enemy is not the cat (which can be belled) or another predator, but the human beings who have destroyed, polluted, and poisoned vast areas of their natural habitats. Wetlands where many birds breed are vanishing at an alarming rate, as are fields, forests, and open pastureland. Down go the trees as new houses and roads are built. A factory rises on a filled-in swamp; a shopping mall replaces a grassy, flowery meadow.

Birds and many other creatures are dispossessed. Some are sickened or killed by ingesting polluted water, chemicals, or contaminated insects. Some are unable to reproduce in sufficient numbers to survive as a species. Some flee to parks and other protected areas. And some learn, or try, to adapt to living in the suburbs.

How can we help them? Besides giving support to worthy wildlife and wilderness organizations, conservation projects, nature centers, and sanctuaries, the naturalist/gardener can create a backyard habitat where plants, birds, and animals can coexist harmoniously in a natural and poison-free environment.

Bringing Back the Bluebird

There's something special about a bluebird. Besides being very beautiful—sky blue, with a brick-red breast and white belly—it's family-minded, tidy, a beneficial grub- and insect-eater, and a singer of sweet songs. Long regarded as a symbol of hope and happiness, the bluebird's lot has not been very happy or hopeful. The population of this lovely bird has been on the decline for decades.

There are three species of bluebird: the western, the mountain, and the eastern. The eastern species has been particularly affected by loss of habitat in its range, which extends from Canada to the Gulf and from the eastern United States to the Rockies. In New York and other northeastern states, where flocks in the hundreds used to arrive from the South in late February or early March to breed and spend the summer, a flock of a dozen is seldom seen and even a pair is an exciting event.

Bluebird Life-style

Once the female has accepted a mate, she does most of the nest building and incubating of eggs. After they hatch, the male shares the feeding chores. When the young are ready to leave the nest in two to two and a half weeks, the parents continue to feed and watch over the fledglings until they can manage on their own. Then the parents build a new nest and have another brood. They may even have a third brood later.

Food for bluebirds consists of grubs, worms, and other insects, replaced by berries in cold weather. Because of the loss of much open land to building, wild berries aren't as common as they used to be, and greedy starlings may gobble most of them in an area where bluebirds live. Furthermore, some of the berries and bugs that the bluebirds eat and feed to their young have been sprayed with harmful, sometimes lethal pesticides.

But the most serious problem for bluebirds is finding places to breed. Bluebirds are cavity-nesters. Old dead trees and wooden fenceposts that provided holes have become a rarity. Orchards are regularly pruned of dead wood and sprayed. More aggressive or larger birds, especially the English sparrow and the starling, preempt any available holes for their nests. Sparrows can even enter the small holes in nest boxes.

Bluebirds and other hole-nesters—woodpeckers, titmice, tree swallows, chickadees, house wrens, crested flycatchers, and nuthatches—have many other enemies, among them raccoon, squirrels, opossums, and snakes, which eat eggs and nestlings when they can get them.

Thus, loss of habitat, competition from sparrows and starlings, and the use of pesticides make it a tough world for the beloved bluebird. Not yet an endangered species, it is close to it in many states. But it may make a comeback, with help from its human friends. The bluebird takes well to nest boxes, and feasts on berries in backyard plantings.

Bluebird Programs

The preservation of the bluebird is a pet project of many wildlife organizations, state park and conservation departments, and concerned individuals. In its booklet "Woodworking for Wildlife," the Missouri Department of Conservation shows how to make a bluebird house, among other birdhouses. It provides helpful tips, such as the fact that the box must be cleaned out after the young have left; sparrow nests must be removed; and grease-coated pipes for mounting boxes and protective metal cones or sleeves should be used to keep predators away. There is also a fact sheet available on feeding and planting for birds. The bluebird is the official state bird of Missouri and a year-round resident.

The Minnesota Department of Natural Resources has a "Bluebird Trail Nest Box" program. In South Carolina, bluebirds are on the increase because of the installation of nest boxes by wildlife groups and individuals.

The Department of Parks and Tourism of Arkansas has a program in Pinnacle Mountain and other state parks for bird housing, feeding, and habitat improvement. According to Jay S. Miller, Administrator of Program Services, a dedicated 90-year-old volunteer, Sam Slagle, has been making, installing, and maintaining nest boxes for bluebirds for many years. Mr. Slagle's "Nest for Success" program suggests placement of the box no lower than 4 feet off the ground to keep it from being easily reached by cats, 'possums, raccoon, and snakes; a 4-by-4-inch floor plan to discourage sparrows, which like space for large nests; a double thickness of wood around the entrance hole to keep out predators reaching for eggs or young; and movement of the box to another location if it doesn't attract bluebirds or other desirable birds after one or two years. Mr. Slagle believes that his swinging front panel makes the box easier to clean than the traditional hinged lid.

Another state claiming the bluebird for its official bird is New York, which is making an intensive effort for its preservation. The New York Nest Box Network program is funded by a $10,000 grant from "Return a Gift to Wildlife," a spe-

Bluebird nest box. Designed by Sam Slagle. Courtesy Arkansas State Parks.

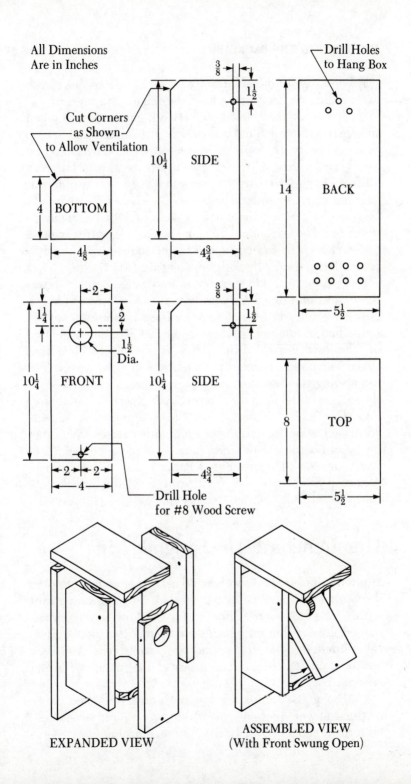

All Dimensions Are in Inches

Drill Holes to Hang Box

Cut Corners as Shown to Allow Ventilation

BOTTOM
4
4⅛

SIDE
10¼
4¾
⅜
1½

BACK
14
5½

FRONT
10¼
1¼
2
2
1½ Dia.
2
2
4

Drill Hole for #8 Wood Screw

SIDE
10¼
4¾
⅜
1½

TOP
8
5½

EXPANDED VIEW

ASSEMBLED VIEW
(With Front Swung Open)

cial line on state income tax forms for contributions to fish and wildlife conservation. Other states have this line also.

The New York Nest Box Network guide gives detailed information about bluebirds and how to make and set up boxes properly. If two or more are installed, they should be about 100 yards apart, for bluebirds are territorial. Nan Chadwick, Project Director, says that the chief problem is keeping sparrows and starlings out of the boxes. This can best be done by making the entrance hole exactly 1½ inches in diameter. The box should be placed on a pole or tree trunk 3 to 5 feet high in an open space facing some cover, which is particularly needed by fledglings learning to fly.

Unassembled kits for boxes and preassembled boxes ready for mounting are offered for sale. With the guide is a Nest Survey Form for notations on the number of boxes the individual installs, where they are placed, whether bluebirds or other birds occupied them, how many eggs hatched, and so on. These reports keep the bluebird volunteer involved in monitoring the boxes, and the project director informed on the success of the network. To participate, write to: Bluebird, P.O. Box 127, Delmar, NY 12054, and enclose a self-addressed, stamped envelope. Many other states have bluebird nest box programs, and volunteers are welcomed. Contact your state's Department of Parks, a local or the national Audubon Society, or the North American Bluebird Society for more information (see Resources).

Hummingbird: The Sprightly Mite

Hummingbirds would surely wind up in the top five, if not as the winner, in a bird popularity poll. A nectar-drinking bird with a long narrow bill adapted for reaching into trumpet-shaped flowers, hummingbirds are among the most beautiful, animated, agile, feisty, and tiny of all birds. And they will be delighted to pay you a visit if the menu is alluring enough.

Among the hummer's favorite entrées are bee balm, cardinal flower, fuchsia, nasturtium, geranium, jewelweed, butterfly weed, coral bells, columbine, morning glory, petu-

FAVORITE FOOD PLANTS FOR HUMMINGBIRDS

Flowers: Bee balm, butterfly weed, cardinal flower, cleome, columbine, coral bells, delphinium, four-o'clock, foxglove, fuchsia, geranium, honeysuckle vine, impatiens, jewelweed, lilies, morning glory, nasturtium, nicotiana, penstemon, petunia, phlox, salvia, trumpet vine

Shrubs: Azalea, flowering quince, honeysuckle, lilac, rhododendron, weigela

Trees: Chinaberry, flowering crabapple, hawthorn, locust, mimosa, tulip tree

Favorites in Woodlands, Desert Areas, and Coastal Areas in the West: Agave, honeysuckle, Indian paintbrush, lily, lobelia, manzanita, ocotillo, penstemon (a great favorite), prickly pear, salvia, scarlet passion flower, wild pink, yucca

nia, trumpet vine, lilies, flowering quince, azalea, honeysuckle, weigela, lilac, locust, and mimosa. Plenty of choice for the gardener! Strong red, yellow, and orange colors attract hummers the most, but I have seen them sip from pink and white cosmos and nicotiana as well. Though not in a league with the bees, the hummingbird's a pollinator too. As it visits these "hummingbird flowers," the hummer transfers pollen on its bill, head, or feathers from flower to flower. It also probes into holes in tree trunks left by insect-hunting sapsuckers, in search of a drink of tree sap. For supplementary protein, it eats insects.

Hummingbird Nectar

Hummingbirds are great tipplers, and like their water spiked with sugar. To attract them to your garden, fill 2- to 4-ounce glass or plastic pill bottles or other small flasks with sugar water—one part sugar to three or four parts water—and hang them from a branch about 5 to 7 feet above the ground, out of direct sun but not in shade. Honey (instead of sugar) is not recommended by some ornithologists, who believe that it may cause bill fungus, tumors, or even fatalities.

Hummers are just wild about the color red. Don't put red coloring in the liquid, but do put a bit of red paint or nail polish on the container, or tie it with a red ribbon. At pet and hardware stores and garden centers, and from specialty catalogs, you can buy hummingbird feeders that are partially made of red plastic with more than one drinking station. Check feeders frequently and keep them filled—once the birds get started, they'll keep coming!

The sweet drink supplements the large amount of flower nectars and insects the little birds must consume in order to maintain their almost constant rapid motion in the air. It's particularly alluring if you don't have enough of their favorite flowers in your garden. It may also attract certain other birds, some long-tongued butterflies, bumblebees, and the beautiful sphinx moth. The hummingbird moth, which bears an uncanny resemblance to the hummingbird, only

Hummingbird feeders made of red plastic and filled with sugar water will give these delightful little birds something to eat when their favorite sources of nectar aren't in bloom.

slightly smaller, is often mistaken for a hummingbird and will also visit the feeder.

You can get surprisingly close to your hummingbird feeder if you let the birds get accustomed to your presence. Sit about 25 to 30 feet away at first, and move your chair a foot or two closer each day. At 6 or 7 feet away, they'll let you gaze your fill as they drink!

The Life of the Hummingbird

There are more than a dozen species of hummingbird, only one of which, the ruby-throated, is found east of the Rockies. The broad-tailed hummingbird is common in the Rockies; the calliope, smallest of all, weighing in at about $\frac{1}{10}$ of an ounce, frequents the Rockies, Sierras, and West Coast up to Canada. Anna's hummingbird is common west of the Sierras; the black-chinned hummingbird is also found in western mountains. Costa's hummingbird appears in the southwestern deserts and southern California. The rufous is abundant throughout the western United States and western Canada. Other species have more limited ranges.

Although different species of hummers are different colors and sizes (the males all wear the brighter, more iridescent colors), they all share certain traits. They feed while hovering in air; they are the only birds that can fly backward; and they can attain speeds of from 30 to 50 miles per hour, with wing beats of from 40 to 80 times a second. Mating season dives and acrobatics of the males are spectacular. And they are pugnacious and territorial.

The males defend their nests and mates fearlessly against intruders, including birds, squirrels, and even cats, regardless of their size or of any danger involved. In fact, with shrill screechy call, speedy attack and pursuit tactics, and long sharp bill as weapon, a hummer can be quite a formidable mite!

Nests are delicate structures about an inch or so in diameter, with spiderwebs often interwoven in the construction. The white eggs (generally two) are the size of peas. Young birds are fed with regurgitated food.

Most western hummers winter in Mexico, some in Central and South America. The ruby-throated winters in Mexico, Central America, and Panama. On its spring flight, it will fly 500 miles or more across the Gulf to southern shores and into southern states. For a while it will rest and feed. Then it moves northward with the advance of spring to the eastern, central, and northern states and eastern Canada, where mating, nesting, and breeding take place.

If you are in your garden when a hummingbird zooms in, stand quietly and relish the pleasure of watching this exquisite little creature hover, wings almost invisible, while drinking from one of your flowers, then dart to another, never alighting.

There may be problems ahead for the hummingbird, for with the widespread destruction of the rainforests and tropical areas where the ruby-throated and others spend their winters, the existence of this beautiful and beguiling featherweight becomes more and more threatened.

Chapter 8

Butterflies and Friends

I'd be a butterfly born in a bower,
Where roses and lilies and violets meet.

Thomas Haynes Bayly,
"I'd Be a Butterfly"

The naturalist/gardener is many things—a gardener, a bird watcher, a butterfly watcher, a wildlife watcher—in effect, an observer and lover of all things in nature. While tending plants and flowers, one notices which creatures visit, take up residence or pass through, and what they like to eat and drink. Perhaps one of the most enchanting visitors is the butterfly. There are ways to attract them to the garden, purely for the pleasure of observing these lovely, delicate creatures, shimmering like stained glass, copper, or the sky itself, as they soar and swoop, rest and feed in the sunlight.

Butterflies will come, as birds do, to an environment where there is a variety of plants and flowers and some moisture. They are sun-lovers, and more of them can be seen on a sunny day than on a cloudy day. (They need to have their wings warmed before they can fly.) In warm climates, more can be observed for longer periods of time throughout the year, but there is almost no place on earth where some species cannot be found. Their prevalence in certain areas is usually linked to larval and adult food preferences.

Butterfly Food Preferences

Butterflies, which subsist mainly on flower nectars, seem to prefer strong colors—red, orange, yellow, and blue—although they will also go to others. Butterfly weed and other milkweeds, zinnias, daisies, mimosa, and buddleia (butterfly bush) are special favorites. In addition to nectar, they feast avidly on rotten or fermented fruit and oozing tree sap. Puddles and muddy ground are important sources of moisture for them. And, incongruous as it may seem, these ethereal creatures have a particular yen for carrion, dung, and traces of urine (your pet's perhaps) to supply moisture and certain minerals, nutrients, and salt not present in their regular diet of sweet liquids. A butterfly's long, coiled tongue, or proboscis, is able to project deep into flowers and other sources.

Different species of butterfly lay their eggs on plants preferred by their larvae. The majority choose deciduous trees, especially willow, elm, ash, hackberry, aspen, poplar, tulip tree, cherry, and birch. Some limit themselves to one plant or a very few; the monarch and queen butterflies choose milkweed, and the swallowtails prefer carrot, dill, and parsley. When the eggs hatch, the foliage of choice is right there for the emerging larvae to eat. However, they have so many predatory and parasitic enemies that rarely are there enough larvae in any one spot to be highly destructive, as some moth caterpillars can be. They are devoured by birds, frogs, toads, some spiders, insects, and small mammals, and parasitized by wasps and flies.

Those that survive grow and molt (shed their skins as they become bigger) four to six times, then enter the chrysalis or pupal stage, in which they may be partly or wholly immobile. Most butterflies do not spin cocoons as moths do but remain in a hard pupal shell or curled inside a leaf, attached to the plant or tree chosen for larval food. When the adult emerges, its growth cycle is finished, and it is ready to breed a new generation. Some butterflies are territorial and can be quite pugnacious, attempting to chase other species from their preferred eating places.

Butterfly Migration

Most of the Lepidoptera (butterflies and moths) remain in the same region where they began life. They winter over as eggs, larvae, pupae, or chrysalids, and some even as adults. A few species migrate. The classic example of migration is the monarch.

Monarchs breed in Canada and northern parts of the United States. In the West, they fly to California and overwinter along the coast and in national parks. Groves of "butterfly trees" can be found in Carmel, Monterey, Pacific Grove, Santa Cruz, and farther south. In the East, some overwinter in Florida, but most of the North American monarch population flies to Mexico to spend the winter near the village of El Rosario in the mountainous state of Michoacán. This is a journey of over 2,000 miles. Critical sites where millions of monarchs converge in winter were dedicated as ecological reserves by the Mexican government in 1986.

There, fir trees cloaked in every bright and soft shade of orange wings with black markings and white dots present an unforgettable spectacle. The hosts of butterflies leave the trees in the sunshine to find food and moisture, return to them at night, and remain and rest when the weather is cloudy. As they fly north in spring, they lay their eggs on milkweed plants, their sole larval food. When the larvae become adults, they journey on to the northern breeding sites, and so the cycle continues.

Butterfly Defenses

Adult butterflies and moths have no means of attack but can take flight or hide when threatened. Many have protective coloration devices. Some can appear to be a part of the leaf, bark, wood, or lichen on which they cling. Others have scare spots or eye spots in gaudy colors on their hind wings to frighten enemies. Butterfly larvae, like those of moths, also have protective devices: camouflage coloration, bristly coats, tricks of concealment, and awful taste.

A few butterflies mimic the appearance of others, in particular the viceroy, which closely resembles the monarch. For this reason, it is avoided by birds and other predators, which have discovered that the monarch tastes terrible and is poisonous because of the toxins in its body from a larval diet of milkweed. Viceroy larvae favor willow and poplar leaves, which don't make them poisonous at all. But the birds don't know that! The queen butterfly shares the monarch's taste for milkweed in the larval stage, though it doesn't resemble the monarch; its wings are a dark reddish brown with white spots. After one taste, a predator usually learns to avoid eating the royalty of the butterfly world.

Butterflies in the Garden

Among the largest and most handsome butterflies you are likely to see in your garden are the swallowtails. Swallowtails' hind wings project in a tip or "tail." The black swallowtail, with two rows of yellow spots and some blue markings on its hind wings, is especially striking, as is its cousin the tiger swallowtail, which is light yellow with black stripes and blue markings on the hind wings. In southern latitudes, the females of both species are often drab brown or black. The spicebush swallowtail, dark brown with yellow spots and greenish blue coloring on its hind wings, is fairly common.

The clouded sulphur, which loves mud puddles, is bright yellow or orange with black-edged wings. The blues, also mud puddlers, include some of the smallest butterflies and the lovely spring azure, the first of our native butterflies to appear in northeastern areas, looking for the earliest spring flowers. Another early visitor may be the mourning cloak, a brown beauty with yellow edges and blue spots.

The large families of fritillaries and crescents are mainly orange-brown or tan, dappled with silvery spots and black markings. Violets are their favorite larval food. The small, bright coppery-orange American copper is quite common in the Northeast, with relatives in the South and West. This is a feisty little creature that not only defends its range from other butterflies, but also will dart pugnaciously at birds, ani-

Butterflies will flock to the naturalist's garden if attractant plants like the butterfly bush are featured in the landscape.

mals, and even intrusive people! And you're very likely to see the pretty painted lady of tawny and salmon hues with black-and-white markings. She lays her eggs primarily on thistles.

If you are growing any member of the Cruciferae, or cabbage family, there is no doubt at all, unfortunately, that you will be visited by the small white cabbage butterfly, which comes early, stays late, and lays innumerable batches of eggs. The green cabbageworms that hatch out are very destructive. Handpicking and several applications of the biological control Bt (see Chapter 11, Battling Bugs and Diseases . . .Naturally) will be necessary.

The Belligerent Larva

I never particularly noticed butterfly larvae until the year I planted carrot seed and saw some small, dark grubs on the tops. As the creatures grew to become inch-long fat caterpillars with bands of black, green, and gold, the carrot tops diminished. Curious to see what would happen to my carrot crop, I left several of the black swallowtail larvae to continue their feasting undisturbed and transferred others by cutting off the leaves on which they were feeding and propping them against a parsley or dill plant, other favorite foods, growing elsewhere.

Two youngsters on a visit one day came racing over to me, shrieking that they had touched "a weird worm" that raised up some kind of smelly antenna and acted ferocious! I went to see. Their "worm" was a swallowtail larva, and when I touched its back, a two-pronged, bright orange "antenna" popped out behind its head, emitting a strong, sweetish yet repellent odor. At the same time, the caterpillar reared up its front end aggressively and turned to face whatever was presumably attacking it. If I had been a small predator, I might very well have been scared off!

The children learned something that day, besides having the fun of pulling and eating delicious homegrown carrots for the first time, and I saw (and smelled) for the first time a fascinating phenomenon: the defense mechanism of this soft, vulnerable creature.

The carrots grew new tops and became perfectly respectable carrots underground, like the others. The larvae gradually disappeared as autumn advanced, to pupate and become "turned-intos" in the spring. . .gorgeous black swallowtail butterflies.

The Butterfly Garden

An assortment of flowering plants, some moisture, and an absence of chemical sprays can make your entire garden attractive to butterflies. To establish a real butterfly garden, dedicate a sunny part of the backyard to wildflowers and certain garden flowers that these winged creatures are partial to, according to your own observations and the box, Plants to Attract Butterflies, in this chapter. Be sure to include a butterfly bush (buddleia) or plant one nearby. Its fragrant pur-

PLANTS TO ATTRACT BUTTERFLIES
NECTAR SOURCES

Garden Flowers
Ageratum
Bee balm
Candytuft
Coneflower
Coreopsis
Cosmos
Daylily
Gaillardia
Lantana
Lobelia
Loosestrife
Marguerite
Marigold
Mignonette
Morning glory
New England aster
Nicotiana
Phlox
Scabiosa
Sedum
Shasta daisy
Sweet alyssum
Sweet william
Verbena
Zinnia

Trees and Shrubs
Beautybush
Blueberry
Buckeye
Bush honeysuckle
Butterfly bush
Fruit trees
Hawthorn
Huckleberry
Lilac
Mockorange
Redbud
Rose of sharon
Spicebush
Spiraea
Sumac
Weigela

Wildflowers
Asters
Black-eyed Susan
Blazing star
Boneset
Butterfly weed
Catnip
Cornflower
Daisy
Dandelion
Goldenrod
Joe-pye weed
Meadowsweet
Nettle
Queen Anne's lace
Red clover
Thistle
Thyme
Vetch
Wild bergamot
Yarrow
(*continued*)

Boldface indicates plants that are highly favored.

PLANTS TO ATTRACT BUTTERFLIES
—*Continued*
LARVAL FOOD SOURCES

Fruit Trees
Apple
Cherry
Pear
Plum
Wild cherry

Deciduous Trees and Shrubs
Ash
Aspen
Birch
Elm
Flowering dogwood
Hackberry
Hawthorn
Poplar

Spicebush
Tulip tree
Viburnum
Willow

Other Larval Food Plants
Bermuda grass
Clover
Dock
Hollyhock
Lupine
Nettle
Plantain
Sorrel
St. Augustine grass
Turtlehead

ple-red flower spikes are an irresistible lure to most species and are in bloom from July until frost. Let the patch get overgrown, a bit wild and weedy, and allow it to self-sow. Keep a spot or two moist or puddly. Include a few flat stones or a slate for the butterflies to sun themselves on.

The adult butterflies will feast on the flower nectars and will find plants, trees, or bushes suitable for their egglaying. Some larvae can be quite voracious, but remember, this is the big feeding stage in the life cycle, so be prepared to share. From hungry caterpillars, beautiful butterflies arise.

For an exciting experience, if you are patient and move slowly, you may be able to approach a perched or feeding butterfly closely. Extend a sweaty finger, and the butterfly, attracted by the salts and moisture, may climb upon it and drink. In fact, if you're a sunbather, you may recall being besieged by butterflies while you were out. If you wondered why the pretty insects were ambling over your arms, wonder no longer: They'd found a human "salt lick."

Moths: The Fly-by-Nights

Since many members of the huge family of moths (which is far larger than that of the butterflies) feed lustily on valued vegetation, stored grains, and fabrics, we tend to look unkindly on moths in general. Certain larvae are indeed extremely destructive. Tent caterpillars, gypsy moth caterpillars, cabbage loopers, and squash borers are as welcome in the home garden as a month-long drought. Even less affection is felt by the farmer for the corn earworm, peach tree borer, codling moth larva (partial to apples and pears), and cotton bollworm, among others.

But as adults, moths are harmless. Many do not feed at all, having only vestigial mouthparts. Those that do feed enjoy the same fare as butterflies: flower nectars, pollen, rotting fruit, dung, and carrion. Most moths, unlike butterflies, are nocturnal, visible only at dusk or later. If they come into your garden, they are attracted by white or pastel-colored flowers with sweet scents, such as petunias and nicotiana. See The Moonlit Garden in Chapter 3, The Naturalist's Flower Garden, for details.

The Gorgeous Silkmoths

Although many moths are rather drab or somber in color, quite a few are spectacularly colorful. Among these are the giant silkworm moths or Saturniids, very distantly related to the Asiatic silkworm. The largest is the handsome russet, red, and grayish brown cecropia, with a wingspread of 5 to 6 inches. Its larvae feed on a wide variety of tree foliage. The polyphemus, with a wingspread of up to 5½ inches, has an eye spot (or scare spot) on each wing. The ones on the hind wings are larger and really seem to stare. An urbanite, the

The lovely luna moth will grace your moonlight garden if you plant fragrant night-blooming flowers like nicotiana.

cynthia, a big olive-brown beauty with white and mauve bands, lays its eggs on the ailanthus (tree of heaven), which grows in metropolitan areas. Perhaps the loveliest of the silkmoths is the luna, with its elegant pale green gossamer wings and long "tails" to the hind wings. Found only in North America, it has become rare because of pesticides and pollution and is now endangered.

The giant silkworms do not feed at all during their short adult life. They may be seen occasionally fluttering against screens in summer, from southern Canada down throughout the eastern half of the United States. These and other moths only seem to be attracted to light or flame. Actually, they are confused and disoriented by it, since they generally fly in dim light or darkness.

Camouflage and Other Tactics

Protective devices of adult moths are similar to those of butterflies. Some have such a bad taste that birds actually spit them out and learn not to eat them again. Big eye spots on wings intimidate some predators; clever camouflage colors are a protection against others. Some caterpillars are very hairy or bristly, such as the woolly bear, often seen in autumn crossing roads or paths on the way to some cozy shelter from winter weather. Birds know—or find out—that these fuzzy creatures do not feel good going down their gullets.

Of the many moths that are adept at camouflage, the catocola is a master. Its hind wings in flight are bright orange, red, and black. At rest on a tree trunk, its dull gray, brown, and white forewings cover the hind wings, and it blends into the tree bark.

The Hummingbird Moth

The family of sphinx or hawk moths is a fascinating one. These moths have stout bodies, very long proboscises, and extremely rapid wing beats. One member of this tribe you should be delighted to see in your garden is the humming-bird moth. Its body is olive green with russet red bands, and its wings are mostly transparent. It bears a startling resemblance to the hummingbird, whose flying and feeding habits it emulates. You may have to look closely to see whether the tiny creature with the fast-beating wings hovering over a flower in the sunlight is a hummer or a hummingbird moth (one of the few moths that feed in daylight) searching for nectar.

Godzilla

In the larval stage, some of the sphinx moths are the hated hornworms, which feed on plants of the nightshade family: potato, tomato, tobacco, pepper, eggplant, and nicotiana. The adult moth is dull gray with black and brown markings, and has a wingspan of 3½ to 4½ inches. Its offspring are green with white lines, black and white dots, and a reddish "horn" at the rear.

A tomato hornworm on the underside of a leaf may look like the Godzilla of caterpillars. A big one can be over 4 inches long and as fat as your thumb. It has a tremendous appetite. But don't panic—something may already be eating *it*. Take a look to see if it is festooned with little white blobs. In spite of their appearance, these are not eggs. The caterpillar has been parasitized by the braconid wasp, a natural enemy, whose eggs, laid on the outside, hatched, burrowed with-in, ate their way out, and are now pupating. They will soon emerge as adults. The caterpillar has been fatally stricken and cannot do much more damage—in fact, it has become a breeding ground for beneficial insects that will patrol your garden for you. Hornworms that have escaped the wasps can be stopped by the biological control Bt sprayed on your tomatoes' foliage before the caterpillars appear. (See Chapter 11, Battling Bugs and Diseases . . . Naturally.)

Bees: The Great Pollinators

The glorious diversity of color, markings, size, shape, and scent of flowers has evolved not by chance but by design, to attract pollinating insects, upon which most plants rely for their very survival. A flower is actually the reproductive organ of a plant, and most of them have both male and female reproductive parts.

The male structures (stamens) produce pollen at their tips (anthers). The female structures (pistils) bear tips (stig-mas) ready to receive pollen, the tiny yellow grains contain-ing male reproductive cells. In its search for food, an insect often gets pollen on its body, which is deposited on another flower it visits. Pollen on the female stigma will fertilize an ovule, and a new seed is born.

A few flowers are self-pollinating, and some, like corn and ragweed, can be fertilized by windblown pollen, but the vast majority need pollinators. These are bees, wasps, butter-flies, moths, hummingbirds, bats, certain beetles, and other insects. The pollinators are well rewarded with sugar-sweet nectars and grains of pollen, rich in vitamins, fats, and pro-tein. The honeybee has evolved to become the champion pol-linator and pollen collector.

Bee Scouts

The female (worker) bee has hollows, or receptacles, on her hind legs for the collection of pollen, which she brings back to the hive. Male (drone) bees do not collect pollen. Every hive has scouts that go out to locate desirable patches of flowers. When they return, they communicate with the food gatherers, indicating location and distance by specific body movements. Then the foragers make their beeline from hive to food and back to the hive. Scouts also have the job of finding a good place for a home for the swarm early in summer. Later in the season when the weather turns cool, the hive stays home and eats its stored honey, first getting rid of the now useless drones, whose only purpose was to fertilize their queen. In cold weather, bees cluster closely together for warmth. Some do very active bee dancing to create more heat inside the hive.

Bee Flowers

The flowers that particularly attract bees produce a lot of pollen and are usually yellow, pink, blue, and lavender, but they will visit flowers of other colors as well, such as rosy magenta lythrum spires. Certain devices have been developed by flowers to lure bees and other insects. Among these are "nectar guides," which may be dots or lines of contrasting color leading inward from the petals, some of which may not be visible to human eyes. Petunias and morning glories have clearly visible nectar lines, whereas dots in the throats of foxgloves invite visitors to enter. Sweet and pungent fragrances, such as those of nicotiana, marigold, and lantana, are an invitation too. Herb flowers, such as basil, marjoram, thyme, lavender, sage, savory, and the mints are very attractive. When my catnip is in bloom, every bee for miles around seems to know it! The same holds true for the early flowering raspberries.

In my garden, the greatest attraction for bees in August and September is the blue cardinal flower with its tall, long-lasting sapphire-blue spires. In September, the bees go wild about the New England aster, with gold-centered purple flower clusters that also draw crowds of monarch butterflies.

FAVORITE FOOD PLANTS FOR BEES

Flowers and Herbs
Anise hyssop
Balsam
Bee balm
Borage
Butterfly weed
Cleome
Coral bells
Cosmos
Globe thistle
Gloriosa daisy
Great or blue lobelia
Hyssop
Lantana
Lavender
Lily
Marigold
Nicotiana
Pitcher's salvia
Rosemary
Salvia
Snapdragon
Sweet alyssum
Sweet rocket
Thyme
Verbena
Zinnia

Trees and Shrubs
Alder
Apple
Autumn olive
Bay laurel
Black locust
Blueberry
Butterfly bush
   (buddleia)
Catalpa
Chastetree (vitex)
English holly

The deliciously scented red-purple sprays of the butterfly bush, which blooms from July to September's end and attracts all butterflies and many other insects, is also a magnet for bees.

The honeybee's role in agriculture is enormous, for many crops are wholly or partly dependent on bee pollination, which is also responsible for the production of honey and beeswax. The home gardener's apple, pear, and peach trees, berry patch, melons, squash, eggplant, and other fruiting vegetables all need the services of bees in order to produce their delicious harvests. Bees are highly vulnerable to pesticides, and even the botanicals pyrethrum and rotenone are lethal to these indispensable insects.

Eucalyptus
Golden-rain tree
Huckleberry
Linden (basswood)
Maple
Mesquite
Peach
Pear
Persimmon
Pin cherry
Plum
Privet
Raspberry
Russian olive
Serviceberry
Siberian peashrub
Spicebush
Sour cherry
Sumac
Tatarian honeysuckle
Tree of heaven
Willow

Wildflowers and
Meadow Plants
Alfalfa
Aster
Birdsfoot trefoil
Buckwheat
Cranberry
Dandelion
Goldenrod
Lupine
Milkweed
Motherwort
Purple loosestrife
White clover
White sweet clover
Wild strawberry

The Burly Bumblebee

The life of the bumblebee is not as social or as complex as that of the honeybee. In spring and early summer, queens lay their eggs alone, in or on the ground, sometimes in an abandoned nesting place of a bird or small animal. When the young hatch, in brood cells built by the queen, they eat from honey pots she has provided for them. They grow, pupate in cocoons, and emerge as infertile worker bees during the summer. The old queen continues laying eggs, all infertile, and the workers take care of them and the larvae. At the end of summer, the queen lays fertile eggs again. Then, her usefulness over, she dies, and so do her worker bees.

Without bees as pollinators, many crops would fail. A bumblebee's long tongue makes it well adapted to feed on and pollinate tubular flowers like the red clover (left), whereas the white clover (right) is more to the liking of the short-tongued honeybee.

The new generation emerges and mates. The males soon die; only the young queens—the mated females—survive. Thus in spring, the bumblebees we see are all queens who have overwintered in the soil and are now feeding on nectar, gathering pollen, and looking for nesting sites.

Bumblebees, except for one short-tongued species, have longer tongues than honeybees and can draw nectar from bee balm, honeysuckle, red clover and other tubular flowers that the shorter-tongued honeybees can't reach.

Mantis Mania

I have often stood entranced for half an hour at a time watching a mantis go about its business of catching and devouring insects. First I have to locate one, but the fully grown, 2½- to

4½-inch-long adult is often big enough to be seen when perched on a leaf or flower surveying its territory. The sharp-eyed mantis remains motionless, hind legs clinging to the plant, forelegs drawn up, waiting for dinner to fly or crawl within reach. Once ensnared within those spiny legs, the victim is doomed, and eaten, still struggling, head first. Rarely does the lightning lunge fail, but when a mantis "strikes out," it merely draws back, resumes the praying position, and waits patiently.

By summer's end or early autumn, any mantids remaining in the garden are quite sure to be females that have eaten their mates and deposited their egg cases, or are about to do so. I kept watch on three of them last year that established themselves in some large cosmos plants near wild asters, where, I am sorry to relate, I saw them consume bees with great relish . . . in addition to flies, wasps, and other bugs.

One day I found a mantis trying to escape from the cat, who was gingerly batting it around on the grass. I picked up the big insect, which promptly turned its head to glare balefully at me and grabbed my hand so hard that its pincers left tiny scratch marks on my skin. The next time a mantis needed rescuing, I wore gloves. I shall never know whether they were hanging on for dear life or actually attacking me! Mantids are known to assault creatures much bigger than themselves.

As the weather cooled, I found my mantids hanging head down, as they often do, facing west and soaking up the warmth of the afternoon sun. I think they knew that their days were numbered. By mid-October they were no longer to be seen, victims doubtless of nights too chilly for them to survive.

I found two egg cases, one on a stem in a precarious spot where it would be thrown out in the fall cleanup. I cut that one off and tied it securely to a twig in a bush nearby. The mantids are gone, but they left me something to look forward to. Should the cases blow away or get eaten by predators over the winter, I can always order a fresh supply through one of the mail-order companies that carry biocontrols (see the Resources list for Chapter 11, Battling Bugs and Diseases . . . Naturally). Spring won't find my garden without mantids!

Chapter 9

Backyard Wildlife

Many creatures may come to visit your garden, some of whom have been deprived of their natural habitat and food sources. They are all interested in finding something good to eat, a safe place to live, or both. Rarely do they present a danger to humans or pets. Some are commonplace—the rabbit, squirrel, chipmunk, field mouse, mole, woodchuck, and opossum. Others, visible in years gone by only in field, forest, swamp, or grassy hillside—including the skunk, raccoon, deer, and fox—have been forced to live in or near the suburbs or built-up areas.

Wildlife in the backyard present a fascinating challenge to the homeowner. These creatures of the wild are trying to get along with us. It is a matter of survival for them in a new environment that is often unnatural and sometimes hostile. We can and should attempt to coexist in harmony with them.

The Rambunctious Rabbit

The most common rabbit is the eastern cottontail, which is grayish brown with a white tail and rust-colored nape. It has 2- to 3-inch-long ears, is 15 to 18 inches long, and weighs 2 to 4 pounds. The cottontail is indeed a prolific breeder, producing three or four litters a year of up to nine bunnies each. However, few survive to maturity, and those that do rarely live more than a year. The range of this rabbit extends from the East Coast to Arizona and North Dakota. Its far-west relatives include the brush rabbit, pygmy rabbit, Nuttal's cottontail, desert cottontail, and the jackrabbits.

The rabbit has many enemies, including weasels, foxes, hawks, owls, skunks, and humans who shoot or trap them for food and fur. Prolific breeders, able to freeze motionless if danger is near, yet also quick to flee and hide in a thicket or burrow, the cottontail flourishes nonetheless.

Usually quite content with buds, leaves, berries, and tender tips of twigs, rabbits can be tempted by garden vegetables in summer and tree bark in winter. If they are a real nuisance—and when food is scarce in winter they *can* be—repellents (see The Adaptable Deer, page 182) can be sprayed or painted on trees and shrubs; 2-foot-high chicken wire can be stretched tight around stakes to protect the vegetables or berry patch. (See Chapter 6, On Growing Vegetables, for further controls.)

The Ingenious Squirrel

The gray squirrel is 17 to 20 inches long, with a tail that can reach 10 inches. It weighs 14 to 25 ounces and has buff underfur; the tail is silvery. In the North, it can be black; and white colonies are scattered throughout its range, which extends from the East Coast to Texas and Oklahoma. This rollicking rodent builds both summer and winter leaf nests in mature trees and occasionally uses holes in trees as dens.

Squirrels bear two or three young in spring, often having a second litter in late summer.

Squirrels, which do not hibernate, are constantly searching for food and become friendly beggars if you offer a nut or cracker now and then. They can smell nuts buried under a foot of snow. Squirrels eat insects, seeds, buds, and berries, as well as nuts, and relish sips of tree sap. Occasionally they may rob birds' nests of eggs or young. They are also skilled in circumventing the most ingenious devices to keep them out of bird feeders.

Most of the squirrels we see are gray; a few are black. Red squirrels, close but often unfriendly and quarrelsome relatives, are less likely to appear in the garden because they prefer woodlands. The largest squirrels, the golden, brown, and orange squirrels, live in the South and West.

When food is very scarce, squirrels, as well as skunks, raccoon, and other hungry critters, may go after garden bulbs. These scroungers may be repelled by mothballs, moth flakes, or cayenne pepper scattered over the bulb bed and renewed after every rain, or possibly by mothballs placed in the bulb hole at planting time and covered with enough dirt to prevent contact with the bottom of the bulb. Well-anchored heavy mulch, chicken wire, branches, and sticks over bulb sites will be deterrents. (Place markers where bulbs are planted.) These measures will also keep squirrels from uprooting garden plants as they dig holes to bury their winter food stashes.

The Cheerful Chipmunk

Our most common chipmunk is the eastern chipmunk (there are 13 specialized western species, usually with very small ranges). It is reddish brown, with a white belly, a dark stripe down its back, and three stripes on each side—a central white stripe surrounded by two black stripes. This ground-dwelling

Diurnal animals like the chipmunk, groundhog, and rabbit will visit the naturalist's garden if shelter such as walls and shrubs is provided.

relative of the squirrel is 8½ to 12 inches long, with a 3- to 5-inch tail. It weighs only 2 to 5 ounces. It lives in open woodland and around bushes or stone walls, where it digs a burrow and bears one litter a year, either in May or midsummer, of three to five young. The eastern chipmunk's range extends from the East Coast west to North Dakota and south to Virginia and Mississippi.

This lively, pert little creature is entertaining and is in no way destructive. Chipmunks eat seeds, nuts, and berries. They will also happily stuff their cheeks with any crumbs, raisins, or crackers you toss out and race like a flash to their burrows. They lay up supplies in an underground storage room and hibernate in the winter, waking up now and then for a nibble or two or a brief foray outside. If you are patient and let an acquaintance develop, Chip may come and eat from your hand, as squirrels will.

The Slandered Skunk

The striped skunk can be found all over the United States and in much of Canada. It is black, with a white stripe down its face and two broad white stripes on its back. This skunk is 20½ and 31½ inches long, with a bushy black tail that can be 7 to 15½ inches long; skunks weigh 6 to 14 pounds. They bear one litter a year of four to seven young, in dens usually made in other animals' abandoned burrows. Like squirrels, skunks do not hibernate. Do not approach one under any circumstance—striped skunks are the major carriers of rabies in the United States. Relatives include the hooded skunk, spotted skunk, and hog-nosed skunk.

Of all the backyard visitors, the skunk is the most undeservedly maligned. Unless you keep chickens, you'll find it a truly peaceful creature. Its menu is mainly insects and their larvae, including Japanese beetles and the gypsy moth caterpillar; mice and other small creatures; fruits, berries, and grains; a frog, snake, or bird if it can catch one; and carrion. The skunk does not feed on crops. If you see a skunk rooting around in your garden, it is doubtless seeking out pesky grubs and beetles.

Contrary to general opinion, skunks don't "attack" without warning. If confronted with an enemy or provoked, they turn around, raise their tails, and stamp their feet first. Then, if the enemy doesn't take the hint and depart, it most assuredly will get sprayed. It's a rare (and foolish!) animal that will face up to a skunk more than once in a lifetime. If your dog does get sprayed, be warned: The terrible smell lingers obstinately for days, despite all efforts to remove it. Tomato juice and carbolic soap do the best job of minimizing the stench.

Skunks feel pretty confident about themselves—with reason!—but unfortunately, are killed on the road quite often because they are not particularly afraid of cars or may be dining on a dead creature and just don't feel like abandoning their meal. Maybe the skunk thinks that the car will show the proper respect and back off, as almost everything else does.

Mainly nocturnal, skunks seldom amble about in the daytime. If you hear them rattling around in your trash cans at night, strap the lids securely on the cans with bungee cords or nylon straps—after, of course, the animals depart!

The White-Footed or Wood Mouse

The white-footed mouse is grayish to orange-brown with a white belly, large ears, and a tail half again as long as it is. It is 6 to 8 inches long, with a $2\frac{1}{2}$- to 4-inch tail, and weighs just $\frac{1}{2}$ to $1\frac{1}{2}$ ounces. White-footed mice are nest-builders, occasionally even appropriating an abandoned bird's nest. They remain active all year. Favorite foods are black cherries and jewelweed seeds. Their range extends from the East Coast west to Montana and Arizona.

If you have a cat that goes outside, you needn't worry about mice on the property. Any mouse within the cat's range will unerringly be tracked down and brought tenderly and dead to the doormat. Lacking a feline, you may find that mice can do some damage in winter when berries, seeds, nuts, and insects are scarce. A nibble or two at a plant root, crown, or stem is not a serious matter. Lots of nibbles at the bark of young trees around their bases can girdle and kill the trees. Bark bites may also be made by deer, voles, rabbits, or other hungry animals. If you notice that this is happening, put up tree guards or tree wrap on trunks. Keep mulches, piles of leaves, and grasses away from the trunks of young trees (especially fruit trees) so that the mice cannot creep through or burrow under cover to the trees. Vegetables such as parsnips and carrots that are often stored in the ground over winter can also be targets for hungry mice. If mice are a problem in your area, cage root crops stored in the ground or bring them into the basement for winter storage.

The white-foot, essentially a nocturnal creature, is rarely responsible for much damage in the garden; in fact, its natural habitat is in the woods and dense bushes. Although very prolific, the mouse has innumerable predators that keep its numbers down. And with its pert, upright posture and huge liquid brown eyes, the white-footed mouse is downright appealing.

The Resourceful Raccoon

The raccoon, with its reddish brown, fluffy body, bushy, black-ringed tail, and distinctive black "mask" over the eyes, is a well-known character all over its range across the entire United States and southernmost Canada. It is 2 to just over 3 feet long, with a 7½- to 16-inch tail, and can weigh from 12 to a whopping 50 pounds. The sedentary raccoon will make a leaf nest in a large hollow tree, where its young—up to seven in a litter—will be born in April or May.

The natural diet of this omnivorous creature includes berries, nuts, grains, insects, birds, bird eggs, grasshoppers, frogs, fish, and snakes. It has a bottomless pit for a stomach, which, like a garbage truck, seems to be able to accommodate anything and everything. That may include much of what is destined *for* the garbage truck. Forced into suburbs and even cities, away from its usual stream or wet woodland habitat, the raccoon will forage in garbage pails, mostly at night. It is incredibly clever at opening things; in fact, its fingers have an almost human dexterity. And it has a favorite vegetable: corn. For a few succulent ears, a 'coon will do all but sell its greedy soul. It even has a corn-detecting radar system: Raccoon can smell ripe ears!

People go to great lengths to discourage this masked bandit. These schemes and more have been tried: bright lights at night, enclosures, mothballs, red pepper, scarecrows, strung-up aluminum foil plates and strips that rattle and clatter, loud rock music, a dog tied to a tree nearby. Nothing works. The dog howls and goes crazy, and so do the neighbors. Not so the raccoon.

The best anti-raccoon measures: Don't leave pet food outside, particularly at night. Package food garbage tightly. If possible, put it out early in the morning before collection time, not the night before. Lysol or Tabasco sauce sprinkled on garbage or inside the containers, and mothballs or moth flakes nearby, are likely to lessen the allure. Place something heavy on the pail lids. But with a nose that knows, and dexterous paws, the raccoon may outwit you after all.

Raccoons are playful and cute, and their antics make them seem almost human. But raccoons are susceptible to rabies and distemper. It is dangerous to attempt to play with, provoke, or corner them. If you have a problem with these animals, call a professional trapper or the animal warden in your area and leave the trapping to them.

The Myopic Mole

The eastern or common mole is not the most photogenic of mammals. Its eyes are invisible in its smooth coat of gray or brownish fur. Its most prominent feature is its long pink snout, followed by its flipperlike forefeet and stubby, almost naked tail. The 3- to 9-inch-long mole, which weighs 3 to 5 ounces, does indeed have very poor vision; it tracks its prey through keen hearing and a superb sense of smell. It can move through loose, well-drained soil at the rate of a foot a minute. Moles have only one litter a year, bearing two to six young in underground nests. The eastern mole's range is from the East Coast west to Wyoming. Relatives include the star mole, which has octopuslike short tentacles on the end of its snout.

The mole is another creature with an undiscriminating appetite, but it does draw the line at raiding garbage pails. Moles live in tunnels that they excavate and are seldom seen aboveground. They do not hibernate and are constantly searching for food, as they use up so much energy digging.

Moles will eat insects and their larvae, slugs and snails, ants, caterpillars, worms and grubs, and occasionally vegetation and leaves. They are beneficial as insect- and grub-eaters and also as lawn aerators. This is not much consolation when part of an elegant lawn is marked by mole tunnels, but it does tell you something useful: more than likely, the lawn is infested with Japanese beetle grubs, which will also draw skunks and other creatures to tear up chunks of sod.

You can get rid of the grubs with an application of the biological control Bp (*Bacillus popilliae*), milky spore disease, sold under the trade names Doom and Japidemic. This method takes longer to be effective than trapping, flooding out, gassing, or poisoning the moles. But it remains in the soil for years and will destroy generations of Japanese beetle grubs. It's also more pleasant for both mole and gardener.

The Adaptable Deer

The white-tailed deer is tan or reddish brown with a white throat and belly. Fawns, born once a year either singly, as twins, or as triplets, are spotted. White-tailed deer are 3 to 3½ feet tall at the shoulder and 4½ to 7 feet long. Males weigh 200 to 300 pounds and may have antlers spread to 3 feet; females weigh 150 to 250 pounds. Deer are nocturnal, retiring to shallow oval "beds" in protected areas at dawn. If alarmed, they can reach speeds of 35 mph. The white-tail is found over most of the United States and southern Canada.

Because of human encroachments into woodland territory, deer are now invading the periphery of the suburbs. When forests go down and buildings and roads replace them, the deer's habitat and food supply are drastically diminished. Deer find themselves perforce in closer proximity to people in their search for edibles, which may include ornamental plantings, food crops, and fruit tree branches and bark. They have been seen contentedly breakfasting on a rosebush or bank of impatiens and other small tender flowers. At times, we must take certain measures to keep these lovely creatures from damaging our valuable property.

Curtailing Deer Damage

Solid fences or walls about 6 feet high will keep deer out. They are more likely to jump over a chain-link or wire fence that they can see through, so those should be higher still. There are other methods available to ward off deer (see the controls listed in Chapter 6, On Growing Vegetables). A fruit tree trunk or precious shrub can be covered with lightweight netting or surrounded by chicken wire staked in place. Taste and smell repellents (sold under the trade names of Deer Away and Chew Not) sprayed or painted on trees or ornamentals are effective for a few months. Loud rock music may be a torment they (along with many other two- and four-footed creatures) cannot endure. One eccentric-looking but effective method makes use of bars of strong-smelling deodorant soap. Hang them in the branches (with wire or in mesh bags or stockings) without removing the soap wrappers.

A repellent spray to apply to vegetation may be made at home with an onion, a garlic bulb, and red pepper mixed with a little water in a blender, then strained and added to about a gallon of water plus a small amount of soap or detergent to help make it stick. Renew after rain.

There is one other natural product that is said to make the hungriest deer quail and turn tail, but it is difficult to obtain unless you are friendly with someone who works in a zoo. This is lion or tiger manure. It is otherwise occasionally available packaged in small quantities combined with organic matter under the trade name of Zoo Doo. The sanitized Zoo Doo may not smell strong enough to signal "Predator!" to deer, but it could be worth trying.

Although all these precautions make the deer seem like man's worst enemy—and the orchardist may feel that it is, with reason—for the naturalist/gardener, the grace and beauty of these animals must be a rich compensation for the trouble involved in protecting crops and ornamentals. The sight of a doe and fawn at a fencerow or field's edge as you look out the window at sunrise brings the serenity of unmarred forests as close as your backyard!

The Woodchuck, or Groundhog

The brown woodchuck is a solid animal, 16½ to 32 inches long, with short legs, a bushy, 4- to 10-inch-long tail, and a weight of 4½ to 14 pounds. It enjoys sunlight, unlike most wild mammals, and can often be seen in the daytime. In April or May, the chuck's one litter of four or five young is born. Woodchucks don't chuck wood, incidentally; their name is derived from an Indian word. They range from the eastern central part of the United States north into Canada.

These fat, bearlike creatures usually stick to fields, woods, and grassy hillsides, but where these open, rural areas have been built up, they are attracted to garden vegetables and roadside areas. They go into a deep winter sleep and need to eat a lot and get fat before hibernating in an underground network of tunnels and dens. These portly, self-important creatures are fun to watch even when they're not predicting the weather. Standing on their hind legs looking over the terrain, they seem lords of all they survey. If you don't want them to be lords of your vegetable patch, however, a 2-foot wire-mesh fence with an additional foot underground will probably keep them out.

In the West, the woodchuck's relative, the rockchuck, or marmot, rarely ventures from its mountainous and rocky habitat into a backyard.

The garden at night hosts a different cast of animals, including the deer, 'possum, and raccoon.

The Entertaining Opossum

The opossum is easy to spot with its long whitish fur, 10- to 21-inch pink tail, and white face mask with black ears, pink snout, and beady black eyes. Opossums are 25½ to 40 inches long and weigh 4 to 14 pounds. They do not hibernate and are often to be seen on the roadsides on winter nights looking for carrion. Opossums live in leaf nests in hollow logs or other shelters, where they bear two or three litters a year. Females may have 20 or more bean-sized infants, which must make their arduous way to the 13 nipples in her pouch. Only the strongest—or luckiest—survive, but it is not unusual to see a mother 'possum carrying six or seven babies on her back.

Formerly a resident of the Deep South, the opossum, the only marsupial in North America and its most ancient mammal, has been extending its range and can now be found as far north as southern Canada and as far west as the West Coast. Like skunks, they are nocturnal and don't see very well in the bright light of day or in the glare of automobile headlights. They eat almost anything, including carrion, frogs, fish, any kind of fruit (but especially persimmons), eggs, mice, insects, birds, worms, and snakes (including poisonous rattlers, copperheads, and cottonmouths; they are immune to snake venom). On occasion, they also eat garbage and birdseed. If you don't relish the idea of opening your trash can and finding a disgruntled opossum inside, secure the lid with nylon straps or bungee cords.

Playing 'Possum

'Possums really do play 'possum, and it's no game to them. When no escape route is available, "playing dead" is a life-saving device to trick predators into thinking that the opossum is dead and maybe rotting and inedible. They can lie in a deathlike stillness for a long, long time. When they are sure that the coast is clear, they spring to life and scamper away or scoot up the nearest tree.

Opossums occasionally visit my backyard at night and scrounge for the crumbs or crackers I put out for the birds. I like to see their funny white triangular faces and bright beady eyes—preferably not too near the garbage pail!

Driver Alert

Grasses and other vegetation along highways and roadside areas are attractive to opossums, woodchucks, skunks, deer, and many other wild animals. There, they often find succulent weeds, grasses, seeds, and other kinds of food. Intent upon feeding, in search of mates, or establishing territory, these creatures are not looking out for cars as they stray on to the edge of the road or decide to cross it. Many do not survive the crossing to find out if the grass is greener. Keeping a sharp lookout, a driver in rural or suburban areas may be able to avoid such fatal encounters.

The Wily Fox

The red fox is usually a rusty red above, with a white throat and belly and black "socks," but there are black and silver forms. All have a white-tipped tail. These foxes are 15 to 16 inches tall at the shoulder and 35½ to 40½ inches long, with 14- to 17-inch tails. They weigh 8 to 15 pounds. The mother fox bears up to ten kits in an earthen den sometime between March and May. Red foxes are omnivorous and principally nocturnal. The slightly smaller gray fox is gray above, reddish below, with a black-topped tail. It forms its den in caves, rock piles, or hollow trees, which it can climb. Like the red fox, it is omnivorous and primarily nocturnal. Its range is limited to the United States, whereas the red fox is also found throughout Canada.

The fox deserves its reputation of wiliness and cunning: It had better, or it will end up in a fur coat. Hunted and trapped to excess, foxes survive by their sharp wits and even manage to exist in suburban or well-populated areas. They usually, but not always, do their hunting for food at night. Their most plentiful food is mice. Seldom will a fox venture into a backyard; if you should see one, it is after a rodent and will not linger.

The Beneficial Bat

There are 39 species of bat in the United States, so you probably have at least one kind of these flying mammals in your area. Like moles, their sight is poor; they guide themselves by sound. Bats can walk and climb as well as fly. They bear one or two young a year. North American bats range from 2½ to 7½ inches long and can weigh over 2 ounces. Ears of long-eared species may be 2 inches long.

The bat's appearance, which many people find repulsive, plus its prominent but totally unrealistic role in horror stories and folklore, has earned it an undeserved bad reputation. The few species of vampire bat live only in Latin America. North American bats rarely carry rabies, do not attack people or suck human blood, and are not desirous of getting entangled in your coiffure. They have highly sensitive auditory equipment and wings splendidly adapted for flight. They do not all live in caves; many roost in barns, shutters, attics, and trees.

Harmless and shy, beneficial in their appetite for insect pests and pollinating fruit crops in some areas, they ask only to be left alone and not persecuted. The bat, a night flyer, can consume several thousand mosquitos and other bugs in one night. And bat dung, or guano, is one of the richest organic sources of nitrogen and minerals.

The Serviceable Snake

Like "bat," the word "snake" evokes instant aversion in most people. This too is unfortunate, for the snake most likely to be seen in your garden is the common garter snake, mostly brown and yellow in color. It is completely harmless and dotes on insects and their larvae, snails, and slugs, as do the brown snake and the green or grass snake. Other snakes that might possibly be found near human habitations are the blacksnake and the milk snake, both beneficial rodent eaters. They are all much more frightened of us than we are of them and do not strike unless provoked.

A Helping Hand

Every creature that visits or resides in your backyard is not as pretty as a butterfly, as cute as a chipmunk, or as beneficial as a ladybird. But all of them, and many more, have their rightful place within the vast ecological web of plant and animal life, where they are dependent on each other and interrelated with their environment. When people destroy natural habitats or make them unlivable by polluting or poisoning them, the ecology is disturbed and the balance of nature is upset.

Remember the flowery meadow or the woods not far from where you live or once lived? Chances are they are gone, and with them the creatures that lived there, who must find shelter and sustenance elsewhere or perish. As they search, many draw closer to our backyards. With an awareness of their plight and needs, we can offer some of these wildlings a sanctuary, and have the pleasure of observing them in the habitat that we have created out of flowers, shrubs, trees, and water.

Part Three

HOW TO KEEP THE GARDEN HEALTHY

Chapter 10

The Stuff of Life

> *Without the microorganisms at work in compost, soil would literally be dead.*
>
> Eleanor Perényi,
> *Green Thoughts: A Writer in the Garden*

You *can* make a silk purse out of a sow's ear. In gardening terms, this means that you can change poor, unproductive soil into a rich, fertile growing medium. Beautiful flowers, strong, healthy plants, and good things to eat cannot be expected to grow in worn-out, exhausted earth. Just as human beings need protein, calcium, vitamins, and other nutrients in their diet in order to be healthy, plants need certain elements to grow and thrive.

The subjects of compost, fertilizer, and mulch sometimes cause readers' eyes to glaze over. But if plants could talk, they would say that it is of supreme interest to them and vital to what they can do for you. So, for the sake of your garden, please read on!

Compost

Of all the soil builders in the world, the best and cheapest is compost, the one fertilizer you can make yourself of organic materials collected and heaped together. Unfortunately, a strange collection of rumors about compost exists. People unfamiliar with it believe that the pile will take up too much space, or space better used for something else; that it will be an eyesore; that it will smell; that it will draw rodents; that it will be difficult to make; and that it won't do anything that chemical fertilizers can't do. None of this is accurate. Here's the truth about compost.

A compost pile can be as large or as small as space and available materials permit, as long as it is at least 3-by-3-by-3 feet. (Smaller piles will dry out or cool off rather than composting.) It can be located in any inconspicuous angle or corner outside the house, porch, or garage, or be conveniently sited in the vegetable garden. Bins can be painted green to blend with the vegetation or designed to look like an extension of a fence or toolshed. Even a small compost pile will have more value for your garden than a shrub that might occupy the same space.

Compost will not smell or draw rodents unless something highly inappropriate, such as meat, fat, or bones, is added to it. If you do add meat scraps to the pile, it will draw not only rodents but maggots, flies, cats, dogs, and a host of other creatures you were not planning to invite to dinner.

A compost pile is not an eyesore. It can be enclosed in handsome brick or plank bins. While ripening, the compost itself has the appearance of a brown leafy mass, with bits of green and other colors that gradually turn brown too.

Compost cannot be considered on terms of equality with chemical fertilizers, because they cannot do what it does. It conditions and improves the tilth, or quality, of the soil, aerates it so that roots and soil life can breathe, and encourages the spread of plant roots and the tunneling of earthworms, which further aerate the earth. Compost increases the capacity of sandy soil to retain water and nutrients and of clay soils to drain and "breathe" properly. It releases nutrients slowly but steadily, so they do not burn or harm plants. It stimulates the spread of beneficial microorganisms in the soil, which are constantly at work improving soil structure and fighting disease-bearing bacteria.

Compost returns to the earth that which came from the earth. Recycling organic matter and wastes is an integral part of natural gardening—and of all life on earth.

What to Put in the Pile

Good compost can be made from the most ordinary materials. The main ingredient in my compost is the leaves I gather in the fall. Bagging leaves and throwing them out is a terrible waste! So is discarding plant refuse from the garden. This includes dead flowers, leaves, stems, trimmings, weeds, pine needles, grass clippings, spent annuals, vegetable plants pulled after autumn harvest, and fallen apples—all grist for future compost. Wood ashes can be added, but not coal or charcoal ashes, which may take centuries to decay.

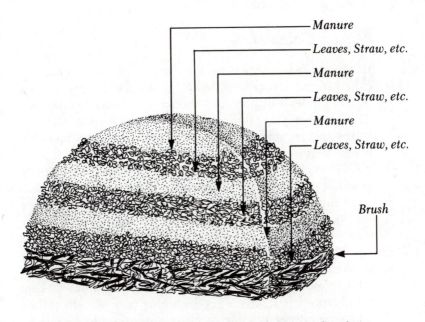

Manure

Leaves, Straw, etc.

Manure

Leaves, Straw, etc.

Manure

Leaves, Straw, etc.

Brush

A well-built compost pile starts with a layer of brush for aeration, then alternates layers of high-carbon leaves and straw with high-nitrogen manure, grass clippings, and kitchen scraps for fast, even heating.

A vast variety of kitchen waste is excellent for composting, including wilted or overripe vegetables and fruit; cores and peels; tea leaves and bags; eggshells; coffee grounds; carrot, beet, and celery tops; peanut shells; and nonmeat leftovers such as bread, rice, and cereal. If you have a shredder or access to one, twigs, branches, stalks, and newspapers can be shredded and added to the pile. The finer everything is chopped or shredded, the quicker the composting proceeds.

Even a small household can fill an empty coffee can every few days with coffee grounds, unused lettuce or celery leaves, an apple core, a mushy grape, and a few table scraps and dump it on the compost pile. If you don't care for the looks of it, bury kitchen waste under some leaves or a sprinkling of dirt. Ask your grocer for the beet and carrot tops and cabbage and lettuce leaves he throws away. Sometimes he has spoiled fruit and vegetables to get rid of. All are grist for the compost mill. Your neighbors may also be willing to contribute their kitchen scraps.

Making Compost

Compost can be made in a pit in the ground (the technique is called trench composting), in a pile on the ground, or in a bin. Bin styles are almost as varied as composters themselves. The simplest is a cylinder of chicken wire held in place by stakes driven into the ground. Others include 55-gallon drums set up on frames, with turning cranks so they can be rotated; rectangular bins made of snow fence, cinder blocks, boards, bricks, or discarded builders' pallets; even galvanized trash cans with holes punched for ventilation. A number of ingenious designs can also be purchased from garden supply catalogs.

Whatever bin you use, if any, the techniques for making good compost are the same. For fast heating (which translates into fast composting), the pile must be aerated, kept evenly moist, and have a good working ratio of high-carbon and high-nitrogen materials (an example would be mixing high-carbon leaves or straw with high-nitrogen kitchen scraps and fresh grass clippings). You can aerate the pile by turning it (forking it over from the top, so you're building a

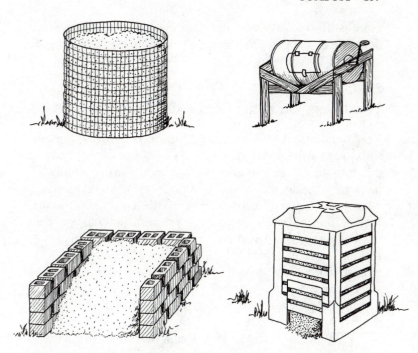

You can make or buy a variety of compost bins. Popular varieties include a simple wire cylinder, a 55-gallon drum and stand, a commercial plastic composter, and a concrete-block bin.

new pile every two weeks or so), building it on a bed of branches or cornstalks, or inserting ventilation poles to open up the pile from inside. The pile should be kept evenly moist—a handful of compost should feel about as damp as a squeezed sponge for optimum decomposition. If the weather has been dry, you may have to hose the pile down. But don't drench it, or you'll drown the microorganisms that are doing the composting for you!

Many composters add a thin layer of soil to their piles to ensure the presence of these microscopic decomposers. Some also add high-nitrogen fertilizers such as bloodmeal, chicken manure, or bat guano to hasten the process. Whatever your technique, unless you're using an intensive method (like the California 14-day composting system), you'll probably have finished compost ready to go in the garden in about three months. If you have enough space, you can start building a new pile as soon as one is completed, so you'll have a steady supply of "black gold."

What Goes On in the Compost Pile

Vast numbers of bacteria, fungi, and other tiny soil organisms are at work breaking down the contents of the compost pile into smaller and smaller parts. If earthworms get in, they help too. Inside the heap, a buildup of heat takes place, which is necessary for bacterial activity. Gradually the texture of the materials becomes finer, and the color darkens until it resembles damp peat moss. The compost begins to remind me of crumbled bittersweet chocolate—it looks almost good enough to eat! Indeed, for the garden, it will be a splendid feast.

If compost is ready, or nearly ready, in fall, spread it in the flowerbed, where it will serve as a mulch over winter and in spring can be turned into the soil. Start a fresh pile with autumn leaves and healthy garden trash. If compost is ready in spring, spread it and dig it in before spring planting. Start a new pile with the spring cleanup.

Organic Fertilizers and Soil Conditioners

Fertilizers contain at least one of the three major elements needed by plants: nitrogen, phosphorus, and potassium. If you buy packaged fertilizer, the percentage of each element is listed in that order on the outside of the bag in a formula such as 5-5-5. Nitrogen stimulates the growth of leaves and stems; phosphorus encourages growth of roots and stems and production of flowers; and potassium helps produce fruit and flowers and builds resistance to disease and cold weather. Organic fertilizers also contain varying amounts of the micronutrients (such as boron and manganese) that are vital to plant growth.

Water-soluble fertilizers such as liquid seaweed, fish emulsion, and compost and manure teas deliver nutrients to your plants much faster than dry fertilizers. They give newly set plants, transplants, and seedlings a quick start and can be reapplied every three weeks in summer as a regular watering to boost growth and flowering. These liquids will not burn plants and may be applied as foliar feeds to leaves for even faster absorption.

The Finest Fertilizers

One of the best organic fertilizers is manure, used by gardeners the world over to enrich their gardens since gardening began. The best soil-building manures are bulky horse and cow manure; the richest in nutrients are high-powered chicken manure and guano (bird and bat manure). The nutrient range is 2-1-1 for composted cow manure to 13-8-2 for bird guano. If you have access to fresh manure, add it to the vegetable garden in fall so that it can decompose before spring planting; fresh manure can burn plants.

If you plan to side-dress ornamentals or other permanent plantings, compost the manure before you use it. You may be able to find a source of aged (well-rotted) manure that can be used immediately. To use as a soil builder, add 40 pounds of composted cow manure per 50 to 100 square feet of ground. Because it's such a concentrated source of nutrients, on the other hand, up to 5 pounds of guano per 100 square feet (or 1 pound per 5 gallons of water for manure tea) should be ample as fertilizer.

Nitrogen

Good sources of nitrogen are bloodmeal (15-1.3-0.7), cottonseed meal (6-2.5-2), and fish meal (10-0.5-1). Bloodmeal will add a quick nitrogen boost and last three to four months in the soil; apply up to 3 pounds per 100 square feet but no more, or you'll burn the plants. Cottonseed meal lasts longer—four to six months—but it acidifies the soil, so it's best for plants like azaleas, rhododendrons, hollies, dogwoods, blueberries, and strawberries. Add 2 to 5 pounds per 100 square feet, or 2 to 4 cups per inch of trunk diameter for trees (put the meal around the dripline of each tree). Use up to 5 pounds of fish meal per 100 square feet in early spring, at transplanting, or as a means of giving plants a boost. It lasts six to eight months.

Phosphorus

The best sources of phosphorus are bonemeal (3-20-0), colloidal phosphate (0-20-0), and rock phosphate (0-33-0). These are also good sources of calcium, so they'll raise soil pH. Use up to 5 pounds of bonemeal per 100 square feet. It's especially good for fruit trees, bulbs, and flowerbeds and lasts six months to a year. Use up to 10 pounds of colloidal phosphate per 100 square feet in the garden in fall and when planting bare-root trees in winter. It breaks down faster than rock phosphate and will continue to release phosphorus for two to three years. Rock phosphate is applied at the same rate as colloidal phosphate. It releases phosphorus best in acid soils with a pH lower than 6.2.

Potassium

For potassium, choose greensand (0-1-6), langbeinite (0-0-22), or kelp meal (1-0-12). Apply up to 10 pounds of greensand per 100 square feet in fall. It is slowly available but lasts up to 10 years and loosens clay soils. Langbeinite (sold as Sul-Po-Mag and K-Mag) is especially rich in potassium, so you'll need less—up to 1 pound per 100 square feet. It's also rich in sulfur and magnesium, so look for it if your soil is deficient in these micronutrients. Apply kelp meal at the same rate as langbeinite. It lasts six months to a year. Because kelp contains natural growth hormones, it's best used sparingly to avoid fast, weak growth.

Building the Soil

The best garden soil is loaded with humus, which is decomposed vegetable matter. To increase the humus content of your soil, add soil conditioners—compost, leaves, grass clippings, pine needles, hay, straw, green manures, even shredded newspaper. Some soil conditioners, such as grass clippings and leguminous green manures like clover and Austrian peas, are also excellent sources of nitrogen.

Peat moss, on the other hand, has very little value as a fertilizer but high value as a soil conditioner when mixed thoroughly with either clay or sandy soil. Gypsum, finely ground white calcium sulfate, is also used to give better drainage in heavy clay soil and is especially useful in damp, low-lying areas where soil is impacted and retains too much water.

In general, soil conditioners are not fertilizers. Their value lies in improving the soil so that the nutrients in it, and those added to it, can be more readily absorbed by plant roots.

Mulches

Now that we have come this far, let's cover the rest of the ground—with mulch. A mulch can be made of virtually anything, from nourishing compost to ugly black plastic. To mulch is to lay the stuff between and around vegetables, flowers, shrubs, and trees.

Why should you mulch? Because it has many virtues for all seasons. In winter, it helps to keep the ground at a uniform temperature, warding off the damaging effects of alternate freezing and thawing, which may force plants up out of the ground and kill their roots. It protects the lower parts of the plant from cold or blustery winds. In summer, mulch keeps weeds down and helps the soil retain moisture and coolness by lessening evaporation and blocking the drying effects of sun and summer wind. It is a boon to the gardener who prefers not to cultivate the soil and yank weeds.

Choosing a Mulch

The best mulch is compost, loaded with nourishment for plants as well as soil-enhancing humus. There are many other good mulches, however, among them peat moss, salt hay (ordinary hay mats down more tightly and can contain weed seeds but is often much less expensive), buckwheat or cocoa hulls, wood chips, bark chips, leaves, pine branches, aged sawdust (fresh sawdust drains soil nitrogen as it decomposes), and seaweed. Salt hay, or seaweed if you can get it (it is rich in micronutrients), is among the best of the lot. Don't use pure peat moss—a thick layer will bake and get crusty in dry weather, so water may run off instead of being absorbed. Peat can be combined with grass clippings or leaves to prevent crusting and increase absorption. Oak leaves, pine needles, and peat are recommended as mulches for azaleas, rhododendrons, woodland wildflowers, and other plants that like acid soil.

Peat, hulls, and chips are attractive but add little nutritive value and are costly. To be suitable for flowerbeds, bark or wood chips should be shredded. Since all wood products are low in nitrogen and draw nitrogen from the soil, it's advisable to mix them with a high-nitrogen fertilizer such as bloodmeal or cottonseed meal to make a satisfactory mulch, which will gradually decompose.

Plastic Mulch

Now, as for that black plastic: It is favored by some gardeners because it warms cold soil early in the season so planting can begin sooner, and it smothers weeds. Some plastic sheets have precut holes for planting; some need to have holes or slits cut in them. What's so bad about plastic? It is not biodegradable, and, unlike organic mulches, it adds nothing to the soil. It needs to be anchored down, must be lifted for fertilizing, and should be removed at season's end.

Because the soil is kept warmer by plastic than if exposed or otherwise mulched, there is a danger of heat buildup in the soil. Clear plastic heats up even faster, and the heat penetrates farther into the soil, but unlike black plastic, it does nothing to reduce weed growth—if anything, it enhances it. Perhaps worst of all, black plastic is just plain ugly, a blight upon the landscape, and clear plastic is not much of an improvement. In the naturalist's garden, these unnatural materials should be reserved for the vegetable plot, where a jump on the season can provide a more plentiful harvest.

Summer Mulch and Winter Mulch

In late spring or early summer, spread several inches of mulch around your plants. Fresh grass clippings and leaves in quantity will mat down, mold, or get soggy and prevent sufficient circulation of air, so use them in combination with other organic materials such as straw or salt hay. Mulch before the sun and hot air cook the earth too much in summer but after the soil has warmed in spring and planting, seeding, and fertilizing are completed. When young plants are a few inches high, pull mulch up to the plants, but don't let it directly touch the stems or the high humidity could foster fungal diseases.

After the ground freezes in cold areas, the summer mulch may need to be replenished if it has partly decomposed or if you've turned it into the soil after harvest and cleanup. Heap fresh material generously around—but not on top of—the crowns of perennials and biennials. Don't wait until the ground is frozen solid, or you may be tempted to skip the job! But wait until some freezing has occurred, or the mulch will prevent ground freeze and plants may start growing again in a warm spell in late autumn, only to be killed by a renewed cold snap. Most organic mulches gradually decay over winter and can be dug into the soil the following spring.

Pine or other branches, chopped-up Christmas trees, and a thick layer of salt hay are fine for winter protection, but must be removed in spring. But the prettiest and least expensive winter mulch is one you can't make or buy. It's a good thick cover of snow that lasts or is regularly renewed. Unfortunately, warm climates don't have it, and temperate zones can't depend on it, so it's best to do your own mulching as insurance, then see if the weather does its part.

In hot and dry climates and desert areas with scant rainfall, a mulch is a necessity to catch and retain every drop of rain, dew, or water and to keep the soil cool. Mulches will also modify the vast temperature shifts that occur between day and night in the desert garden.

Cultivation

There is an alternative to summer mulching—cultivation. Use a long-handled, three- or four-pronged cultivator or a hoe to scratch up the surface of the soil around plants, taking care not to cut too deeply, as some flower and vegetable roots are quite near the surface. This light scuffling provides a loose earth or dust mulch and destroys germinating weeds that you may not even see. Pull up larger weeds, break off their roots and flowers or seed heads, and toss weeds into the compost or back into the garden where they will enrich the soil. Cultivation every week or ten days keeps weeds from growing big.

To discourage weeds further, space plants closely enough so that the ground between them is shaded. This deprives the young weeds of light, making them spindly, weak, and easy to uproot.

Cultivating on a regular basis can replace summer mulching in most, but not all, ways; it certainly can't keep plant roots cool and moist, it adds nothing to the soil, and it does entail work. But for many gardeners it's enjoyable exercise and a way of feeling closer to their soil and their plants. And in very short-season areas, where the main concern is heating the soil as fast as possible and keeping it warm as long as possible, cultivation may be the only viable alternative.

The Gardener's Tools

In order to till the soil, add soil builders and fertilizers, irrigate, weed, and even plant, the naturalist/gardener needs tools. Top-quality garden equipment is more economical in the long run because it will last for many years, perhaps a lifetime. Before buying, heft and feel a tool in your hand, making sure that it feels comfortable, not too heavy, not too light. Pretend to use the tool to see how it feels "in action." The most important factor is the quality of the steel. Look for drop-forged, heat-treated steel, which is resistant to the ravages of wear and weather and tends to hold a sharp cutting edge. The most durable tools are forged with solid sockets, rather than seamed welding. The handle should be unpainted, so you can make sure that the grain is fine and smooth. The strongest handles are white ash.

Other than willing hands and a strong back, every gardener needs a minimal assortment of tools. A spade or shovel and a spading fork are needed to loosen and turn over the soil and to heft compost, manure, and mulching materials. A metal rake is helpful to level off the surface of the flowerbed, once dug and prepared for planting. A long-handled cultivator keeps the soil loose and aerated and uproots weeds. (Long-handled tools in general make it easier to garden without stooping and bending.) For getting out pesky weeds close to plant stems and vegetables, you have a choice of hoes with sharp, flat edges or sharp points. A trowel for digging small planting holes is a necessity, and so are strong, sharp clippers. You may also want long-handled pruning shears. A lightweight leaf rake is handy for fall and spring cleanups.

Lightweight plastic hoses and rubber, plastic, or canvas soakers that release droplets of water at ground level come in various lengths. Two nozzles for the hose, one that can be adjusted to a fine spray and one that shuts off the flow of water when you release your grip (automatic shut-off), are both valuable. Unless you have enough stakes saved from last year, you will need a supply of stakes of various lengths, as well as twistems, cord, and plant labels. A wheelbarrow or garden cart is a great convenience for lugging tools, fertilizers, and plants about.

Other Useful Tools

Garden centers and catalogs offer a wide variety of other garden equipment. A set of tools for cultivating, crumbling, breaking up soil, and weeding comes with a removable handle that fits them all. A long-bladed weeder makes digging up dandelions and other deep-rooted weeds easier. A bulb planter—which can also make holes for seedlings—bites sharply into the earth, removing a neat cylinder of soil (almost like coring an apple), and expedites this tough job.

For marking and making rows for seeds, you can buy a row marker with a retractable cord that you can mount on two plastic stakes; a furrow maker, which draws one to five furrows in the soil, spaced as you desire; and seeders to deposit seeds at precise intervals. Netting of various types and sizes can be purchased at garden centers, hardware stores, or fabric shops and attached to stakes for the support of vine crops, tomatoes, and climbing flowers. For properties with a lot of garden waste, leaves from big deciduous trees, and space for a sizable compost pile, an electric shredder may be a good investment.

Long-time gardeners usually have favorite tools that seem to last forever. My favorites are a long-handled, four-pronged cultivator, my faithful 30-year companion in the garden; Grandma's flour scoop, long out of the flour bin and into bags of bonemeal and fertilizer; and a World War II entrenching shovel, courtesy of the U.S. Army, which still digs a darn good hole!

Keeping Tools in Shape

To keep garden equipment in tip-top shape, remove dirt, bits of grass, and other debris after using and wipe with an oily rag. Don't leave tools out in the yard. Make sure they're clean and dry before you put them away. Apply an occasional drop of oil to hinged or movable parts and screws. The best tools may have the fewest moving parts and should be able to be easily dismantled for cleaning, oiling, and replacing of parts if necessary. For easy cleaning and oiling, a bucket of greasy sand in the toolshed or garage is an excellent device; plunge each tool in and out after use. When the season is over, all equipment should be cleaned, and oiled where necessary, before storing over the winter.

A Healthy Garden and How to Achieve It

The health of your garden is as much "the stuff of life" as the compost, fertilizer, and mulch that sustain it. A clean, well-nourished, and adequately watered garden is a healthy garden. You get no guarantees that the weather will cooperate (it seldom does) or that no weeds or harmful insects will appear (they always do). But certain basic gardening practices will maintain good growing conditions, promote vigorous plants, and provide attractions for wildlife.

I have discussed these practices, where appropriate, throughout *The Naturalist's Garden*, but they bear repeating. So here are ten steps on the path to garden health.

1. Sanitation: Add only healthy garden trash to the compost pile; burn or throw out any sickly or diseased vegetation. Keep the backyard litter-free in order to make it harder for bugs, slugs, and diseases to sneak in.

2. Nutrition: Make sure your plants are well fed. Plants use up nutrients in the soil as the season advances, and need supplementary feedings for continued growth and bloom. The best and least costly fertilizer is compost.

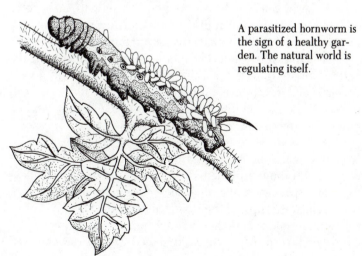

A parasitized hornworm is the sign of a healthy garden. The natural world is regulating itself.

3. Mulching: A layer of organic matter in the flower and shrub borders helps to keep weeds down, retain soil moisture, maintain even soil temperatures, reduce soil erosion, and lessen the gardener's work load. As the mulch decays, it also enriches and improves the quality of the soil.

4. Watering: Soaker hoses deliver water to the root zone, where it's needed, with no waste. If you use a sprinkler or conventional hand-held hose, water in the morning so that foliage can dry off during the day. Leaves that stay wet overnight encourage mildew and disease. Water should penetrate the ground several inches deep; otherwise, plants form shallow roots and are vulnerable to drought. Don't forget your trees and shrubs! To do their best, they need deep, regular waterings.

5. Rotation: Rotation is the practice of planting a certain vegetable or family of vegetables in different parts of the garden rather than in the same spot every year. This practice prevents a buildup of soilborne insect pests and diseases to which these plants are susceptible. Rotation can be used with mildew-prone flowers such as zinnias too.

6. Interplanting: In the informal naturalist's garden, flowers, vegetables, and herbs are not necessarily separate and distinct units that never meet or merge. Interplanting is another form of natural control: A slightly mixed-up garden, where flowers, herbs, and vegetables are interspersed with one another, tends to limit the onslaught of pests and diseases that affect a particular species. The visual effect is attractive and colorful.

7. Diversification: The more variety in your garden, the better. Many different shrubs, trees, and flowering plants encourage the presence of birds, pollinating and beneficial insects, butterflies, chipmunks, and other small creatures, and discourage the spread of plant pests and diseases.

8. Weeding: Weeds draw nourishment and moisture from your soil, robbing your garden plants. Hand-pulling is the oldest and, I think, still the best way to get rid of them. Mulching, close spacing, tilling, and hoeing are other effective controls. Tear weeds up and toss them back into the flowerbed or on the compost pile, where they will decompose and add nutrients. Try to pull weeds *before* they go to seed. Do not recycle weed seeds or their ripe flower heads back into the garden, unless you want to grow a new crop of weeds!

9. Replacing Chemicals with Natural and Biological Controls: There are many ways to avoid the use of chemical sprays and dusts to kill insect pests. Natural predators and parasites can be encouraged to live in your garden or even purchased by mail-order and released in your yard. Handpicking is often effective. Readily available bacterial diseases can be used to control caterpillars and grubs. Cloth or plastic barriers, beer and pheromone traps, and botanical sprays and dusts are all part of the naturalist/gardener's arsenal. And new controls are being developed by researchers all over the country. (For more, see Chapter 11, Battling Bugs and Diseases . . . Naturally.)

10. Introducing Healthy Plants and Seeds into the Garden: Examine any plant carefully for signs of ill health or poor condition before you buy it (see Chapter 3, The Naturalist's Flower Garden, for further details). Read seed packets and catalog descriptions to see if seed is disease- and mildew-resistant. If you are saving seed from plants in your garden, collect seed only from healthy plants for next year's sowing.

Chapter 11

Battling Bugs and Diseases ...Naturally

Fortunately for man, the insect world is divided against itself. It is a realm of endless struggle, of fierce and deadly competition. . . . It is estimated that far more than half the insects prey upon other insects.

Edwin Way Teale,
The Strange Lives of Familiar Insects

It is one of the purposes of this book to provide a wide spectrum of information on the beneficial role Nature, and the home gardener working along with her, plays in the control of plant pests, diseases, and weeds. You need not panic and run for the spray gun or other chemical offensive weapon the moment a bug, weed, or sickly leaf comes into view. Some such cures may be worse than the disease. In any event, no garden can be or need be completely blemish-free. Furthermore, a certain number of insect pests are even desirable, to provide food for beneficial predatory and parasitic insects, many birds, and other small creatures.

Back in the fifties, DDT, a highly effective insecticide used in World War II, was applied by farmers and home gardeners without a care. Little was known about its toxic side effects and persistence in the environment. But by the sixties,

Rachel Carson and other scientists were becoming increasingly uneasy about the long-term effects of DDT and related chemicals—long-lasting chemical substances called chlorinated hydrocarbons—on the chain of life. Their research led them to conclude that the environment was being polluted and altered by the massive use of these pesticides. The buildup in the tissues of fish and wildlife made many creatures ill and caused innumerable deaths. The survival of many species was threatened; human health and safety were also at serious risk.

Unmasking DDT

Carson's book *Silent Spring*, published in 1962, revealed the horrifying facts about chemical poisons and started a revolution against their indiscriminate use. The message of *Silent Spring* was clear. All life is interrelated; harm one form or aspect and the entire web of life is affected. Concern must be shown for the safety of human beings and *all* forms of life. People must learn about the toxic effects of chemicals and what the alternatives to them are.

DDT was banned in the United States in 1972. Since 1972, when health and safety testing was mandated, other agricultural chemicals have been removed from the market, but hundreds of them are still in use and available to the home gardener as well as the farmer. Many contain ingredients that are acutely toxic, causing damage to wildlife and people on contact or as long-lasting residues in soil, water, and food. Many have been found to cause genetic and nerve damage, cancer, birth abnormalities, and sterility.

Effective insecticides kill pests, but they also kill beneficial insects. The remaining pests, and others coming into the area, are able to multiply freely since fewer of their natural enemies are about. The surviving pests are more likely to be resistant to the next dose of insecticides, so the sprayer may turn to a stronger chemical. Residues of the poisons continue to seep into the soil and groundwater, adversely affecting many kinds of wildlife and disrupting the natural balance.

Until the happy day when chemical products for pest and disease control can be made without hazardous side effects, the gardener and the ecology will benefit by the use of other means of control.

The Helping Hand—Yours

You can encourage and increase the presence of beneficial creatures in your garden, and fight back at the injurious ones, in a number of environmentally safe ways. One of the best natural controls, insect-eating birds, can be encouraged to come to the backyard. To attract them, you must provide trees, shrubs, and flowering plants in sufficient variety for food, shelter, and nesting, and water for drinking and bathing. Such a setting will also lure beneficial insects, which help control the pests. How· to create this pleasing setting is discussed in Chapter 7, Birds in the Backyard.

The good fight against the bad bugs involves some of the least pleasurable but most important tasks in the garden. Handpicking bugs is one of them. Although the mere thought of grabbing bugs with your bare hands may turn your stomach, it's a simple and effective technique. And you can always use tweezers.

The Rogues' Gallery

High on the unwanted list is the Japanese beetle, one of the most ubiquitous and ruthlessly destructive of all backyard pests. If you do not recognize this rogue, he is ½ inch long and metallic blue or green with coppery wing covers. I think if sheer hatred could kill, all our worries about Japanese beetles would be over! But unfortunately, we have to do more than fume.

The most direct method of control is to walk around with a can of water topped with oil, kerosene, or charcoal lighter fluid and pick or tap the bugs off into it. A great many can be caught, as they are so busy gobbling your flowers that they are usually unaware of impending doom. They will drown in plain water, too, but more slowly. I stamp firmly on those that fall to the ground. Cut roses early in the day, and before they are fully open, in order to thwart the beetle's villainous attacks.

Japanese beetle traps baited with floral lures can also be set up, but there is some argument that they work so well that they actually bring in beetles. If you use traps, remember to empty them regularly. You can control beetle grubs in your lawn with milky spore disease. (See Biological Controls in this chapter.)

Aphids are tiny ($\frac{1}{12}$- to $\frac{1}{5}$-inch-long) green, blue-black, red, brown, or pinkish insects. They cluster in hordes on buds and tender tips of rosebushes and many other plants and suck out the juices. The most direct control is to remove and squash them between your fingers whenever you see them. Don't be faint of heart—just think of all the harm they do! Aphids can also be dislodged by a forceful stream of water from the hose or destroyed by a spray of insecticidal soap. Their worst garden enemies are ladybugs and aphid lions, the larvae of the lacewing. For both, they are gourmet fare.

One of the most undesirable and repulsive pests is the slug, a mainly nocturnal shell-less mollusk that devours leaves and can defoliate plants. Slugs range from $\frac{1}{2}$ inch to a whopping 3 inches long and can be pink, gray, black, or brown, sometimes with mottled patterns. Rain and lush growth encourage their proliferation. The time-honored method for trapping slugs is to set out shallow saucers of beer in the garden. The creatures are attracted by the scent, crawl in, get sloshed, and drown. Sometimes, however, more of them can be found beneath the saucer than in it.

Ashes or gravel near plant stems may keep slugs away, as they dislike crawling on rough surfaces. Smashing them with a foot or stone can replace handpicking, but squashing a large slug underfoot is undeniably slimy. Instead, lift it with a trowel or tongs, or clip a leaf with slug attached, and drop it into a tin half filled with salty water (hold the beer). This will deliver the *coup de grâce*. But nothing eliminates slugs as efficiently as a toad. If there is a toad on your property, cherish it. There is nothing a toad relishes more for breakfast, lunch, or dinner than a slug, unless it is a caterpillar, cutworm, or other horrid grub. Toads and frogs devour many other insects and spiders, too.

Bug Fights Bug

In the ceaseless battle against harmful insects waged by the human race, nature lends a hand with battalions of beneficial insects, too often unknown for what they are and what good actions they perform. It is astonishing to discover how many insects seem to have been created for a specific purpose: to search and destroy their target pest victims. Nature tends to keep things in balance, and when certain pests are numerous, their natural enemies increase; when fewer of these pests are in a given area, fewer of their enemies appear there.

Beneficial insects are divided into two groups: predatory and parasitic. Predatory insects eat their prey. Parasitic insects parasitize their prey by laying their eggs inside, on the surface of, or close to their victims. The emerging larvae destroy the unwitting and unwilling host, eating their way in or out, sometimes both.

A great many of these natural controls are out in your garden right now, working for you industriously. In case you don't know all of them, let me introduce you.

Insect Predators

Almost everyone recognizes a ladybug, or lady beetle, whether two-spotted, seven-spotted, or nine-spotted (and there are others). Their larvae can eat two dozen or more aphids a day, and the adults a great deal more than that, plus mites and other tiny insects. But do you know a lacewing when you see one? The lacewing, ⅜ to ¾ inch in length, is one of the prettier insects. It is easily recognizable by its delicate light green gossamer wings and golden eyes. It lives mainly on flower nectars and honeydew, a liquid secreted by aphids. You can draw and keep both lacewings and ladybugs in your

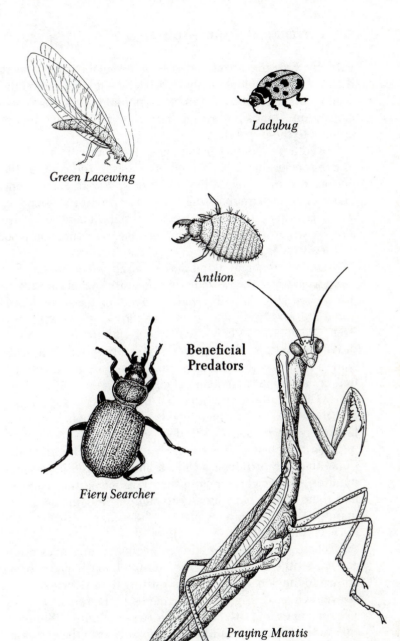

Green Lacewing

Ladybug

Antlion

Beneficial Predators

Fiery Searcher

Praying Mantis

yard by growing an abundance of nectar-bearing flowers that bloom over a long season. The lacewing larva, called the aphid lion, is indeed a ferocious predator, gorging voraciously on aphids and other harmful small insects before going into the pupal stage.

Another predatory insect "lion" is the antlion. The larva of one species digs a pit in sand or loose soil and waits at the bottom for an unsuspecting insect or spider to come along and fall in, whereupon the victim is promptly seized in strong jaws and drained like a bottle of soda. These larvae are also known as doodlebugs. Another species pounces on prey on the surface.

One of the biggest and fiercest of all insect predators is the praying mantis, a fascinating creature. Adults are 2½ to 4½ inches long, superbly camouflaged in green and tan. Some are mostly brown; others are mostly green with jade eyes. The mantis lies in wait for dinner with forelegs held in a prayerful position. Those powerful legs, equipped with sharp spines, are ready to make a lightning strike at any insect, spider, or caterpillar that comes along.

Mantids attack anything that moves within their sight, and their sight is extremely good. The triangular head on a flexible neck can swivel 180 degrees, and if those big eyes seem to be looking directly at you, they are. It's the only insect that can turn its head like a human being! If you find mantids in your garden, note their position so that you can find them again. They usually remain in the same area. My mantids favor big cosmos plants, where many insects come for nectar and pollen.

These carnivores are also cannibals. Young ones often eat each other when hungry. Mature females have been known to dine on apparently unresisting males after mating, or even while mating. Before laying eggs, the female creates a foamy mass and attaches it to a twig or branch. She lays eggs in the foam, then adds finishing touches to the egg case, which will harden, becoming a protective shell for the eggs over the winter. The female herself will not survive the cold weather.

If you don't have mantids in your garden, you can "import" them (see Buy a Bug in this chapter). You may not be able to spot the young mantids, but by late summer some of the big adults should be visible. Watching a mantis catch and consume a meal, then fastidiously clean each foreleg almost like a cat cleans its legs and paws, is an unforgettable experience. So is watching a mantis watching you. (See Mantis Mania in Chapter 8, Butterflies and Friends.)

Fireflies, or lightning bugs, shine like tiny shooting stars over the dark grass on summer nights. Their blinking lights are signals to attract mates. They are useful as well as beautiful. Adults eat nothing, but the larvae feed on assorted slugs, snails, and insects.

Dragonflies and damselflies are swift-flying, predatory beauties that like to be near a pond, pool, or marsh. Their larvae (called naiads) feed mainly on mosquito wigglers in the water. Some live underwater for a year or two, preying on tiny fish, aquatic insects, and even each other. Adult darners, the big, fast North American dragonflies, are brilliantly colored in blue, green, purplish, and brown and have a wingspan of up to 6 inches. The wings are transparent. In their relentless war on mosquitoes, which they catch in the air, these insects swoop, dive, fly backward, and hover very much as hummingbirds do. And like mantids, they have excellent vision and fierce appetites. In autumn, the females lay their eggs in water or on vegetation near water. With the arrival of cold weather, the adults perish.

Hosts of other predatory insects help keep injurious insects and other pests in check and pollinate some flowers. The beetle family, the largest order in the entire animal kingdom, contains many predators. One of the ground beetles has the splendid name of fiery searcher. Gleaming in greenish gold, black, and copper, it attacks and eats caterpillars. Both larva and adult will climb trees in search of prey.

Insect Parasites

A number of insects in the adult stage eat nothing at all, and others subsist on flower nectars and pollen. Among these are the parasitic beneficial flies, wasps, and beetles, which lay their eggs inside or on the outside of the host's body or on nearby foliage that the victim eats. The eggs hatch into lar-

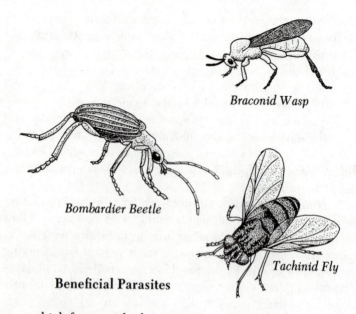

Braconid Wasp

Bombardier Beetle

Tachinid Fly

Beneficial Parasites

vae, which feast on the host insect, itself usually in an immature (egg or larval) stage, and kill it.

More than likely, the tomato hornworm you see festooned with little white "cocoons" on a partly denuded plant is half dead and doesn't know it. The braconid wasp has laid eggs on it that hatched, entered the big caterpillar and ate heartily, burrowed to the outside, and are now in the pupal stage. Soon the hornworm will die. The tiphia wasp, the trichogramma wasp, and the tachinid fly parasitize aphids, cutworms, borers, cabbageworms, and many other kinds of pesky caterpillars.

In the enormous family of ground beetles, the bombardier beetle, averaging ½ inch in length, blue winged with head and legs of tan or yellowish brown, is outstanding for its unique defense mechanism. The bombardier can eject a scalding hot toxic puff that makes a popping noise, audible to human ears if you're close enough. This must sound like the roar of a cannon to a small approaching enemy or prey, and it is accompanied by a foul smell. The bombardier aims well, and a direct hit can leave a startled victim with severely irritated eyes or mouth. If you handle a bombardier, expect to be blasted with a hot substance that may stain your skin! But don't hold self-defense against them—their larvae feed enthusiastically on pupating insects. Bombardiers are found in wet or moist places throughout the United States and southern Canada.

Buy a Bug

Yes, you can! Several of the beneficial predatory insects and their eggs or larvae are available commercially, as well as the parasitic trichogramma wasp, which attacks many harmful caterpillars (see the Resources list for this chapter). The mail-order companies that sell beneficials will deliver your insects at the best times for you to release them, with instructions on how to set them out. This varies from insect to insect and area to area. General recommendations are to set out mantis egg cases in late winter or early spring, to release lacewing larvae in early summer and again two weeks later, and to release ladybugs in summer.

Ladybugs are shipped as adults, and some may decide to wander off. They're more likely to stay in your yard if you water the area well just before releasing them and only release them in the cool of the evening. Aphid lions, the larvae of lacewings, will pupate and become adults in one to three weeks, but before then they are ferociously hungry predators. Praying mantids hatch out of roundish walnut-sized brown egg cases in May and June and usually remain in the area where they emerge. Firmly tie the egg cases earlier in the season to shrubs in various spots in the garden.

Some of these imported helpers may be eaten by birds and other predators (or each other). The first three mantis egg cases I received either hatched and were all eaten by predators and each other, or the cases were ripped away by the wind and disappeared. It was late winter. I tried another batch in early spring, and several survived. The mortality rate of the juveniles may be very high, but those mantids that survive will be very useful to you in the war on harmful insects.

Nematodes, Protozoans, and a Snail

For control of a wide variety of soil-dwelling pests, parasitic nematodes can be purchased, placed in water, and sprayed or sprinkled on crops and in the garden. These minute creatures kill insects underground and are not harmful to anything else. As parasites, they infest, kill, and consume host pests such as borers, cutworms, weevils, and maggots. The dreaded iris borer is a favorite target. They are not to be confused with the injurious plant nematode.

If grasshoppers are a bane in the summer garden, there is a protozoan parasite, *Nosema locustae*, which may be purchased and applied in spring or summer to control the nymphs and young grasshoppers that are less than 1 inch long. The disease continues to be spread by infected grasshoppers, so it is even more effective the second summer after application. It is sold as Grasshopper Attack.

There's even a mail-order predator for slugs and garden snails, the decollate snail. These cannibalistic snails will reduce the ranks of their vegetarian brethren. And *Pediobius folveolatus*, a predatory wasp that scientists have used to effectively control the Mexican bean beetle, looms on the gardener's horizon.

Botanical Insecticides

These insecticidal poisons are called botanicals because they are derived from plants. Botanical sprays and dusts break down, or biodegrade, in nature much more quickly than synthetic chemical pesticides and, unlike them, do not accumulate in the soil or in human or animal tissues. However, they are far from completely safe. Therefore, they should be used only after other techniques have failed. Botanicals include:

Pyrethrum: This is one of the least toxic to humans and animals of all insecticides. It is derived from the petals of a species of chrysanthemum. It is lethal to many injurious insects and, unfortunately, to beneficial ones, including bees, as well. It can kill fish. Pyrethrum is widely available; brand names include Raid Tomato and Vegetable Fogger and Perma-Guard.

Rotenone: Rotenone is produced from the roots of two legumes, *Derris* and *Lonchocarpus*. Like pyrethrum, rotenone can knock out many harmful insects, including aphids, thrips, and a number of beetle pests, but it will affect harmless ones as well and is lethal to bees and fish. Some plant life, such as certain ferns, roses, lantanas, and others, can be damaged by rotenone dust or spray. Brand names include Safer's Japanese Beetle Spray and Bonide Liquid Rotenone/Pyrethrins Spray.

Ryania: This botanical is made from powdered stems of the ryania scrub. It is used chiefly for the control of the codling moth larvae on fruit trees. It is of slight toxicity to humans. Ryania is also sold combined with rotenone and pyrethrum as a dust or spray.

Sabadilla dust: Made from the seeds of a South American lily, this botanical helps to control many adult insects but is particularly effective against the dreaded squash bug.

Nicotine: Although its residual effect is very short, nicotine (derived from tobacco) is highly poisonous to humans and animals. For this reason, although it is very effective as an insecticide, nicotine is not recommended under any circumstances.

Homemade Botanicals

Other botanicals can be made at home. A tea brewed from cedar chips is said to be effective against most garden pests, including potato beetles and squash bugs. Tomato- or rhubarb-leaf tea will control blackflies, whiteflies, aphids, leafminers, and caterpillars. Reserve any containers you use for these brews only for this purpose and that no one mistakenly tastes a toxic tea. Keep out of reach of children.

The botanical standby for the home gardener is a hot pepper spray. Hot peppers contain capsaicin, the same inflaming agent that makes us reach for the water after downing a jalapeño. Ground fresh or dried peppers steeped in water for 24 hours should control pests if the brew is strained and a bit of dishwashing detergent is added to help it adhere to plants. Apply regularly until the problem is brought under control.

Mechanical Controls

Mechanical controls include traps like the previously described beer trap for slugs and other control techniques, such as placing cardboard collars around the stems of transplants to prevent cutworm damage. Many have suggested themselves to ingenious gardeners and scientists. One of the most effective is the yellow sticky trap. These can be purchased or made of yellow plastic strips or wooden stakes painted yellow and coated with a sticky substance such as Tanglefoot. Aphids, leafminers, thrips, whiteflies, and other small insects are drawn to the color yellow and get stuck on the trap.

Another effective mechanical control is diatomaceous earth (DE), a powder made from the shells of fossilized microscopic ocean plants called diatoms. The sharp edges of these shells pierce the skin of soft-bodied insects such as aphids, caterpillars, and mites, as well as slugs, drying them out and killing them. Wood ashes can also be used against soft-bodied insects, though they are less effective than DE. Spread either substance on the ground around seedlings; dust the foliage of mature plants.

Biological Controls

Biocontrols are the wave of the future in nontoxic pest controls, and on its crest ride laboratory-developed bacteria, fungi, and viruses that attack only their specific target pests and leave no harmful residues. A number of them are available now.

One of the earliest and best-known biocontrols is a caterpillar-destroying bacterium, *Bacillus thuringiensis* (Bt), sold as Dipel, Thuricide, Attack, Biotrol, and Bactur. It kills tomato hornworms, cabbage loopers, cabbageworms, leaf rollers, gypsy moth larvae, and any other caterpillar that comes in contact with it. Furthermore, infected caterpillars become breeding grounds for the bacteria, spreading the disease among their brethren.

A related bacterium, *Bacillus popilliae* (Bp), sold as Japidemic and Doom, infects Japanese beetle grubs with the fatal milky spore disease. Applied just once to the lawn in early or late summer, according to directions on the label, it is active for years and even grows more effective with time, infecting and killing many generations and freeing your lawn of destructive grubs and moles.

Still in the research stage is a fungal disease, *Beauveria bassiana*, which has proved effective in tests as a control for the Colorado potato beetle. And Bt is constantly being refined as new strains are isolated to make it even more pest-specific.

Pheromones are another major kind of biocontrol. They imitate the sex hormones of the target insect, luring it to a trap instead of its intended mate. Japanese beetles meet their end in the famous Bag-a-Bug traps. Some traps, including Bag-a-Bug and the Blitz-a-Beetle Japanese beetle traps, are baited with a floral lure as well as the pheromone to make them doubly inviting. Pheromones are nontoxic and specific to the target insect.

A twist in pheromone research is the use of the sex attractants to lure in *good* bugs—without the traps, of course! Scientists at the USDA's research center in Beltsville, Maryland, used pheromones successfully to bring spined soldier bugs, vicious insect predators that feed on more than 100 insect species, into the test plots.

Scientists are developing still more biocontrols, including growth retardants, juvenile hormones that prevent pests from maturing and breeding, and laboratory-induced sterility of male insects, which are then released to mate with females of their species. And they're perfecting a sweet-smelling lure to attract and trap the hated yellowjackets. Who knows what tomorrow's garden supply stores and nurseries may carry on their shelves?

As more and more agents for safe control are being researched and marketed, the naturalist/gardener will want to keep up with these developments away from harmful chemical pesticides. To stay informed about exciting developments in laboratory and field work in the battle against injurious insects, look for updates in gardening magazines, check with your county agent, and/or subscribe to a journal specifically about biocontrols. (See the Resource listings for this chapter.)

Read and Heed Label Instructions

Read all label information carefully before using any botanical or biological control, and follow all instructions for use to the letter. Even if the label doesn't say so, you would be wise to wear long sleeves, long pants, and gloves. Try to avoid breathing spray or dust or getting any of it on your face or in your eyes. If any part of the body has been exposed, wash well, and flush your eyes with water immediately if they have been affected. Pyrethrum dust in particular can cause allergic reactions, skin rash, and respiratory irritations if inhaled, especially in asthma sufferers. Wash contaminated clothing.

Environmental statements on labels are there to alert you to take extra precautions. They may warn that the product is or may be toxic to bees, fish, birds, and other wildlife, or certain kinds of plants. To be on the safe side, don't apply any botanical when bees or other wildlife are present or may be affected by drift from the area being treated. Store separately from food and well out of the reach of children. When applying them, take care to keep botanical sprays or dust away from any body of water.

If the product you are using is to be applied on or near food crops, look for information on the label as to how many days must pass between the last application and the harvest.

Integrated Pest Management (IPM)

More and more, professionals are using natural enemies and biological controls in an effort to avoid chemicals or significantly decrease their use in agriculture, orcharding, and forestry, as well as in the home garden. This new approach is called integrated pest management (IPM). IPM takes into consideration the entire ecosystem in determining which are the most effective and, at the same time, the least hazardous tactics to use in solving problems caused by injurious pests and diseases. The key is to reduce pest damage to tolerable levels rather than eliminate pests entirely.

IPM is a combination of all the efficient, benign, and nonpolluting methods and agents that have been presented to the reader: selection of pest- and disease-resistant cultivars (cultivated varieties) of plants and seeds; good cultural practices in the garden, including sanitation, humus-enriched soil, interplanting, handpicking, and traps; recognition and encouragement of insect predators and parasites, the natural enemies of insect pests; and use of biological controls. To these ecologically sound methods, professional growers may add an extremely limited use of carefully chosen chemicals to be used as a last resort. For the naturalist/gardener, however, chemicals would be self-defeating, polluting the natural world he or she has worked so hard to enhance. Our goal is to use an IPM approach without carrying it to a chemical extreme.

Most nurseries do not have or dispense sufficient information about alternatives to chemicals, because their pest-control information is derived from the companies that manufacture and supply chemical products. Dislodging aphids with strong spurts of water from the hose, or handpicking Japanese beetles, for example, would hardly be a good sales pitch! It's up to the gardener to be well informed about nonchemical alternatives and make good use of them so that no environmental damage will result. And that's a lot healthier for the gardener as well as the garden.

Resisting Disease

There are three steps the naturalist/gardener can take to keep disease out, or at least minimize it in the garden: Grow resistant varieties, build the soil, and practice good garden sanitation. Seed and nursery catalogs list resistance or tolerance to disease, if any, with each entry. Resistance is a strong ability to withstand or repel the disease; tolerance is an ability to survive and produce flowers and/or fruit in spite of infection.

Vegetable breeding programs have focused on combating diseases in cucumbers, melons, peas, and tomatoes, but resistant varieties of bean, celery, corn, pepper, potato, spinach, turnip, and even Chinese cabbage are available (for some examples, see Chapter 6, On Growing Vegetables). Vigorous fruit breeding programs have produced resistant varieties such as Prima, Priscilla, Sir Prize, Liberty, and Freedom apples; Luscious pear; Indian Summer and Royalty raspberries; and a host of strawberries, including Allstar, Earliglow, Guardian, Lester, Redchief, Scott, and Surecrop.

Ornamentals have also been bred to resist disease. Powderpuff asters, Giant Pacific delphiniums, Ming Yellow lilies, Crystal Bowl pansies, Rose Pinwheel and Ruffles Hybrid zinnias, and numerous roses—America, Bonica, Climbing Don Juan, Honor, Intrigue, Olympiad, Seashell, Touch of Class, Tropicana, and Voodoo are just a sampling—have some resistance to the diseases that generally plague their fellows.

Soil building combats disease by encouraging strong, vigorous growth. Plants that are not stressed for nutrients and have plenty of water are less likely to succumb than weak, half-starved plants. The nuts and bolts of soil building are given in Chapter 10, The Stuff of Life.

Practicing good garden sanitation is mostly a matter of common sense. Remove debris (weeds, spent plants, old mulch, and so on) from the garden and compost it. But if you find diseased plants, remove any affected parts and throw them in the trash—don't take chances on the disease surviving in the compost pile. When cutting off diseased stems and branches, disinfect your pruners between cuts with undiluted rubbing alcohol or a solution of 10 percent bleach in water. Don't handle a diseased plant and then touch a healthy one without washing or disinfecting your hands.

Growing vegetables and annual flowers in different parts of the garden each year—rather than always growing onions in the same place, for example—can keep diseases from getting a foothold in the soil. But if a disease has established itself, you can combat it with a technique called soil solarization. Four to six weeks before you plant, saturate the soil you want to disinfect with water, then lay a single layer of clear plastic sheeting directly on the soil. The plastic raises the temperature of the soil, destroying bacteria, fungi, weed seeds, and nematodes. Beneficial soil organisms are more tolerant of high soil temperatures and take over once their malevolent brethren are dispatched. Naturally, the stronger the sunlight, the hotter the soil will become, but the technique will work before spring planting if you're lucky enough to get a month of mostly clear, sunny weather.

Chapter 12

Weather or Not

The thirsty earth soaks up the rain,
And drinks, and gapes for drink again.
The plants suck in the earth, and are
With constant drinking fresh and fair.

Abraham Cowley,
"Drinking"

Weather is the greatest uncertainty in the naturalist's garden. Your job as gardener is to try to keep things running smoothly for the plants and animals that live in or visit your yard, whatever the weather decides to do. Tips for helping wildlife survive are found in Chapter 1, Landscaping for Wildlife, and Part Two, The Garden as Backyard Nature Center.

A good way to ensure the survival of perennials, shrubs, and trees is to plant only those that are hardy in your area. Refer back to Chapter 3, The Naturalist's Flower Garden, and consult the USDA Hardiness Zone Map on page 238 for more on hardiness. To make sure you get a bumper crop of annual flowers and vegetables, check the days to maturity of the variety you're considering on the seed packet or in a catalog, and be certain that it has time to mature in your growing season.

Of course, from time to time you may want to take a chance on something that's considered risky in your area just for the fun of it. If you want a particular plant badly enough, there are plenty of tricks you can use to speed up "production." Determined gardeners have grown cantaloupes in Vermont by starting the fastest-maturing varieties indoors, then transplanting them out into a black-plastic-covered raised bed under a clear plastic tunnel! If this seems like a bit more trouble than a trip to the farmers' market, there are plenty of plants that flourish in every part of the country. A look back over the tree and shrub charts (Chapter 2) and the Minimanuals (Chapters 3 and 4) should convince you of that!

But average length of growing season, heat, and cold aren't the only factors the naturalist/gardener must take into account. Your fickle weather may flood the garden every day in May, when plants are trying to get a foothold, then throw a drought at you in July, when crops need water most. Fortunately, there *are* techniques to help your plants and wildlife cope with these unfriendly extremes.

When in Drought

Be prepared for a dry spell, and the garden will be better able to cope with a drought. When rainfall is insufficient, the soil feels dry an inch or more below the surface, and tender plants begin to wilt, it's time to give nature a hand. Water deeply every five to seven days. Soil should be wet to a depth of 6 to 8 inches or more. Late afternoon or early evening watering lessens evaporation and promotes retention of water. Light, sandy soil will dry out faster than heavy clay soil, which tends to retain moisture.

If you have a good, loamy soil in a mulched, well-watered garden, your plants will be vigorous and able to cope better with a dry spell. But anything recently planted or transplanted will be vulnerable and must be given first water rights. This applies also to shrubs and trees planted the previous season or even the previous year, for they are not yet well enough rooted or toughened up enough to endure very dry conditions.

Germinating seeds, young seedlings, and vegetables must have water. Plants that went in bare-root or without a good root system will be the first to hang their heads. Old, established perennials and sturdy annuals will withstand a dry period longer, and older trees and shrubs longer still. Wildflowers want water like everything else, though many are native to dry waste places and can make do with a short supply for quite a long time. Most perennial wildflowers have extensive root systems and can continue to perform after the cultivated flowers begin to wilt.

In a severe drought, if you live where local regulations curtail watering, use the allotted time to water one or two sections or plantings thoroughly. Sprinkling lightly here and there does more harm than good, encouraging roots to reach toward the surface, where they dry out faster. Expect the unwatered lawn to go dormant and gradually turn brown and unattractive. But it will not die, and when it finally does rain, the grass will green up again, so don't waste precious water on it. *Do* set mowers extra high: At 2½ to 3 inches, the grass can help shade its own roots. And leave grass clippings on the yard as a shading, moisture-retentive mulch.

Beating a Drought

Now that you have become economy-minded about water, you can make some of it do double duty. Save water from cooked vegetables. Keep the pan of rinse water from dishes (not the sudsy water)—plants will tolerate a very slight amount of well-diluted soap or detergent. Every little drop helps your garden survive.

The most valuable drought-beater after rain is mulch, mentioned so often in these pages. A mulched garden flouts drought far better than an unmulched garden. The mulch retains whatever moisture is in the soil, smothers greedy

Use water wisely during a dry summer. Easy methods of conserving water include planting a drought-resistant wildflower meadow instead of a lawn, mulching flower and vegetable beds, and using water-saving drip irrigation instead of wasteful sprinklers. Don't forget to provide water for birds and animals when a dry spell strikes.

weeds, and shades plants' roots to keep them cool. The more mulch, the merrier your garden will be under a glaring sun.

If you think a drought is likely, rake up all the leaves and twigs on your property, add grass clippings and weeds (remove their flowers or seeds first) and odds and ends from pruning. Add packing materials if you have them. Even small stones and pebbles can be used in a makeshift mulch. Raid the local garden store for straw, hay, or salt hay, and spread it thickly.

During this trying time, the birds and other backyard creatures will be thirsty too. Keep the birdbath filled with clean water. If you don't have a birdbath, make a watering hole. Let the hose trickle slowly into a shallow pan, or even into a hollow in the ground. A puddle of muddy water is still better than none, and butterflies and other insects will enjoy it too! Drought is also the time when wildlife will be most grateful for the shade and shelter of a mixed tree and shrub border, where they can hide from direct sunlight.

If drought seems to be a problem for you every summer, consider featuring drought-tolerant plants in your landscape (see the box Perennials for Difficult Sites). If you live in an arid area, you might even want to take this one step further and try xeriscaping.

Xeriscaping: Dryland Horticulture

Much of the western United States has a perpetual water problem, which is worsening in some areas and is compounded by the heavy drain of midsummer watering to keep Kentucky bluegrass and exotic or nonnative plantings fresh and green. Xeriscape—a word derived from the Greek word *xeros*, meaning dry, and *landscape*—is being used to define dryland gardening or horticulture. It began in Denver in the summer of 1985, when Water Department officials became seriously alarmed about the amount of water being sprinkled away.

Xeriscaping uses trees, shrubs, ornamentals, and grasses native to dry climates, not merely cacti, yucca, and the like.

PERENNIALS FOR DIFFICULT SITES

Swamps, Bogs, Wet Places
Blue flag (*Iris versicolor*)
Japanese iris (*Iris ensata*)
Marsh marigold (*Caltha palustris*)
Purple loosestrife (*Lythrum salicaria*)
Swamp milkweed (*Asclepias incarnata*)
Swamp rose mallow (*Hibiscus moscheutos*)
Yellow flag (*Iris pseudacorus*)

Purple Flag

Swamp Rose Mallow

Drought-Tolerant
Balloon flower (*Platycodon grandiflorus*)
Black-eyed Susan (*Rudbeckia hirta*)
Butterfly weed (*Asclepias tuberosa*)
Coreopsis (*Coreopsis grandiflora*)
Daylily (*Hemerocallis* hybrids)
Evening primrose (*Oenothera* spp.)
Gaillardia (blanket flower) (*Gaillardia* ×*grandiflora*)
Gloriosa daisy (*Rudbeckia hirta*, cultivated form)
Goldenrod (*Solidago* spp.)
Penstemon (*Penstemon gloxinioides*)
Phlox (*Phlox paniculata*)
Pitcher's salvia (*Salvia azurea*)
Purple coneflower (*Echinacea purpurea*)
Sedum (stonecrop) (*Sedum* spp.)
Sundrop (*Oenothera tetragona*)
Yucca (*Yucca filamentosa*)

(continued)

Blue Sage

Purple Coneflower

Sedum

Gaillardia

PERENNIALS FOR DIFFICULT SITES—*Continued*

Lily-of-the-Valley

Moist Shade

Astilbe (*Astilbe* ×*arendsii*)
Bee balm (*Monarda didyma*)
Blue lobelia (*Lobelia siphilitica*)
Cardinal flower (*L. cardinalis*)
Forget-me-not (*Myosotis silvatica*)
Joe-pye weed (*Eupatorium maculatum*)
Lily-of-the-valley (*Convallaria majalis*)
Primrose (*Primula* spp.)
Sensitive fern (*Onodea sensibilis*)
Trollius (globe flower) (*Trollius europaeus* and *T. ledebourii*)
Virginia bluebell (*Mertensia virginica*)

Virginia Bluebell

Primrose

Cold Winters

Bleeding heart (*Dicentra spectabilis* and *D. eximia*)
Columbine (*Aquilegia* spp.)
Coral bells (*Heuchera sanguinea*)
Delphinium (*Delphinium* spp.)
Loosestrife (*Lythrum salicaria*)
Lupine (*Lupinus polyphyllus*)
Oriental poppy (*Papaver orientale*)
Peony (*Paeonia lactiflora*)
Yarrow (*Achillea* spp.)

Coralbells

Oriental Poppy

Ken Ball, of the Denver Water Department, a conservation specialist working on the xeriscaping project, promotes heat- and drought-resistant buffalo grass and other native prairie grasses for lawns and groundcovers. Buffalo grass needs almost no watering and has to be mowed only twice a year. The Denver Botanic Gardens are experimenting with a number of drought-resistant shrubs and perennials and creating highly acclaimed xeriscapes.

Homeowners and nurseries in water-thirsty western and southwestern areas, as well as in Texas, Florida, and other dry southern areas, are urged to favor Rocky Mountain and other indigenous trees and plants that can survive on rainfall alone. Plants native to arid climates elsewhere in the world are being investigated for suitability to our own arid climates. Remember too that the use of native plants will encourage the unique wildlife of arid areas to make themselves at home in your yard. Xeriscaping can create an inviting natural landscape of the plants these creatures eat and nest in right around your house. (For more information on xeriscaping, check the Resource listings and the bibliography for this chapter.)

Moisture— Too Much of a Good Thing?

In the throes of a period of drought, the gardener may be further hampered by water restrictions and can only hope for that "gentle rain from heaven" as flowers droop, leaves wilt, lawns turn brown, and trees look dusty and parched. When a soaking rain finally comes along, it is a time of ecstasy for gardener and garden alike, to say nothing of thirsty birds and animals, and it's hard to believe there could ever be too much of the lovely water. But overabundant rainfall can be as bad as drought.

Plants can be said to be drowning when their roots lie in water too long (unless they are water plants, of course). They must have air; the earth must "breathe." Heavy clay soil holds more water, a plus in time of drought but a liability in torrential rains. Another problem is a hard subsoil or hardpan layer beneath a thin layer of loam. Roots can't develop properly; water can't penetrate deeply and tends to run off, carrying the shallow topsoil with it. On the other hand, soil that is sandy and light doesn't retain water well and often dries out too fast. Excessive rain or moisture causes precious nutrients, particularly nitrogen, to leach or flow away, out of the reach of plant roots. Leaching is less often a problem in soil that has been organically enriched. More organic matter, plus fertilizer rich in nitrogen, can be added after the deluge.

Prolonged spring rains slow the growth of seedlings and may cause seeds to rot. Young plants cannot thrive in soggy, chilly soil. Some early plantings may have to be replaced. This is a good reason not to rush spring planting, thinking that you will get a head start on the season. It could be a washout!

Low-lying, permanently damp or wet places on some properties can be a real headache if you're determined to fight the moisture, for good drainage in such an area is difficult and costly to obtain. Raised beds can sometimes help, but for really soggy soil, expensive systems of drainage pipes and tiles may be necessities. I say, if you can't lick 'em, join 'em. Why not make this seemingly undesirable spot uniquely attractive as a bog garden or a place for plants that thrive in wet soil? Add humus and peat moss for enrichment and conditioning, and many delightful perennials will be happy there, requiring little additional care. Or proceed to the next step and make a pool or pond (see Chapter 5, Pools and Water Gardens).

A Last Word

Fickle weather and a harsh climate or less-than-ideal site are just some of the challenges you may face. Many gardeners are devastated when their tender seedlings are nipped by a late frost, their carefully planted seeds drowned in torrential spring rains, or their precious rosebushes pine away and die (as mine did), unable to compete successfully with encroaching conifers for nourishment and sunlight. When expectations for flawless performances by flowers, fruit, and vegetables are not all fulfilled despite the most painstaking efforts, it can indeed be frustrating.

But naturalist/gardeners take nature's vagaries and pranks in their stride and are never disappointed, for there are always enough rewards in a blossoming border and attractive backyard to be joyful about. What excitement you feel when a pair of bluebirds finally decides to rear their young in your nest box, two years after it was put up! The wildflower meadow you started last year is coming into its own, and the delightful mixture of blooms attracts monarchs, two kinds of swallowtail, and innumerable bees and other insects. There's a robin's nest in the old lilac—the one you've always been meaning to prune back and never did (and now you're glad). And the toad that found a congenial nook under some bushes apparently survived the winter—welcome back!

Naturalist/gardeners love gardening; we also love wildlife, the endlessly interesting and entertaining activities of the birds, mammals, reptiles, amphibians, butterflies, and other insects that visit us or come to stay. I hope *The Naturalist's Garden* encourages you to invite many more of them to make their home in your backyard.

USDA Hardiness Zone Map

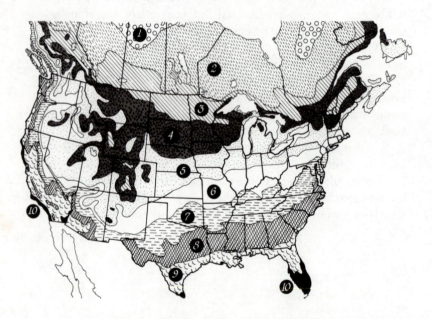

Average Minimum Temperatures for Each Zone

	Zone 1	below −50°F		Zone 6	−10 to 0°F
	Zone 2	−50 to −40°F		Zone 7	0 to 10°F
	Zone 3	−40 to −30°F		Zone 8	10 to 20°F
	Zone 4	−30 to −20°F		Zone 9	20 to 30°F
	Zone 5	−20 to −10°F		Zone 10	30 to 40°F

Note: Where zones are indicated in charts and Minimanuals, they represent the northernmost area where a plant can usually be grown.

Resources

General

High-quality tools, transplants, fruit and ornamental cultivars, vegetable seed, biocontrols, and soil amendments are often available locally. If you can't find what you want, would like a larger selection, or just enjoy armchair shopping, there are myriad seed and nursery catalogs to tempt you. Several guides to who has what are available:

"Gardening by Mail: Where to Buy It"
The Mailorder Association of Nurserymen
210 Cartwright Blvd.
Massapequa Park, NY 11762
(send business-sized SASE)

Seed, Bulb and Nursery List
ROG
33 E. Minor St.
Emmaus, PA 18098
(send business-sized SASE with two first-class stamps)

The National Gardening Association Directory of Seed & Nursery Catalogs
CATALOGS
National Gardening Association
180 Flynn Ave.
Burlington, VT 05401
(NGA members $3, nonmembers $4)

The resources listings that follow also list representative catalogs for appropriate chapters. (For example, the listing for Chapter 6, On Growing Vegetables, features catalogs of mail-order vegetable seed.) Not all catalogs are free—though many are—but because catalog prices change, no prices are listed. Write the companies and request a catalog or current price. Companies that charge for their catalogs will often credit the catalog price toward an order.

Virtually every garden magazine periodically reviews new varieties. In addition, such magazines as *American Horticulturist, Flower & Garden, Harrowsmith, Horticulture, National Gardening,* and *Rodale's Organic Gardening* devote a major section of one of their winter issues (typically the January issue) to the year's new vegetables, flowers, herbs, fruits, trees, and shrubs. Read up before you reach for the catalogs!

These magazines are also entertaining, informative guides to the world of gardening. Write for current subscription prices:

American Horticulturist
The American Horticultural
  Society
7931 E. Boulevard Dr.
Alexandria, VA 22308

The Avant Gardener
P.O. Box 489
New York, NY 10028

Flower & Garden
Modern Handcraft Inc.
4251 Pennsylvania Ave.
Kansas City, MO 64111

Harrowsmith
The Creamery
Charlotte, VT 05445

Horticulture
Subscription Department
P.O. Box 51455
Boulder, CO 80321

HortIdeas
Rt. 1, Box 302
Gravel Switch, KY 40328

National Gardening
The National Gardening
  Association
Depot Square
Peterborough, NH 03458

Rodale's Organic Gardening
33 E. Minor St.
Emmaus, PA 18098

Sunset
3055 Wilshire Blvd.
Los Angeles, CA 90010
(especially for western states)

Chapter 2: Trees and Shrubs—Sources of fruit, nut, and ornamental trees and shrubs

Bear Creek Nursery
P.O. Box 411
Northport, WA 99157

Chestnut Hill Nursery Inc.
Rt. 1, Box 341
Alachua, FL 32612

Emlong Nurseries Inc.
2671 W. Marquette Woods Rd.
Stevensville, MI 49127

Inter-State Nurseries Inc.
P.O. Box 208
Hamburg, IA 51640

Kelly Brothers Nursery Inc.
100 Maple St.
Dansville, NY 14437

Lawson's Nursery
Rt. 1, Box 294, Yellow Creek Rd.
Ball Ground, GA 30107

Henry Leuthardt Nurseries
Montawk Hwy., P.O. Box 666-0
East Moriches, NY 11940

J. E. Miller Nurseries Inc.
5060 W. Lake Rd.
Canandaigua, NY 14424

Musser Forests Inc.
P.O. Box 15 MA
Indiana, PA 15701

National Arbor Day Foundation
100 Arbor Ave.
Nebraska City, NE 68410

Pacific Tree Farms
4301 Lynwood Dr.
Cula Vista, CA 92010

Raintree Nursery
391 Butts Rd.
Morton, WA 98356

Stark Bro's Nurseries & Orchards
Co.
Box 2281G
Louisiana, MO 63353

Wayside Gardens
Garden La.
Hodges, SC 29695

Refer also to: Brooklyn Botanic Garden Record, Plants and Gardens. *Nursery Source Manual.* Handbook no. 99., vol. 38, no. 3. Edited by Frederick McGourty, Jr. Autumn 1982.

There are a number of societies devoted to trees and their culture. For more information, write to any of the following:

American Pomological Society
103 Tyson Bldg.
University Park, PA 16802

California Rare Fruit Growers,
Inc.
The Fullerton Arboretum
California State University
Fullerton, CA 92634

Friends of the Trees Society
P.O. Box 1064
Tonasket, WA 98855

Home Orchard Society
P.O. Box 212
Portland, OR 97202

North American Fruit Explorers
(NAFEX)
c/o Robert Kurle
10 S. 055 Madison St.
Hinsdale, IL 60521
(publishes informative quarterly,
Pomona)

Northern Nut Growers
  Association Inc.
John English, Treasurer
R.R. #3
Bloomington, IL 61701

Tree People
12601 N. Mulholland Dr.
Los Angeles, CA 90210

Chapter 3: The Naturalist's Flower Garden—Sources of annuals, biennials, and perennials

Bluestone Perennials
7235 Middle Ridge Rd.
Madison, OH 44057

McClure & Zimmerman
1422 W. Thorndale
Chicago, IL 60660

Daffodil Mart
Rt. 3, Box 794
Gloucester, VA 23061

Milaeger's Gardens
4838 Douglas Ave.
Racine, WI 53402

Dutch Gardens
P.O. Box 400
Montvale, NJ 07645

Shady Oaks Nursery
700 19th Ave. N.E.
Waseca, MN 56093
(plants for shady gardens)

Far North Gardens
16785 Harrison
Livonia, MI 48154

Wayside Gardens
Garden La.
Hodges, SC 29695

Klehm Nursery
Rt. 5, Box 197
South Barrington, IL 60010

White Flower Farm
Rt. 63
Litchfield, CT 06759

Many general seed catalogs, including Burpee's, Park's, and Thompson & Morgan, carry extensive flower listings. For their addresses, see the source listing for Chapter 6, On Growing Vegetables.

Chapter 4: Wildflowers in the Garden— Sources of wildflowers

Applewood Seed Co.
5380 Vivian St.
Arvada, CO 80002

Conley's Garden Center
Boothbay Harbor, ME 04538

Botanic Garden Seed Co., Inc.
9 Wyckoff St.
Brooklyn, NY 11201

Midwest Wildflowers
Box 64
Rockton, IL 61072

Moon Mountain Wildflowers
P.O. Box 34
Morro Bay, CA 93442

Clyde Robin Seed Co., Inc.
Box 2366
Castro Valley, CA 94546

Native Plants, Inc.
9180 S. Wasatch Blvd.
Sandy, UT 84092

Southwestern Native Seeds
Box 50503
Tucson, AZ 85703

Native Seeds
14590 Triadelphia Mill Dr.
Dayton, MD 21036

The Vermont Wildflower Farm
P.O. Box 5, Rt. 7
Charlotte, VT 05445

Orchid Gardens
6700 Splithand Rd.
Grand Rapids, MN 55744
(very informative Wildflower
    Culture Catalog)

Wildflower Source
Box 312
Fox Lake, IL 60020

Wildseed
16810 Barker Springs
Houston, TX 77084

Plants of the Southwest
1812 Second St.
Santa Fe, NM 87501

More complete listings may be had from:

"Nursery Sources—Native Plants
    and Wild Flowers"
New England Wild Flower
    Society
Garden in the Woods
Framingham, MA 01701
$4.50 postpaid

"Sources of Native Seeds and
    Plants"
Soil Conservation Society of
    America
7515 N.E. Ankeny Rd.
Ankeny, IA 50021
$3.00 postpaid

Wildflower mixes are also often offered by companies that sell garden flowers. (See the listings for Chapter 3, The Naturalist's Flower Garden.)

Questions about wildflowers and their care may be directed to: National Wildflower Research Center, 2600 FM, 973 North, Austin, TX 78725, a nonprofit wildflower research center established in 1983 by Mrs. Lyndon B. Johnson and associates to investigate and promote research on wildflowers and disseminate information about their use in the landscape. Enclose SASE with your query.

Chapter 5: Pools and Water Gardens—Sources of pools, plants, and equipment

Bee Fork Water Gardens
Rt. 1, Box 115
Bunker, MO 63629

Lilypons Water Gardens
312 Flower Rd., P.O. Box 10
Lilypons, MD 21727
and
P.O. Box 188, 312 Lilypons Rd.
Brookshire, TX 77423

Paradise Gardens
14 May St.
Whitman, MA 02382

Slocum Water Gardens
1101 Cypress Gardens Rd.
Winter Haven, FL 33880

William J. Tricker & Sons
74 Allendale Ave., P.O. Box 398
Saddle River, NJ 07458

Van Ness Water Gardens
2460 N. Euclid Ave.
Upland, CA 91786

Wicklein's Aquatic Farm &
Nursery
1820 Cromwell Bridge Rd.
Baltimore, MD 21234

Detailed information on growing waterlilies can be obtained from the Water Lily Society, P.O. Box 104, Buckeystown, MD 21717.

Exceptionally fine waterlily pools can be viewed at the Missouri Botanical Garden in St. Louis and at Longwood Gardens, Kennett Square, Pennsylvania.

Chapter 6: On Growing Vegetables—Sources of vegetable seeds

Burgess Seed & Plant Co.
905 Four Seasons Rd.
Bloomington, IL 61701

W. Atlee Burpee Co.
300 Park Ave.
Warminster, PA 18974

The Cook's Garden
Box 65
Londonderry, VT 05148

Farmer Seed & Nursery
818 N.W. Fourth St.
Faribault, MN 55021

Henry Field Seed & Nursery Co.
Dept. 87, 2176 Oak St.
Shenandoah, IA 51602

Gurney Seed & Nursery Co.
Second and Capitol
Yankton, SD 57079

Harris Seeds
Morton Farm
3670 Buffalo Rd.
Rochester, NY 14624

H. G. Hastings Co.
P.O. Box 4274
Atlanta, GA 30302

Johnny's Selected Seeds
310 Foss Hill Rd.
Albion, ME 04910

Jung Seed Co.
335 S. High St.
Randolph, WI 53957

Mellinger's Inc.
2310 W. South Range Rd.
North Lima, OH 44452

Nichols Garden Nursery
1190 N. Pacific Hwy.
Albany, OR 97321

Park Seed Co. Inc.
Hwy. 254 North
Greenwood, SC 29647

Seeds Blüm
Idaho City Stage
Boise, ID 83706

Stokes Seeds Inc.
Box 548
Buffalo, NY 14240
and
28 Water St.
Fredonia, NY 10463

Thompson & Morgan Inc.
Farraday and Gramme Ave.
P.O. Box 1308
Jackson, NJ 08527

Otis S. Twilley Seed Co.
P.O. Box 65
Trevose, PA 19047

Vermont Bean Seed Co.
Garden La.
Fair Haven, VT 05743

If you're looking for heirloom or nonhybrid seeds or would just enjoy reading about them, join The Seed Savers Exchange (P.O. Box 70, Decorah, IA 52101), which publishes the hefty *Garden Seed Inventory* (telling where you can find open-pollinated varieties), as well as its informative *Winter Yearbook* and *Fall Harvest Edition*.

For sources of tools, fertilizers, and soil builders, see sources for Chapter 10, The Stuff of Life. For pest-control sources, see the listing for Chapter 11, Battling Bugs and Diseases . . . Naturally.

Chapter 7: Birds in the Backyard—Sources of bird supplies

Audubon Workshop, Inc.
1501 Paddock Dr.
Northbrook, IL 60062

Barzen Enterprises, Inc.
455 Harrison St., N.E.
Minneapolis, MN 55413

Bird n' Hand Inc.
73 Sawyer Passway
Fitchburg, MA 01420

Bower Bird Feeders
P.O. Box 92
Elkhart, IN 46515

The Crow's Nest Bookshop
Laboratory of Ornithology
159 Sapsucker Woods Rd.
Ithaca, NY 14850

Droll Yankees, Inc.
Mill Rd.
Foster, RI 02825

Duncraft
33 Fisherville Rd.
Penacook, NH 03303

Heath Manufacturing Co.
140 Mill St.
Coopersville, MI 49404

Hummingbird Haven
1255 Carmel Dr.
Simi Valley, CA 93065

Hyde Bird Feeder Co.
56 Felton St., P.O. Box 168
Waltham, MA 02254

Jerry Janicki
6657 W. 111th St.
Worth, IL 60482

National Audubon Society Wild
  Bird Food
Box 207
Bristol, IL 60512

Wells L. Bishop Co., Inc.
464 Pratt St.
Meriden, CT 06450

Wild Bird Supplies
4815 Oak St.
Crystal Lake, IL 60014

Many flower and garden catalogs feature bird feeders, birdseed, hummingbird feeders, and birdbaths. Look for them when you're ordering plants. Local garden centers and hardware stores also stock many of these products. For other sources, check classified and other advertisements in garden and nature magazines.

A number of bird lovers' societies publish magazines and offer programs for fellow enthusiasts. Some of these are:

Bird Feeders Society
P.O. Box 225
Mystic, CT 06355
(publishes the quarterly
  magazine *Around the Bird
  Feeder*)

Bird Friends Society
Essex, CT 06426
(publishes the quarterly
  magazine *Wild Bird Guide*)

National Audubon Society
950 Third Ave.
New York, NY 10022
(publishes the monthly *Audubon*
  magazine; has 450 local
  chapters)

North American Bluebird
  Society
Box 6295
Silver Spring, MD 20906
(publishes the quarterly journal
  Sialia)

There is also a magazine exclusively for backyard bird watchers:

Bird Watcher's Digest
Box 110, Dept. AJ3
Marietta, OH 45750

To learn more about birds, join your local bird club. Most have lectures, slide shows, and field trips, and some stock field guides, other bird books, and bird call records.

Government publications are also a great source of information about birds. Write the Superintendent of Documents (U.S. Government Printing Office, Washington, DC 20402) for a current price list. Some of the most helpful include: "Homes for Birds" (Stock No. 1980-0-301-753); "Attracting and Feeding Birds" (Stock No. 1973-727-375/202-3-1); "Relative Attractiveness of Different Foods at Wild Bird Feeders" (Stock No. 024-010-00587); "Invite Birds to Your Home: Conservation Plantings for the Northeast" (Stock No. PA-840); "Invite Birds to Your Home: Conservation Plantings for the Southeast" (Stock No. 0100-00316); "Invite Birds to Your Home: Conservation Plantings for the Midwest" (Stock No. 0100-1450); and "Invite Birds to Your Home: Conservation Plantings for the Northwest" (Stock No. 0100-03307). State government publications can often be extremely helpful in suggesting regional plants, discussing local birds, and so forth. Write your state's Soil Conservation Service, Cooperative Extension Service, Department of Fish and Game, and Department of Natural Resources for publications lists.

Sources of trees, shrubs, and herbaceous plants for birds can be found in the Resource lists for Chapter 2, Trees and Shrubs, Chapter 3, The Naturalist's Flower Garden, and Chapter 4, Wildflowers in the Garden.

Chapter 8: Butterflies and Friends

Butterfly Organizations

The Butterfly Club of America
736 Main Ave.
Suite 200, Box 2257
Durango, CO 81302

The Lepidopterists' Society
Secretary, Julian P. Donahue
Natural History Museum of Los
  Angeles County
900 Exposition Blvd.
Los Angeles, CA 90007

Southern Lepidopterists' Society
Secretary-Treasurer, Tom Neal
3820 N.W. 16th Place
Gainesville, FL 32605

Bees in Your Backyard

Most states have apiary inspection programs and state apiarists. Consult these apiarists or your Cooperative Extension Service agent for advice and information on beekeeping in your state. Many states also have statewide and local beekeepers' associations, with meetings and short courses on beekeeping. Penn State, Cornell, and

Ohio State universities offer home correspondence courses in bee-keeping. The USDA maintains a laboratory for the study of honey-bees, The Carl Hayden Bee Research Center (2000 E. Allen Rd., Tucson, AZ 85719). The USDA publishes *Beekeeping for Beginners* (pamphlet Stock No. 001-000-03936-9), available from the Superintendent of Documents, U.S. Government Printing Office, Washington, DC 20402.

Sources of Beekeeping Supplies

Brushy Mountain Bee Farm
Rt. 1, Box 1350G
Moravian Falls, NC 28654

Hubbard Apiaries
P.O. Box 160
Onsted, MI 49265

W. Atlee Burpee Co.
300 Park Ave.
Warminster, PA 18974

Walter T. Kelley Co.
Clarkson, KY 42726

A. I. Root Co.
623 W. Liberty St.
Medina, OH 44258
(also publishes the monthly
  Gleanings in Bee Culture)

Dadant & Sons, Inc.
Hamilton, IL 62341
(also publishes the monthly
  American Bee Journal)

Diamond International Corp.
Apiary Department
P.O. Box 1070
Chico, CA 95927

Nectar-producing plants are available from nurseries and catalogs that sell flowers and fruit trees (see the source lists for Chapter 3, The Naturalist's Flower Garden, and Chapter 4, Wildflowers in the Garden). A company that specializes in "bee plants" is Bee Pasture Seeds, R.R. 2, Sabetha, KS 66534.

Chapter 9: Backyard Wildlife

Helpful Organizations

National Institute for Urban
  Wildlife
10921 Trotting Ridge Way
Columbia, MD 21044
(quarterly newsletter; write for
  publications list)

National Wildlife Federation
1412 Sixteenth St., N.W.
Washington, DC 20036
(*National Wildlife* magazine;
  Ranger Rick, a magazine for
  children; Gardening with
  Wildlife Kit, $16.95)

Wildlife Management Institute
709 Wire Bldg.
1000 Vermont Ave., N.W.
Washington, DC 20005
(brochures such as "Helping
    Wildlife: Working with
    Nature;" write for
    publications list)

The government publishes any number of valuable booklets and bulletins on wildlife. For a current price list, write: Superintendent of Documents, U.S. Government Printing Office, Washington, DC 20402. A sampling of interest: "Planning for Wildlife in Cities and Suburbs" (Stock No. 024-010-00471); "Plant Materials for Conservation" (Stock No. 001-000-03867); "Conservation Plants for the Northeast" (Stock No. 001-000-03605-0); "More Wildlife through Soil and Water Conservation" (Stock No. 001-000-01425-1); and "Making Land Produce Useful Wildlife" (Stock No. 001-000-0021-7). State governments are excellent sources of bulletins with local applicability. Check with your state's Soil Conservation Service, Department of Environmental Conservation, Department of Fish and Game, Cooperative Extension Service, and Department of Natural Resources to see what's available.

Chapter 10: The Stuff of Life
Sources of Organic Fertilizers and Soil Amendments

Blue Ridge Agri-Service
Rt. 2, Box 582
Knoxville, MD 21758

Necessary Trading Company
New Castle, VA 24127

Peaceful Valley Farm Supply
11173 Peaceful Valley Rd.
Nevada City, CA 95959

Progressive Agri-Systems, Inc.
201 Center St.
Stockertown, PA 18083

Ringer Research
Eden Prairie, MN 55343

For a more complete, state-by-state listing, write *Rodale's Organic Gardening* Readers' Service, 33 E. Minor St., Emmaus, PA 18098, and request their "Soil Builders & Organic Fertilizers" listing. Enclose a business-sized SASE and two first-class stamps.

Sources of Tools, Composters, and Other Gardening Supplies

Brookstone Co.
127 Vose Farm Rd.
Peterborough, NH 03458

Clapper's Garden Catalog
1125 Washington St.
West Newton, MA 02165

Gardener's Supply Co.
128 Intervale Rd.
Burlington, VT 05401

Green River Tools
Box 1919
Brattleboro, VT 05301

A. M. Leonard, Inc.
6665 Spiker Rd.
Piqua, OH 45356

Walter F. Nicke
Box 667G
Hudson, NY 12534

Smith & Hawken
25 Corte Madera
Mill Valley, CA 94941

Chapter 11: Battling Bugs and Diseases ... Naturally

Sources of Biocontrols

Beneficial Insects Co.
P.O. Box 323
Brownsville, CA 95919

Beneficial Insects Ltd.
P.O. Box 154
Banta, CA 95304

Bio-Resources
1210 Birch St.
Santa Paula, CA 93060

Integrated Pest Management
305 Agostino Rd.
San Gabriel, CA 91776

Mellinger's Nursery
2310 W. South Range Rd.
North Lima, OH 44452

Natural Pest Controls
9397 Premier Way
Sacramento, CA 95826

The Necessary Trading Co.
New Castle, VA 24127

The Nematode Farm
2617 San Pablo Ave.
Berkeley, CA 94702

Peaceful Valley Farm Supply
11173 Peaceful Valley Rd.
Nevada City, CA 95959

Rincon-Vitova Insectaries, Inc.
P.O. Box 95
Oak View, CA 93022

For more complete listings,
write:

Biological Control Services
    Program
3288 Meadowview Rd.
Sacramento, CA 95832
(request a free copy of *Suppliers
    of Beneficial Organisms in
    North America* by Larry G.
    Bezark and Helen Yee)

Rodale's Organic Gardening
  Readers' Service
33 E. Minor St.
Emmaus, PA 18098
(request their pamphlet,
  "Resources for Organic Pest
  Control"; enclose a
  business-sized SASE and two
  first-class stamps)

For more information, write:

International Organization of
  Biological Control
1050 San Pablo Ave.
Albany, CA 94706

Two of the most informative publications on IPM and biocontrols
are *The IPM Practitioner*, a monthly magazine, and *Common
Sense Pest Control Quarterly*. Both are available from Bio Integral
Resource Center, Box 7414, Berkeley, CA 94707.

Sources of Earthworms

Cape Cod Worm Farm
30 Center Ave.
Buzzards Bay, MA 02532

The Worm Factory
Rt. 3, Box 351
Atkins, AR 72823

Chapter 12: Weather or Not

Sources of Weather Data

American Meteorological Society
45 Beacon St.
Boston, MA 02108
(publishes the journals
  Weatherwise and the *Bulletin
  of the American
  Meteorological Society*)

National Climatic Center
Federal Bldg.
Asheville, NC 28801
(request publications list and
  prices for their *Selective
  Guide to Climatic Data
  Sources* and *Climatic Atlas of
  the United States*)

National Oceanic and
  Atmospheric Administration
  (NOAA)
Weather Radio
(continuous weather information
  broadcasts; to receive them,
  you must buy a special
  "weather radio," but these are
  not prohibitively
  expensive—they can be found
  for under $25; weather
  channels on cable television
  also give continuous weather
  broadcasts)

Sources of Weather Instruments

Weather Measure
Qualimetrics, Inc.
P.O. Box 41257
Sacramento, CA 95841
(free catalog)

Weatherwise Instruments
68 Browning Ave.
Nashua, NH 03062

Sources of Plants for Difficult Climates

Abundant Life Seed Foundation
P.O. Box 772
Port Townsend, WA 98368
(for the Pacific Northwest and
    damp climates)

Garden City Seeds
Box 297
Victor, MT 59875
(for the North)

Johnny's Selected Seeds
310 Foss Hill Rd.
Albion, ME 04910
(for the North)

Larner Seeds
P.O. Box 407
235 Fern Rd.
Bolinas, CA 94924
(for the West)

Native Seeds SEARCH
3950 W. New York Dr.
Tucson, AZ 85745
(for the Southwest)

Plants of the Southwest
1812 Second St.
Santa Fe, NM 87501

Prairie Nursery
P.O. Box 365-R
Westfield, WI 53964
(for the Midwest)

Prairie Ridge Nursery
R.R. 2, 9738 Overland Rd.
Mt. Horeb, WI 53572
(for the Midwest)

Prairie Seed Source
P.O. Box 83
North Lake, WI 53064
(for the Midwest)

Bibliography

General References

Audubon Society Nature Guides. New York: Chanticleer Press/Knopf, 1985. Field guides to seven ecological habitats of the United States.

Brooklyn Botanic Garden Record, Plants and Gardens. Special Issues (Handbooks). Brooklyn, N.Y.: Brooklyn Botanic Garden, Inc.

Bush-Brown, James and Louise. *America's Garden Book*. Rev. ed. by The New York Botanical Garden, Bronx. New York: Charles Scribner's Sons, 1980.

Creasy, Rosalind. *The Complete Book of Edible Landscaping*. San Francisco: Sierra Club Books, 1982.

_____. *Earthly Delights*. San Francisco: Sierra Club Books, 1985.

Editors of *Reader's Digest*. *Illustrated Guide to Gardening*. New York: Random House, 1978.

Editors of Sunset Books and *Sunset* magazine. *New Western Garden Book*. 4th ed. Menlo Park, Calif.: Lane Publishing Co., 1979.

Faust, Joan Lee, ed. *The New York Times Garden Book*. New York: Ballantine Books, 1977.

Garden and Landscape Staff, *Southern Living* magazine. *Southern Living Gardening Guide*. Birmingham, Ala.: Oxmoor House, 1981.

Johnson, Hugh. *The Principles of Gardening*. New York: Simon & Schuster, 1979.

Leighton, Phebe, and Simonds, Calvin. *The New American Landscape Gardener*. Emmaus, Pa.: Rodale Press, 1987.

Perényi, Eleanor. *Green Thoughts: A Writer in the Garden.* New York: Random House, 1983.

Powell, Thomas and Betty. *The Avant Gardener: A Handbook and Sourcebook of All That's New and Useful in Gardening.* Boston: Houghton Mifflin, 1975.

Staff of *Organic Gardening* magazine. *The Encyclopedia of Organic Gardening.* Emmaus, Pa.: Rodale Press, 1978.

Taylor, Norman. *Taylor's Encyclopedia of Gardening.* Boston: Houghton Mifflin, 1961.

Wyman, Donald. *Wyman's Gardening Encyclopedia.* Rev. ed. New York: The Macmillan Publishing Co., 1977.

Wyman, Donald, and Prendergast, Curtis. *Easy Gardens.* Time-Life Encyclopedia of Gardening. New York: Time-Life Books, 1978.

Chapter 1: Landscaping for Wildlife

Agriculture Handbook PA 940. *Conservation Plantings for the Northeast.* Soil Conservation Service, U.S. Department of Agriculture, 1969.

Agriculture Handbook PA 982. *Conservation Plantings for the Midwest.* Soil Conservation Service, U.S. Department of Agriculture, 1976. Excellent guides for shrubs and trees with flowers and berries. Ornamental value and bird use. Valuable regional information.

Agriculture Handbook PA 1093. *Conservation Plantings for the Southeast.* Soil Conservation Service, U.S. Department of Agriculture, 1975.

Agriculture Handbook PA 1094. *Conservation Plantings for the Northwest.* Soil Conservation Service, U.S. Department of Agriculture, 1975.

Cornell Cooperative Extension Bulletin. *Enhancement of Wildlife Habitat on Private Lands.* No. IB 181, n.d.

Missouri Department of Conservation. *Fact Sheet: Recommended Backyard Wildlife Plants for Food, Cover, and Nesting.* St. Louis, Mo.: n.d.

Scott, Jane. *Botany in the Field: An Introduction to Plant Communities for the Amateur Naturalist.* Englewood Cliffs, N.J.: Prentice-Hall, 1984.

Smyser, Carol A., and the Editors of Rodale Press Books. *Nature's Design: A Practical Guide to Natural Landscaping.* Emmaus, Pa.: Rodale Press, 1982.

Chapter 2: Trees and Shrubs

Courtright, Gordon. *Trees and Shrubs for Western Gardens.* Forest Grove, Oreg.: Timber Press, 1979.

DeWolf, Gordon P., Jr., et al. *Taylor's Guide to Shrubs.* Boston: Houghton Mifflin, 1987.

Dirr, Michael A. *Manual of Woody Landscape Plants.* Champaign, Ill.: Stipes Publishing Co., 1983.

Frederick, William H., Jr. *100 Great Garden Plants.* Portland, Oreg.: Timber Press, 1986.

Hudak, Joseph. *Trees for Every Purpose.* New York: McGraw-Hill Book Co., 1980.

_____. *Shrubs in the Landscape.* New York: McGraw-Hill Book Co., 1984.

Petrides, George A. *A Field Guide to Trees and Shrubs.* 2nd ed. Boston: Houghton Mifflin, 1973.

Walker, Laurence C. *Trees: An Introduction to Trees and Forest Ecology for the Amateur Naturalist.* Englewood Cliffs, N.J.: Prentice-Hall, 1984.

Whitcomb, Carl E. *Know It and Grow It II.* Stillwater, Okla.: Lacebark Publications, 1983.

Wyman, Donald. *Trees for American Gardens.* New York: The Macmillan Co., 1965.

_____. *Shrubs and Vines for American Gardens.* Rev. ed. New York: The Macmillan Co., 1969.

Chapter 3: The Naturalist's Flower Garden

Ball, Jeff, and Cresson, Charles. *The 60-Minute Flower Garden.* Emmaus, Pa.: Rodale Press, 1986.

Cox, Jeff and Marilyn. *The Perennial Garden.* Emmaus, Pa.: Rodale Press, 1985.

Damrosch, Barbara. *Theme Gardens.* New York: Workman Publishing, 1982.

De Wolf, Gordon P., Jr., et al. *Taylor's Guide to Annuals.* Boston: Houghton Mifflin, 1986.

_____. *Taylor's Guide to Perennials.* Boston: Houghton Mifflin, 1986.

Editors of Sunset Books and *Sunset* magazine. *Garden Color: Annuals and Perennials.* Menlo Park, Calif.: Lane Publishing Co., 1981.

Grounds, Roger. *Ornamental Grasses*. New York: Van Nostrand Reinhold Co., 1981.

Harper, Pamela, and McGourty, Frederick. *Perennials: How to Select, Grow and Enjoy*. Tucson, Ariz.: HP Books, 1985.

Hudak, Joseph. *Gardening with Perennials Month by Month*. New York: Demeter Press Book, Quadrangle, The New York Times Book Co., 1976.

Loewer, Peter. *Gardens by Design*. Emmaus, Pa.: Rodale Press, 1986.

McNair, James. *All about Bulbs*. San Francisco: Ortho Books, 1981.

Schenk, George. *The Complete Shade Gardener*. Boston: Houghton Mifflin, 1984.

Sinnes, A. Cort. *All about Annuals*. San Francisco: Ortho Books, 1981.

Time-Life Book Editors and Crockett, James U. *The Time-Life Book of Annuals*. New York: H. Holt & Co., 1986.

——. *The Time-Life Book of Perennials*. New York: H. Holt & Co., 1986.

Verey, Rosemary. *The Scented Garden*. New York: Van Nostrand Reinhold Co., 1981.

Chapter 4: Wildflowers in the Garden

Aiken, George D. *Pioneering with Wildflowers*. Woodstock, Vt.: Countryman Press, 1984.

Art, Henry W. *A Garden of Wildflowers*. Pownal, Vt.: Storey Communications, 1986.

Brooklyn Botanic Garden Record, Plants and Gardens. *Gardening with Wildflowers*. Handbook no. 38, 1979.

Crockett, James U., and Allen, O. *Wildflower Gardening*. Time-Life Encyclopedia of Gardening. Alexandria, Va.: Time-Life Books, 1977.

Headstrom, Richard. *Suburban Wildflowers*. Englewood Cliffs, N.J.: Prentice-Hall, 1984.

Martin, Laura C. *The Wildflower Meadow Book*. Charlotte, N.C.: East Woods Press, Fast and MacMillan Publishers, 1986.

Peterson, Roger Tory, and McKenny, Margaret. *A Field Guide to Wildflowers of Northeastern and North-Central North America*. Boston: Houghton Mifflin, 1968.

Phillips, Harry R. *Growing and Propagating Wild Flowers*. Chapel Hill, N.C.: The University of North Carolina Press, 1985.

Scott, Jane. *Botany in the Field*. Englewood Cliffs, N.J.: Prentice-Hall, 1984.

Steffek, Edwin F. *The New Wild Flowers and How to Grow Them*. Portland, Oreg.: Timber Press, 1983.

Taylor, Kathryn S., and Hamblin, Stephen F. *Handbook of Wild Flower Cultivation*. Toronto: The Macmillan Co., 1970.

Tenenbaum, Frances. *Gardening with Wild Flowers*. New York: Charles Scribner's Sons, 1973.

Chapter 5: Pools and Water Gardens

Brooklyn Botanic Garden Record, Plants and Gardens. *Water Gardening*. Handbook no. 106. Vol. 41, no. 1. Edited by Barbara Pesch. Spring 1985.

Editors of Sunset Books and *Sunset* magazine. *Garden Pools, Fountains and Waterfalls*. Menlo Park, Calif.: Lane Publishing Co., 1975.

Heritage, Bill. *The Lotus Book of Water Gardening*. London: The Hamlyn Publishing Group, 1973.

_____. *Ponds and Water Gardens*. Poole, Dorset: Blandford Press, 1981.

Kramer, Jack. *Water Gardening*. New York: Charles Scribner's Sons, 1971.

Ledbetter, Gordon T. *Water Gardens*. New York: W. W. Norton & Co., 1979.

Matson, Tim. *Earth Ponds: The Country Pond Maker's Guide*. Woodstock, Vt.: Countryman Press, 1982.

Swindells, Philip. *The Overlook Water Gardener's Handbook*. New York: The Overlook Press, 1984.

Chapter 6: On Growing Vegetables

Ball, Jeff. *Jeff Ball's 60-Minute Garden*. Emmaus, Pa.: Rodale Press, 1985.

Bartholomew, Mel. *Square Foot Gardening*. Emmaus, Pa.: Rodale Press, 1981.

Bennett, Jennifer. *Harrowsmith Northern Gardener*. Camden East, Ontario: Camden House Publishing, 1982.

Bubel, Nancy. *The Seed-Starter's Handbook*. Emmaus, Pa.: Rodale Press, 1978.

Carr, Anna. *Good Neighbors: Companion Planting for Gardeners*. Emmaus, Pa.: Rodale Press, 1985.

Cox, Jeff, and the Editors of *Rodale's Organic Gardening. How to Grow Vegetables Organically*. Emmaus, Pa.: Rodale Press, in press.

Crockett, James U. *Vegetables and Fruits*. The Time-Life Encyclopedia of Gardening. New York: Time-Life Books, 1972.

Cruso, Thalassa. *Making Vegetables Grow*. New York: Alfred A. Knopf, 1975.

Doscher, Paul; Fisher, Timothy; and Kolb, Kathleen. *Intensive Gardening Round the Year*. Brattleboro, Vt.: The Stephen Greene Press, 1981.

Editors of Sunset Books and *Sunset* magazine. *Vegetable Gardening*. Menlo Park, Calif.: Lane Publishing Co., 1975.

Hill, Lewis. *Cold-Climate Gardening*. Pownal, Vt.: Storey Communications, 1987.

Hunt, Majorie B., and Bortz, Brenda. *High-Yield Gardening*. Emmaus, Pa.: Rodale Press, 1986.

Jeavons, John. *How to Grow More Vegetables Than You Ever Thought Possible on Less Land Than You Can Imagine*. Rev. ed. Berkeley, Calif.: Ten Speed Press, 1982.

London, Sheryl. *Anything Grows!* Emmaus, Pa.: Rodale Press, 1984.

Newcomb, Duane. *Growing Vegetables the Big Yield–Small Space Way*. Los Angeles: Jeremy P. Tarcher, 1981.

Philbrick, Helen, and Gregg, Richard B. *Companion Plants*. New York: Devin-Adair Co., 1966.

Raymond, Dick. *Wide-Row Planting: The Productive Miracle*. Charlotte, Vt.: Garden Way Publishing, 1977.

———. *The Joy of Gardening*. Charlotte, Vt.: Garden Way Publishing, 1982.

Reilly, Ann. *Park's Success with Seeds*. Greenwood, S.C.: George W. Park Seed Co., 1978.

Staff of *Organic Gardening* magazine. *The Encyclopedia of Organic Gardening*. Emmaus, Pa.: Rodale Press, 1978.

Chapter 7: Birds in the Backyard

The Audubon Society Guides to North American Birds: Eastern Region. Vol. 1. New York: Alfred A. Knopf, 1977.

Briggs, S. A., ed. *Landscaping for Birds*. Washington, DC: Audubon Naturalist Society of the Central Atlantic States, 1973.

Burke, Ken, ed. *How to Attract Birds*. San Francisco: Ortho Books, 1983.

DeGraaf, R. M., and Witman, G. M. *Trees, Shrubs, and Vines for Attracting Birds*. Amherst, Mass.: University of Massachusetts Press, 1979.

Dennis, John V. *A Complete Guide to Bird Feeding*. New York: Alfred A. Knopf, 1975.

———. *Beyond the Bird Feeder*. New York: Alfred A. Knopf, 1981.

Harrison, G. H. *The Backyard Birdwatcher*. New York: Simon & Schuster, 1979.

Kress, Stephen W. *The Audubon Society Handbook for Birders*. New York: Charles Scribner's Sons, 1981.

———. *The Audubon Society Guide to Attracting Birds*. New York: Charles Scribner's Sons, 1985.

Layton, R. B. *Thirty Birds That Will Build in Bird Houses*. Jackson, Miss.: Nature Book Publishers, 1977.

Mace, Alice E., ed. *The Birds around Us*. San Francisco: Ortho Books, 1986.

McElroy, T. P., Jr. *The New Handbook of Attracting Birds*. Rev. ed. New York: Alfred A. Knopf, 1978.

Mahnken, Jan. *Feeding the Birds*. Pownal, Vt.: Garden Way Publishing, 1983.

National Geographic Society. *Field Guide to the Birds of North America*. Washington, DC: National Geographic Society, 1983.

Peterson, Roger Tory. *A Field Guide to Western Birds*. Boston: Houghton Mifflin, 1972.

———. *A Field Guide to the Birds East of the Rockies*. Boston: Houghton Mifflin, 1980.

Proctor, Noble. *Garden Birds*. Emmaus, Pa.: Rodale Press, 1986.

Reilly, Edgar M., and Carruth, Gordon. *The Bird Watcher's Diary*. New York: Harper & Row Publishers, 1987.

Robbins, Chandler S.; Bruun, Bertel; and Zim, Herbert S. *Birds of North America*. New York: Golden Press, 1966.

Schutz, W. *How to Attract, House and Feed Birds*. New York: The Macmillan Publishing Co., 1974.

Simonds, Calvin. *Private Lives of Garden Birds*. Emmaus, Pa.: Rodale Press, 1984.

Terres, John K. *Songbirds in Your Garden*. New York: Harper & Row Publishers, 1987.

Tyrrell, Esther Quesada. *Hummers, Their Life and Behavior: A Photographic Study of the North American Species*. New York: Crown Publishers, 1985.

USDA Soil Conservation Service. *Invite Birds to Your Home*. Washington, DC: U.S. Government Printing Office, 1980.

U.S. Fish and Wildlife Service. *Relative Attractions of Different Foods at Wild Bird Feeders*. Report no. 233. Washington, DC: U.S. Government Printing Office, n.d.

Wood, Richard H. *Wood Notes: A Companion & Guide for Bird-watchers*. Englewood Cliffs, N.J.: Prentice-Hall, 1984.

Zeleny, Lawrence. *The Bluebird: How You Can Help Its Fight for Survival*. Bloomington, Ind.: Indiana University Press, 1976.

Chapter 8: Butterflies and Friends

Aebi, Ormond and Harry. *The Art & Adventure of Beekeeping*. Emmaus, Pa.: Rodale Press, 1975.

Klots, Alexander B. *A Field Guide to the Butterflies of North America, East of the Great Plains*. Boston: Houghton Mifflin, 1951.

Milne, Lorus and Margery. *The Audubon Society Field Guide to North American Insects and Spiders*. New York: Alfred A. Knopf, 1980.

Morse, Roger A. *The Complete Guide to Beekeeping*. New York: E. P. Dutton Co., 1974.

Pyle, Robert Michael. *The Audubon Society Handbook for Butterfly Watchers*. New York: Charles Scribner's Sons, 1984.

Reilly, Norman, ed. *Butterflies and Moths*. Rev. ed. New York: Viking Press, 1965.

Tekulsky, Mathew. *The Butterfly Garden*. Boston: Harvard Common Press, 1985.

Chapter 9: Backyard Wildlife

Chambers, Kenneth A. *A Country-Lover's Guide to Wildlife*. Baltimore, Md.: The Johns Hopkins University Press, 1979.

Dennis, John V. *The Wildlife Gardener*. New York: Alfred A. Knopf, 1985.

Durrell, Gerald, with Lee Durrell. *A Practical Guide for the Amateur Naturalist*. New York: Alfred A. Knopf, 1983.

Headstrom, Richard. *Suburban Wildlife*. Englewood Cliffs, N.J.: Prentice-Hall, 1984.

Lawrence, Gale. *A Field Guide to the Familiar: Learning to Observe the Natural World*. Englewood Cliffs, N.J.: Prentice-Hall, 1984.

Logsdon, Gene. *Wildlife in Your Garden*. Emmaus, Pa.: Rodale Press, 1983.

Martin, A. C.; Zim, H. S.; and Nelson, A. L. *American Wildlife and Plants*. New York: Dover Publications, 1951.

Mitchell, John, and the Massachusetts Audubon Society. *The Curious Naturalist*. Englewood Cliffs, N.J.: Prentice-Hall, 1980.

National Wildlife Federation. *Gardening with Wildlife*. Washington, DC: National Wildlife Federation, 1974.

Ricciuti, Edward R. *The New York City Wildlife Guide*. New York: Schocken Books, Nick Lyons Books, 1984.

Shuttlesworth, Dorothy. *Exploring Nature with Your Child*. New York: Harry N. Abrams, Publishers, 1977.

Chapter 10: The Stuff of Life

Apelhof, Mary. *Worms Eat My Garbage*. Kalamazoo, Mich.: Flower Press, 1982.

Brooklyn Botanic Garden Record, Plants and Gardens. *Handbook on Mulches*. Vol. 13, no. 1. Edited by Paul Frese. 1978.

Campbell, Stu. *Let It Rot! The Gardener's Guide to Composting*. Charlotte, Vt.: Garden Way Publishing, 1975.

Logsdon, Gene. *The Gardener's Guide to Better Soil*. Emmaus, Pa.: Rodale Press, 1975.

Minnich, Jerry; Hunt, Marjorie; and the Editors of *Organic Gardening* magazine. *The Rodale Guide to Composting*. Emmaus, Pa.: Rodale Press, 1979.

Ortloff, H. Stuart, and Raymore, Henry B. *A Book about Soils for the Home Gardener*. New York: William Morrow & Co., 1972.

Sinnes, A. Cort. *All about Fertilizers, Soils and Water*. San Francisco: Ortho Books, 1979.

Stout, Ruth. *How to Have a Green Thumb without an Aching Back*. New York: Cornerstone Library, 1973.

Stout, Ruth, and Clemence, Richard. *The Ruth Stout No-Work Garden Book*. Emmaus, Pa.: Rodale Press, 1978.

Sussman, Vic. *Easy Composting*. Emmaus, Pa.: Rodale Press, 1982.

Chapter 11: Battling Bugs and Diseases ... Naturally

Borror, Donald J., and White, Richard E. *A Field Guide to the Insects of America North of Mexico*. Peterson Field Guide Series. Boston: Houghton Mifflin, 1974.

Carr, Anna. *Rodale's Color Handbook of Garden Insects*. Emmaus, Pa.: Rodale Press, 1979.

Carson, Rachel L. *Silent Spring*. Boston: Houghton Mifflin, 1962.

Cravens, Richard H., and the Editors of Time-Life Books. *Pests and Diseases*. The Time-Life Encyclopedia of Gardening. Alexandria, Va.: Time-Life Books, 1977.

Debach, Paul. *Biological Control by Natural Enemies*. New York: Cambridge University Press, 1974.

Graham, Frank, Jr. *Since Silent Spring*. Boston: Houghton Mifflin, 1970.

――――. *Dragon Hunters: The Coming Victory over Man's Ancient Enemies—the Superpests*. New York: E. P. Dutton Co., 1984.

Metcalf, C. L., and Flint, W. P.; revised by Metcalf, R. L. *Destructive and Useful Insects: Their Habits and Control*. 4th ed. New York: McGraw-Hill Book Co., 1962.

Philbrick, John and Helen. *The Bug Book: Harmless Insect Controls*. Charlotte, Vt.: Garden Way Publishing, 1974.

Pirone, Pascal P. *Diseases and Pests of Ornamental Plants*. 5th ed. New York: Wiley-Interscience, 1978.

Westcott, Cynthia. *Plant Disease Handbook*. Rev. 3rd ed. New York: Van Nostrand Reinhold Co., 1971.

――――. *The Gardener's Bug Book*. 4th ed. Garden City, N.Y.: Doubleday & Co., 1973.

Yepsen, Roger B., Jr., ed. *The Encyclopedia of Natural Insect & Disease Control*. Emmaus, Pa.: Rodale Press, 1984.

Chapter 12: Weather or Not

Colebrook, Binda. *Winter Gardening in the Maritime Northwest.* Rev. 2nd ed. Everson, Wash.: Maritime Publishers, 1984.

Editors of Sunset Books and *Sunset* magazine. *Desert Gardening.* Menlo Park, Calif.: Lane Publishing Co., 1967.

Foley, Daniel J. *Gardening by the Sea, from Coast to Coast.* Philadelphia: Chilton Books, 1965.

Head, William. *Gardening under Cover.* Eugene, Oreg.: Amity Foundation, 1984.

Jennings, Charles. *Drought Gardening.* Portland, Oreg.: Victoria House, 1977.

Kaiser, Diane. *A Book of Weather Clues.* Washington, DC: Starrhill Press, 1986.

Kramer, Jack. *Drip System Watering for Bigger and Better Plants.* New York: W. W. Norton and Co., 1980.

Ludlum, David, and the Editors of *Country Journal* magazine. *The New England Weather Book.* Boston: Houghton Mifflin, 1976.

Nehrling, Arno and Irene. *Easy Gardening with Drought-Resistant Plants.* New York: Dover Publications, 1975.

Olgyay, Victor. *Design with Climate.* Princeton, N.J.: Princeton University Press, 1967.

Schaefer, V. J., and Day, John A. *A Field Guide to the Atmosphere.* Boston: Houghton Mifflin, 1981.

Simonds, Calvin. *The Weather-Wise Gardener.* Emmaus, Pa.: Rodale Press, 1983.

Index

A

Acer spp. *See* Maple
Achillea millefolium. See Yarrow
Actaea spp. *See* Baneberry
Adder's tongue. *See* Trout lily
Ageratum houstonianum (ageratum), 33, 63, 124
Ailanthus, 166
Albizzia julibrissin. See Mimosa
Alisma natans. See Water plantain
Allegheny serviceberry, 14–15
Althaea rosea. See Hollyhock
Alyssum, 33, 59–60, 63, 72
Amelanchier laevis. See Allegheny serviceberry
Angel's trumpet, 70
Animal deterrents, 115–18, 181, 183–85
Annual Minimanual, 62–69
Annuals, 33, 35, 43, 57–69, 72
    wildflower, 88–91
Annual Wildflowers for Sunny Sites Minimanual, 88–91
Anthracnose, 120
Antirrhinum majus. See Snapdragon
Antlion, 216
Aphid lion, 219
Aphid, 213
Aquilegia spp. *See* Columbine
Arctostaphylos uva-ursi, 97
Arisaema triphyllum, 95
Arrowhead, 108
Asclepias incarnata. See Swamp milkweed
Asclepias tuberosa. See Butterfly weed
Aster novae-angliae (New England aster), 49, 86, 169
Astilbe arendsii (astilbe), 43

Autumn olive, 22–23
Azalea, 22–23

B

Baby's breath, 43
Bachelor's button. *See* Cornflower
Bacillus popilliae. See Bp
Bacillus thuringiensis. See Bt
Balloonflower, 43–44
Balsam, 60, 63, 124
Baneberry, 97
Basil, 122, 169
Bat, 188
Bayberry bush, 22–23
Bearberry, 97
Beauveria bassiana, 223
Bee balm, 33, 44, 84, 172
Beech, 9, 14–15
Bee, 38, 39, 168–72
Beetle, ground, 218
Begonia semperflorens (begonia), 63
Bellis perennis, 53
Berberis thunbergii, 24–25
Betula spp. *See* Birch
Biennial Minimanual, 53–56
Biennials, 33, 52–56
Biocontrols, 209, 222–24
Birch, 14–15
Birdbaths, 143–44, 232
Bird feeders, 136–37, 147–48, 154–56
Birdhouses, 122, 144–47
Birds, 13, 129–42, 148–49, 211–12
    diet and feeding of, 133–49
Bishop's flower. *See* Queen Anne's lace
Blackberry, 22–23
Black-eyed susan, 84, 115

264

Black gum, 20–21
Black haw, 22–23
Black walnut, 14–15
Blanket flower. *See Gaillardia*
Blazing star. *See Liatris*
Bleeding heart, 44, 96
Bloodroot, 93
Blueberry, 12, 24–25
Bluebird, 13, 133, 145, 148–52
  nest box for, 131
  preservation programs for,
    150–52
Bluebonnet, 90
Blue cardinal flower. *See* Lobelia
Blue fescue, 51
Blue flag, 108
Blue jay, 135, 139
Blue toadflax, 88
Bombardier beetle, 218–19
Botanicals, 220–22
Bp, 182, 223
Browallia speciosa (browallia), 63
Bt, 121, 161, 168, 222–23
Buckthorn, 22–23
Buddleia davidii. See Butterfly
  bush
Bumblebee, 171–72
Bunchberry, 97
Butter-and-eggs, 88
Butterflies, 38, 39, 157–65
  larvae of, 121, 159, 161–62
  plants to attract, 163–64
Butterfly bush, 22–23, 73, 170
Butterfly flower, 68
Butterfly weed, 44, 84

C
Cabbageworm, 120–21, 218
Calendula officinalis (calendula),
  63
Callery pear, 14–15
Caltha palustris. See Marigold,
  marsh
Campanula medium, 53
Campion. *See* Catchfly
Campsis radicans. See Trumpet
  vine
Candytuft, 44, 59
Canterbury bells, 53
Cardinal flower, 34, 44, 84
Cardinal, 132, 136, 138–39
Carnation, 47, 64

Carrot, 124, 161–62
Carya ovata. See Shagbark hickory
Carya pecan. See Pecan
Catchfly, 88
Caterpillars, 161–62, 164–68, 218,
  222–23
Cattail, 107
Cecropia, 165
Celtis occidentalis, 16–17
Centaurea cyanus. See Cornflower
Cereus, night-blooming, 70
Checkerberry. *See* Wintergreen
Cheiranthus allionii. See Wall-
  flower, Siberian
Cheiranthus cheiri. See Wall-
  flower
Cherry, 11, 16–17
Chickadee, 13, 132, 139, 145
China pink. *See* Dianthus
Chipmunk, 176–78
Chrysanthemum, 44
Chrysanthemum frutescens. See
  Marguerite daisy
Chrysanthemum leucanthemum.
  See Ox-eye daisy
Chrysanthemum ×morifolium.
  See Chrysanthemum
Cicada, 74
Clarkia amoena (clarkia), 88
Cleome hasslerana (cleome), 33,
  64
Climate, 29–32
Clover, 82, 172
Columbine, 45, 96
  Rocky Mountain, 96
Companion plants, 113–15
Compost, 12, 36, 38, 62, 193–98,
  201
  bins, 196, 197
  pile, 37, 185–96, 198
Consolida ambigua. See Larkspur
  rocket
Coral bells, 33, 45
Coreopsis spp. (coreopsis), 45, 64,
  88
Cornflower, 64, 88, 115
Corn poppy. *See* Poppy, Shirley
Cornus canadensis. See Bunch-
  berry
Cornus florida. See Dogwood,
  flowering
Cornus kousa. See Dogwood,
  kousa

Cortaderia selloana. See Pampas grass
Cosmos spp. (cosmos), 33, 34, 60, 64, 115
Cowslip. *See* Marigold, marsh; Virginia bluebell
Crabapple, 11, 16–17
Crane's bill. *See* Geranium
Crataegus spp. *See* Hawthorn
Cricket, 74
Crocus, 92
Currant, 12

D

Daisy, 33–34, 47–51, 53, 86, 115
Dame's rocket, 51
Damselfly, 217
Dark-eyed junco, 132
Datura. *See* Angel's trumpet
Daucus carota. See Queen Anne's lace
Daylily, 33, 45, 70–71
DDT, 210–12
Deer, 115–16, 182–85
    curtailing damage of, 182–85
Delphinium elatum (delphinium), 33, 34, 47
Deutzia, 33
Dianthus, 47, 64
Dianthus barbatus. See Sweet william
Dianthus caryophyllus. See Carnation; Dianthus
Dianthus chinensis. See Dianthus
Dicentra cucullaria. See Dutchman's-breeches
Dicentra spp. *See* Bleeding heart
Digitalis purpurea. See Foxglove
Dimensions for Birdhouses, 146
Dogtooth violet. *See* Trout lily
Dogwood, 11
    flowering, 16–17
    kousa, 18–19, 73
Doodlebug, 216
Douglas fir, 15
Dragonfly, 217
Drought, 229–35
Drought-resistant plants, 233, 235
Dryland horticulture, 232–35
Dutchman's-breeches, 93
Dyer's mignonette. *See* Weld

E

Eastern hackberry, 16–17
Eastern hemlock, 16–17
Eastern red cedar, 16–17
Echinacea purpurea. See Purple coneflower
Echinops ritro, 47
Eel grass, 108
Egyptian paper plant, 107
Elaeagnus umbellata. See Autumn olive
Elderberry, 22–23
Elodea, 108
Endangered plants, 99–100
English daisy, 53
Equisetum hyemale. See Horsetail
Erianthus ravennae. See Plume grass
Erythronium americanum. See Trout lily
Eschscholzia californica. See Poppy, California
Evergreen groundcovers, 97–99

F

Fagus spp. *See* Beech
Farewell-to-spring. *See* Clarkia
Favorite Foods of Some Common Wild Birds, 142–3
Favorite Food Plants for Bees, 170–71
Fertilizers, 38, 62, 80. *See also* Compost; Manure
    organic, 198–200
Festuca caesia var. *glauca. See* Blue fescue
Fiery searcher, 215, 217
Finch, 132, 138–39
Firefly, 217
Fire pink. *See* Catchfly
Firethorn, 24–25
Flicker, 138–39
Flowering tobacco. *See Nicotiana*
Flowers, 3–4, 29–40, 69–74. *See also* Annuals; Perennials
    climate and, 30–31
    night-blooming, 69–74
    pollination of, 168–69
    with vegetables, 113–15
Flower volunteers, 59–60
Forget-me-not, 33, 53–54, 93, 109
Forsythia, 33

Fountain grass, 51–52
Four-O'clock, 64–66, 71
Fox, 187–88
Foxglove, 33, 54
Fritillary, 160–61
Frog, 74, 110, 214

G
Gaillardia aristata (gaillardia), 84
Garden health, 207–9
Gardening tools, 204–6
Garden sanitation, 207, 226
Gaultheria hispidula. See Snow-
   berry, creeping
Gaultheria procumbens. See Win-
   tergreen
Gayfeather, 33, 51, 71, 86
Gazania rigens (gazania), 66
Gentiana andrewsii (gentian), 93
Geranium, 66, 96
Geranium maculatum. See Geran-
   ium
Gerbera jamesonii (African ger-
   bera), 47
Globe thistle, 47
Gloriosa daisy, 33–34, 47–48, 60
Glyceria maxima Variegata. *See*
   Manna grass
Goldenrod, 33, 48, 86, 115
Goldfinch, American, 132
Goldfish, 110, 111
Gooseberry, 12
Grapevine, 26–27
Grasses, ornamental, 51–52
Grasshopper, 220
Groundcovers, 97–99, 234
Groundhog. *See* Woodchuck
Gypsophila paniculata. See Baby's
   breath

H
Hardiness Zone Map, USDA, 29,
   228, 238
Hawk moth, 167
Hawthorn, 11, 16–17
Hazelnut, 12
Helianthus annuus. See Sunflower
Hemerocallis hybrids. *See* Daylily
Hepatica spp. (hepatica), 93
Herbs, 72, 123, 169
Hesperis matronalis. See Sweet
   rocket

Heuchera sanguinea. See Coral
   bells
Hibiscus, 71–72
Hibiscus moscheutos. See Swamp
   rose mallow
Hollyhock, 33, 34, 54
Holly, 14–15, 16–17
Honesty, 54
Honeybee. *See* Bee
Honeysuckle, 24–25
Honeysuckle vine, 172
   Hall's, 26–27
   trumpet, 26–27
Horsetail, 107
Hottonia palustris, 108
Hummingbird moth, 167
Hummingbird, 38, 61, 133, 152–56
   favorite food plants of,
      152–53
Humus, 37, 200–201
Hydrocleys numphoides, 107

I
Iberis sempervirens. See Candy-
   tuft
Ilex spp. *See* Holly
Impatiens balsamina. See Balsam
Impatiens capensis. See Jewel-
   weed
Impatiens wallerana (impatiens),
   66
Indian blanket. *See Gaillardia*
Insecticides, 121, 210–12, 224
   botanical, 220–22
Insects. *See also* Butterflies; Moths
   beneficial, 214–20
   control of, 213–14, 219–27
   damaging, 212–14
Interplanting, 208
Ipomoea tricolor. See Morning
   glory
Iris, 48, 108
Iris ensata. See Iris
Iris pseudacorus. See Wild yellow
   flag
Iris sibirica. See Iris
Iris versicolor. See Blue flag
Isatis tinctoria. See Woad

J
Jack-in-the-pulpit, 95
Japanese barberry, 24–25
Japanese beetle, 212–13

Japanese silver grass, 52
Jessamine, 70
Jewelweed, 90
Johnny-jump-up, 59, 60
Juglans nigra, 14–15
Juniperus virginiana, 16–17

K
Kinnikinnick. *See* Bearberry

L
Lacewing, 214–16, 219
Lacy phacelia, 90
Ladybug, 214–16, 219
Lantana camara (lantana), 33, 66
Larkspur rocket, 54
Lepidoptera. *See* Butterflies;
    Moths
Leucanthemum maximum. See
    Shasta daisy
Liatris spp. (liatris). *See* Gay-
    feather
Lightning bug, 217
Ligularia stenocephala (ligularia),
    48
Lilac, 11, 22–23, 33
Lily, 33, 48–49, 70, 95
    Canada, 93
Lilium canadense, 93
Lilium spp. *See* Lily
Lilium superbum. See Turk's cap
    lily
Lily-of-the-valley, 92
Linaria canadensis. See Blue toad-
    flax
Linaria vulgaris. See Butter-and-
    eggs
Linden, 18–19
Liquidambar styraciflua. See
    Sweet gum
Liriodendron tulipifera. See Tulip
    (poplar) tree
Lobelia, 48, 66, 86
Lobelia cardinalis. See Cardinal
    flower
Lobelia erinus. See Lobelia
Lobelia siphilitica. See Lobelia
Lobularia maritima. See Alyssum
Lonicera japonica. See Honey-
    suckle vine, Hall's
Lonicera sempervirens. See Hon-
    eysuckle vine, trumpet

Lonicera tatarica. See Honey-
    suckle
Lotus, 106–7
Lunaria annua. See Honesty
Lupine, 71, 90
Lupinus spp. *See* Lupine
Lupinus subcarnosa. See Blue-
    bonnet
Lythrum salicaria. See Purple
    loosestrife

M
Malus spp. *See* Crabapple
Mandrake. *See* Mayapple
Manna grass, 52
Mantis, 172–73, 215–17, 219
Manure, 36, 62, 199, 201
Maple, 9, 18–19
Marguerite daisy, 49, 71
Marigold, 33–34, 59, 67, 115
    African, 67
    French, 67
    marsh, 95, 108
Marjoram, 169
Marvel-of-Peru. *See* Four-O'clock
Matthiola incana. See Stock
Mayapple, 95
Mertensia virginica. See Virginia
    bluebell
Mexican sunflower. *See Tithonia*
Michaelmas daisy, 49
Microclimates, 29–30
Mimosa, 18–19
Mint, 123, 169
Mirabilis jalapa. See Four-O'clock
Miscanthus sinensis. See Japanese
    silver grass
Mitchella repens, 99
Mockorange, 11, 24–25, 33, 73
Mole, 116, 181–82
Monarch butterfly, 159, 160, 169
Monarda didyma. See Bee balm
Moonflower vine (moonvine), 72
Morning glory, 26–27
Morus spp. *See* Mulberry
Moths, 39, 73, 165–68
    larvae of, 165
Mountain ash, 18–19
Mouse, white-footed, 179–80
Mulberry, 18–19
Mulches, 12, 91–92, 201–4, 208,
    230–32
Mullein, 56, 86

Myosotis sylvatica. See Forget-me-not
Myrica pensylvanica. See Bayberry

N
Nasturtium, 67
Native plants, protected, 99–100
Nelumbium speciosum. See Lotus
Nelumbo lutea, 107
Nematode, 119, 220
Nest boxes, 144–47
Nicotiana alata (nicotiana), 60, 67, 71
Night-blooming plants, 69–73
Nuthatch, 13, 135, 145
Nymphaea spp. *See* Waterlily
Nymphoides indicum, 108
Nyssa sylvatica. See Sour gum

O
Oak, 9, 18–19, 91–92
Oenothera fruticosa. See Sundrop
Oenothera biennis. See Primrose, evening
Opossum, 73, 186–87
Owl, 74, 132–33
Ox-eye daisy, 86

P
Paeonia lactiflora. See Peony
Painted tongue. *See* Salpiglossis
Pampas grass, 52
Pansy, 33, 56
Papaver spp. *See* Poppy
Papyrus. *See* Egyptian paper plant
Parasites, 217–19
Parsleyworm, 120–21
Parthenocissus quinquefolia. See Virginia creeper
Partridgeberry, 99
Pecan, 18–19
Pediobius foveolatus, 220
Pelargonium hortorum. See Geranium
Pennisetum alopecuroides. See Fountain grass
Penstemon gloxinioides (penstemon), 49, 86–87
Peony, 40, 50
Perennial Minimanual, 43–52

Perennials, 33–35, 38–52, 71–72, 109, 123
for difficult sites, 233–34
dividing, 41, 42–43
wildflower, 82, 84–87
Perennial Wildflowers for Sunny Sites Minimanual, 84–87
Pesticides, 80, 111
Pest management, 115–16, 224–27
Petunia hybrida (petunia), 67, 115, 169
Phacelia tenacetifolia. See Lacy phacelia
Pheromones, 223
Philadelphus spp. *See* Mockorange
Phlox paniculata (phlox), 33–34, 50, 71
Picea spp. *See* Spruce
Pickerel weed, 108
Pine
Ponderosa, 15
white, 9–11, 20–21
Pinus strobus. See Pine, white
Pistia stratiotes. See Water lettuce
Pitcher's salvia, 50
Plant rotation, 208, 226–27
Plants to Attract Butterflies, 163–64
Platycodon grandiflorus. See Balloonflower
Plume grass, 52
Plum, 11, 18–19
Podophyllum peltatum. See Mayapple
Pontederia cordata, 108
Pool plants, 104–9
Pools, 101–4
Poppy
annual, 90
California, 63–64, 90
Iceland, 54
oriental, 49
Shirley, 68, 90
water, 107
Praying mantis. *See* Mantis
Predators, beneficial, 215
Primrose, 33
evening, 88, 90
polyanthus, 50
Primula ×polyantha. See Primrose, polyanthus
Pruning, 12–13, 53, 57
Prunus spp. *See* Cherry; Plum

Purple coneflower, 87
Purple loosestrife, 87
Purple martin, 132, 145
Pyracantha spp. *See* Firethorn
Pyrus calleryana. See Callery pear

Q
Queen Anne's lace, 90, 115
Quercus spp. *See* Oak
Quince, 11

R
Rabbit, 175
Raccoon, 73, 111, 180–81
　deterrents for, 115, 118, 181
Rain, excessive, 235–36
Raspberry, 12, 24–25
Ravenna grass. *See* Plume grass
Red-winged blackbird, 132
Repellent sprays, 118, 183
Rhamnus cathartica. See Buck-
　　thorn
Rhododendron, 24–25
Rhododendron spp. *See* Azalea;
　　Rhododendron
Rhubarb, 123
Robin, 135
Rockchuck, 185
Rocket. *See* Ligularia
Rosa rugosa, 24–25
Rosa spp. *See* Rose
Rose, 50, 87
Rosebush, 9–11, 24–25
Rose campion, 88
Roseda luteola. See Weld
Rubus allegheniensis. See Black-
　　berry
Rubus idaeus. See Raspberry
Rubus occidentalis. See Raspberry
Rudbeckia hirta. See Black-eyed
　　susan; Gloriosa daisy

S
Sage, 169
　blue, 33, 50
　mealy-cup, 49
Sagittaria latifolia. See Arrowhead
Salpiglossis sinuata (salpiglossis),
　　67–68
Salvia azurea. See Pitcher's salvia
Salvia farinacea. See Sage, mealy-
　　cup
Sambucus canadensis. See Elder-
　　berry

Sanguinaria canadensis. See
　　Bloodroot
Savory, 169
Scarecrow, 116
Schizanthus spp. (schizanthus), 68
Scilla, 92
Sedum spectabile. See Showy
　　stonecrop
Seeds, 61–62, 79, 82
　healthy, 119–20, 209, 225–26
Shadbush. *See* Allegheny service-
　　berry
Shagbark hickory, 18–19
Shasta daisy, 34, 50–51
Showy stonecrop, 51
Shrubs, 9–15, 20–27, 73
　deciduous, 11–12
　evergreen, 11
　flowering, 9, 14–15, 33
　planting and pruning of,
　　9–12, 13
Shrubs for the Naturalist's Garden,
　　20–25
Silene. *See* Catchfly
Silene armeria. See Sweet william
　　catchfly
Silene coronaria. See Rose cam-
　　pion
Silene spp. *See* Catchfly
Silent Spring, 211
Silkmoth, 165–66
Silver dollar. *See* Honesty
Skunk, 73, 178–79
Slug, 57, 213, 214, 220
Snail, 110, 220
Snake, 116, 188–89
Snapdragon, 68
Snowberry, creeping, 97
Snowberry, 24–25
Snowdrop, 92
Soil, 36, 79, 92
　building of, 36–38, 200–201
Solidago spp. *See* Goldenrod
Sorbus spp. *See* Mountain ash
Sour gum, 20–21
Sparrow, 132, 149
Sphinx moth, 167
Spider flower. *See* Cleome
Spike gayfeather, 51
Spruce, 15, 20–21
Squirrel, 31, 141, 175–76
Starling, 132
Stock, 56

Sundrop, 88, 90
Sunflower, 33, 68, 91
Swallow, 132, 145–47
Swallowtail butterfly, 160
     larvae of, 120, 162
Swamp milkweed, 87, 109
Swamp plants, 233
Swamp rose mallow, 87
Sweet grass. *See* Manna grass
Sweet gum. 9, 20–21
Sweet rocket, 51, 71
Sweet william, 56
Sweet william catchfly, 88
Symphoricarpos albus. See Snow-
     berry
Syringa vulgaris. See Lilac

T
Tachinid fly, 218
Tagetes spp. *See* Marigold
Tape grass, 108
Teaberry. *See* Wintergreen
Thyme, 123, 169
Tilia spp. *See* Linden
Tithonia rotundifolia (tithonia),
     33, 68
Titmouse, 13, 132, 139, 145
Toadflax. *See* Blue toadflax; But-
     ter-and-eggs
Toad, 74, 110, 214
Tomato hornworm, 218
Touch-me-not. *See* Jewelweed
Transvaal daisy. *See Gerbera*
Trees, 3, 9, 13–21
     deciduous, 3, 9
     evergreen, 3, 9
     ornamental, 11
     planting and pruning of, 9–12
Trees for the Naturalist's Garden,
     14–21
Trillium spp. (trillium), 95
Tropaeolum majus. See Nastur-
     tium
Tropical plants, 70, 105–6
Trout lily, 95
Trumpet vine, 26–27
Tsuga canadensis. See Eastern
     hemlock
Tulip (poplar) tree, 20–21
Tupelo. *See* Sour gum
Turk's cap lily, 95, 100
Turtle, 110

Typha latifolia. See Cattail
Typha minima, 107

V
Vaccinium corymbosum. See
     Blueberry
Vallisneria spiralis. See Eel grass
Vegetable breeding programs, 226
Vegetables, 5, 112–15, 121–25
     protection of, 115–20
Verbascum spp. *See* Mullein
Verbena hybrida (verbena), 33,
     68–69
Veronica, 33
Verticillium, 119
Viburnum, 33
     cranberry bush, 20–21
     doublefile, 22–23
Viburnum plicatum. See Vibur-
     num, doublefile
Viburnum prunifolium. See Black
     haw
Viburnum trilobum. See Vibur-
     num, cranberry bush
Viceroy butterfly, 160
Vines, 26–27, 72–73
Vines for the Naturalist's Garden,
     26–27
Viola pedata. See Violet
Viola spp. *See* Pansy; Violet
Violet, 92, 96, 108
Virginia bluebell, 96
Virginia creeper, 26–27
Vitis spp. *See* Grapevine

W
Wakerobin, 95
Wallflower, 56
     Siberian, 91
Wasp, 168, 218, 220
Water conservation, 230–32
Water gardening, 4–5. *See also*
     Pools
Water lettuce, 108
Waterlily, 70, 103–6, 108
Water plantain, 108
Water plants, 104–9
Water snowflake, 108
Water violet, 108
Weather, 228–29
Weeding, 120–21, 208–9
Weld, 56
Wetland plants, 235–36

Wild carrot. *See* Queen Anne's
    lace
Wildflowers, 75–84, 93–99
    annual, 88–91
    perennial, 84–87
    programs for, 83
    protected, 99–100
    woodland, 93–99
Wildlife, 110–11, 174–89
    climate and, 31–32
    landscaping for, 1–7
Wild yellow flag, 108
Winter aconite, 92
Wintergreen, 99
Woad, 56
Woodland Evergreen Groundcov-
    ers Minimanual, 97–99
Woodland Wildflowers Miniman-
    ual, 93–96

Woodchuck, 31, 185
Wood mouse. *See* Mouse, white-
    footed
Woodland groundcovers, 97–99
Woodpecker, 13, 135, 139–40, 145
Wren, 132, 145

X
Xeriscaping, 232–35

Y
Yarrow, 87, 115
Yucca, 73

Z
Zinnia elegans (zinnia), 33, 58, 60,
    69, 115